BEYOND
CORPORATION

THE AMAZING SPIDER-MAN

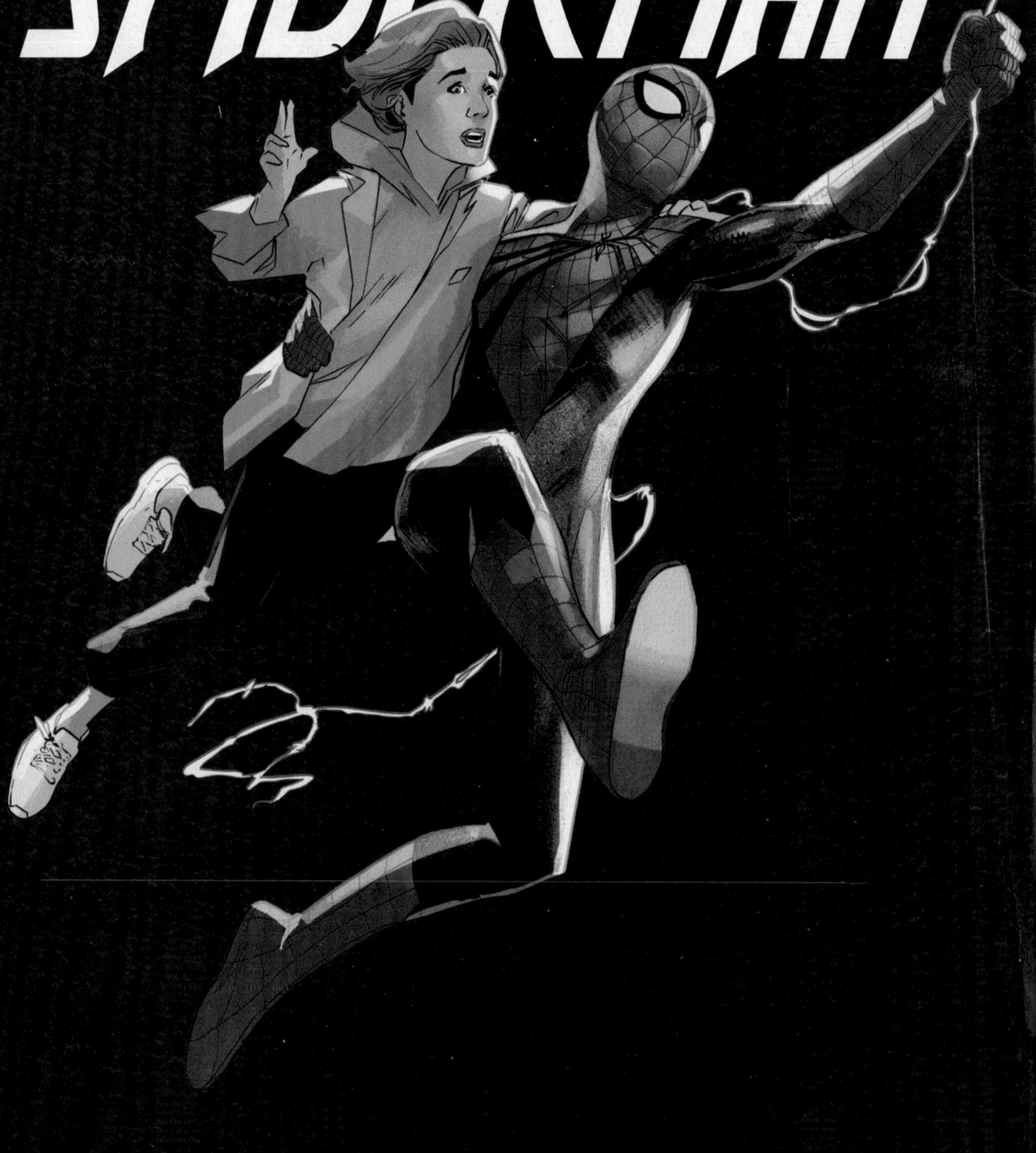

THE AMAZING *SPID*

Ben Reilly is a clone of the original Spider-Man, **PETER PARKER**, who is in the hospital after a grueling fight. Luckily for New York, Ben has taken on the mantle of **SPIDER-MAN**. Backed by the **BEYOND CORPORATION** and their Head of Super Hero Development, **MAXINE DANGER**, Ben has access to all the things your friendly neighborhood Spider-Man could only dream of: a swanky apartment that he shares with his girlfriend, **JANINE GODBE**, an upgraded Spidey-suit and a brilliant support team led by Marcus Momplaisir.

But Ben is beginning to learn that Beyond isn't all that it seems. After duking it out with **DOCTOR OCTOPUS**, Ben came into possession of a top-secret data drive full of Beyond's darkest secrets—secrets Doc Ock promised would topple the foundations of Ben's belief in his corporate backers. That drive, as Ben told Maxine, was destroyed in the battle with Ock.

AMAZING SPIDER-MAN #86, #88

ZEB WELLS/WRITER

MICHAEL DOWLING/ARTIST

BRYAN VALENZA/COLOR ARTIST

VC's **JOE CARAMAGNA**/LETTERER

ARTHUR ADAMS & **ALEJANDRO SÁNCHEZ**/COVER ART

LINDSEY COHICK & **KAEDEN McGAHEY**/ASSISTANT EDITORS

NICK LOWE/EDITOR

AMAZING SPIDER-MAN #87

JED MacKAY/WRITER

CARLOS GÓMEZ/ARTISTS

BRYAN VALENZA/COLOR ARTIST

VC's **JOE CARAMAGNA**/LETTERER

ARTHUR ADAMS & **ALEJANDRO SÁNCHEZ**/COVER ART

LINDSEY COHICK & **KAEDEN McGAHEY**/ASSISTANT EDITORS

NICK LOWE/EDITOR

#86 VARIANT BY
MIGUEL MERCADO

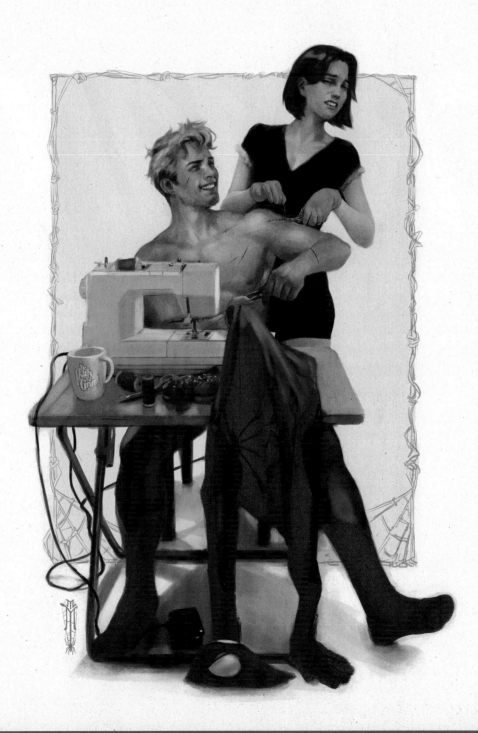

BEN REILLY has the proportional speed, strength, and agility of a **SPIDER**, adhesive fingertips and toes, and the unique precognitive awareness of danger called "**SPIDER-SENSE**"! After the tragic death of his **Uncle Ben**, Ben Reilly understood that with great power there must also come great responsibility. He became the crimefighting super hero called…

ER-MAN

MARY JANE & BLACK CAT: BEYOND

JED MacKAY/WRITER

C.F. VILLA/ARTIST

ERICK ARCINIEGA/COLOR ARTIST

VC's **TRAVIS LANHAM**/LETTERER

J. SCOTT CAMPBELL & **SABINE RICH**/COVER ART

LINDSEY COHICK & **KAEDEN McGAHEY**/ASSISTANT EDITORS

NICK LOWE/EDITOR

AMAZING SPIDER-MAN #88.BEY

GEOFFREY THORNE/WRITER

JAN BAZALDUA & **JIM TOWE**/ARTISTS

JIM CAMPBELL/COLOR ARTIST

VC's **JOE CARAMAGNA**/LETTERER

NICK BRADSHAW & **RACHELLE ROSENBERG**/COVER ART

DANNY KHAZEM/EDITOR

NICK LOWE/EXECUTIVE EDITOR

KELLY THOMPSON, CODY ZIGLAR, SALADIN AHMED, PATRICK GLEASON & **ZEB WELLS**/BEYOND BOARD

SPIDER-MAN CREATED BY
STAN LEE & **STEVE DITKO**

JENNIFER GRÜNWALD/COLLECTION EDITOR
DANIEL KIRCHHOFFER/ASSISTANT EDITOR
MAIA LOY/ASSISTANT MANAGING EDITOR
LISA MONTALBANO/ASSOCIATE MANAGER, TALENT RELATIONS
JEFF YOUNGQUIST/VP PRODUCTION & SPECIAL PROJECTS
DAVID GABRIEL/SVP PRINT, SALES & MARKETING
SARAH SPADACCINI WITH **JAY BOWEN** & **ANTHONY GAMBINO**/BOOK DESIGNERS
C.B. CEBULSKI/EDITOR IN CHEIF

AMAZING SPIDER-MAN: BEYOND VOL. 3. Contains material originally published in magazine form as AMAZING SPIDER-MAN (2018) #86-88 and #88.BEY, and MARY JANE & BLACK CAT: BEYOND (2022) #1. First printing 2022. ISBN 978-1-302-93258-9. Published by MARVEL WORLDWIDE, INC., a subsidiary of MARVEL ENTERTAINMENT, LLC. OFFICE OF PUBLICATION: 1290 Avenue of the Americas, New York, NY 10104. © 2022 MARVEL No similarity between any of the names, characters, persons, and/or institutions in this book with those of any living or dead person or institution is intended, and any such similarity which may exist is purely coincidental. **Printed in Canada.** KEVIN FEIGE, Chief Creative Officer; DAN BUCKLEY, President, Marvel Entertainment; JOE QUESADA, EVP & Creative Director; DAVID BOGART, Associate Publisher & SVP of Talent Affairs; TOM BREVOORT, VP, Executive Editor; NICK LOWE, Executive Editor, VP of Content, Digital Publishing; DAVID GABRIEL, VP of Print & Digital Publishing; MARK ANNUNZIATO, VP of Planning & Forecasting; JEFF YOUNGQUIST, VP of Production & Special Projects; ALEX MORALES, Director of Publishing Operations; DAN EDINGTON, Director of Editorial Operations; RICKEY PURDIN, Director of Talent Relations; JENNIFER GRUNWALD, Director of Production & Special Projects; SUSAN CRESPI, Production Manager, STAN LEE, Chairman Emeritus. For information regarding advertising in Marvel Comics or on Marvel.com, please contact Vit DeBellis, Custom Solutions & Integrated Advertising Manager, at vdebellis@marvel.com. For Marvel subscription inquiries, please call 888-511-5480. **Manufactured between 2/4/2022 and 3/8/2022 by SOLISCO PRINTERS, SCOTT, QC, CANADA.**
10 9 8 7 6 5 4 3 2 1

#86 BEYOND CORPORATION

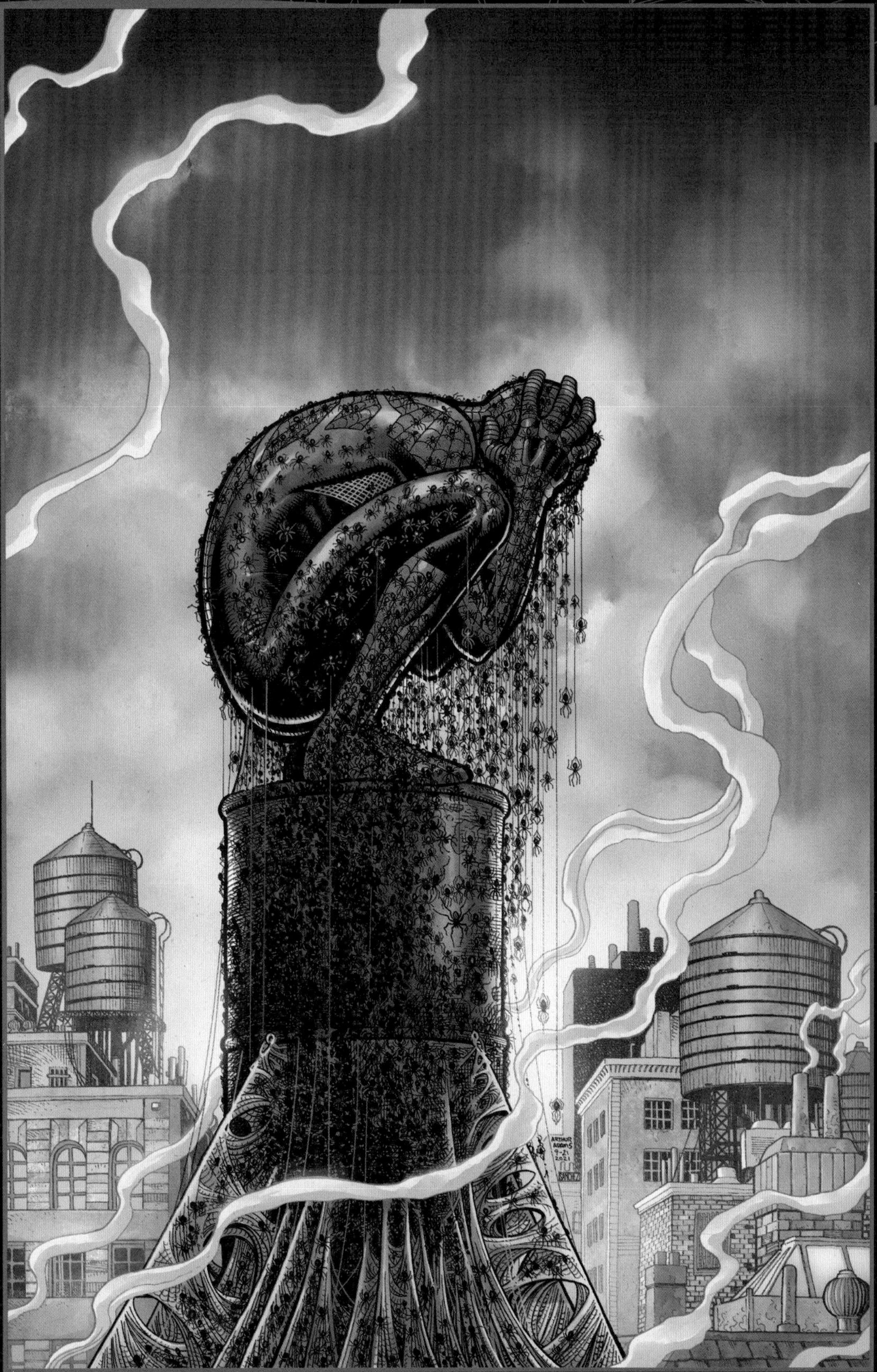

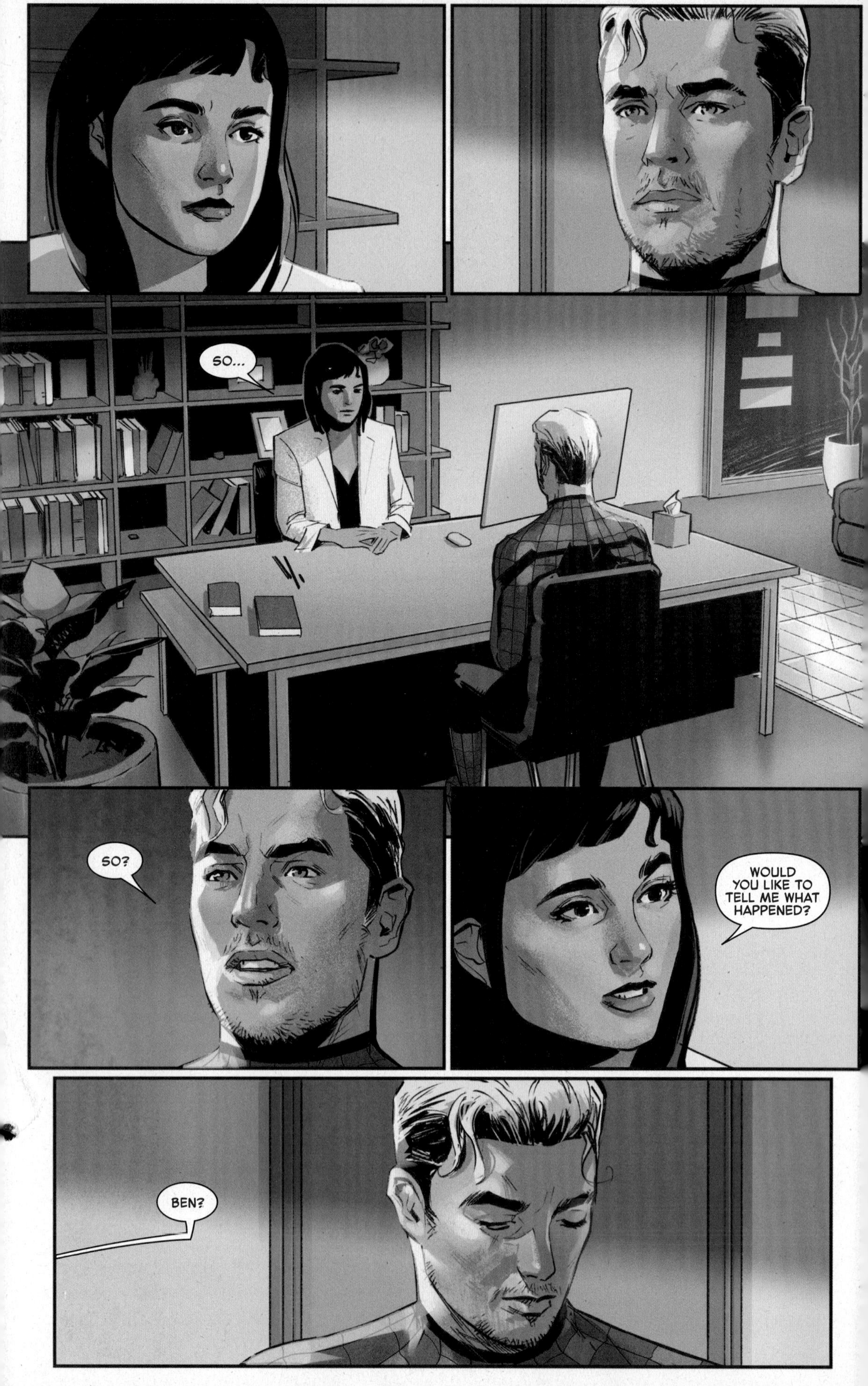
SO...
SO?
WOULD YOU LIKE TO TELL ME WHAT HAPPENED?
BEN?

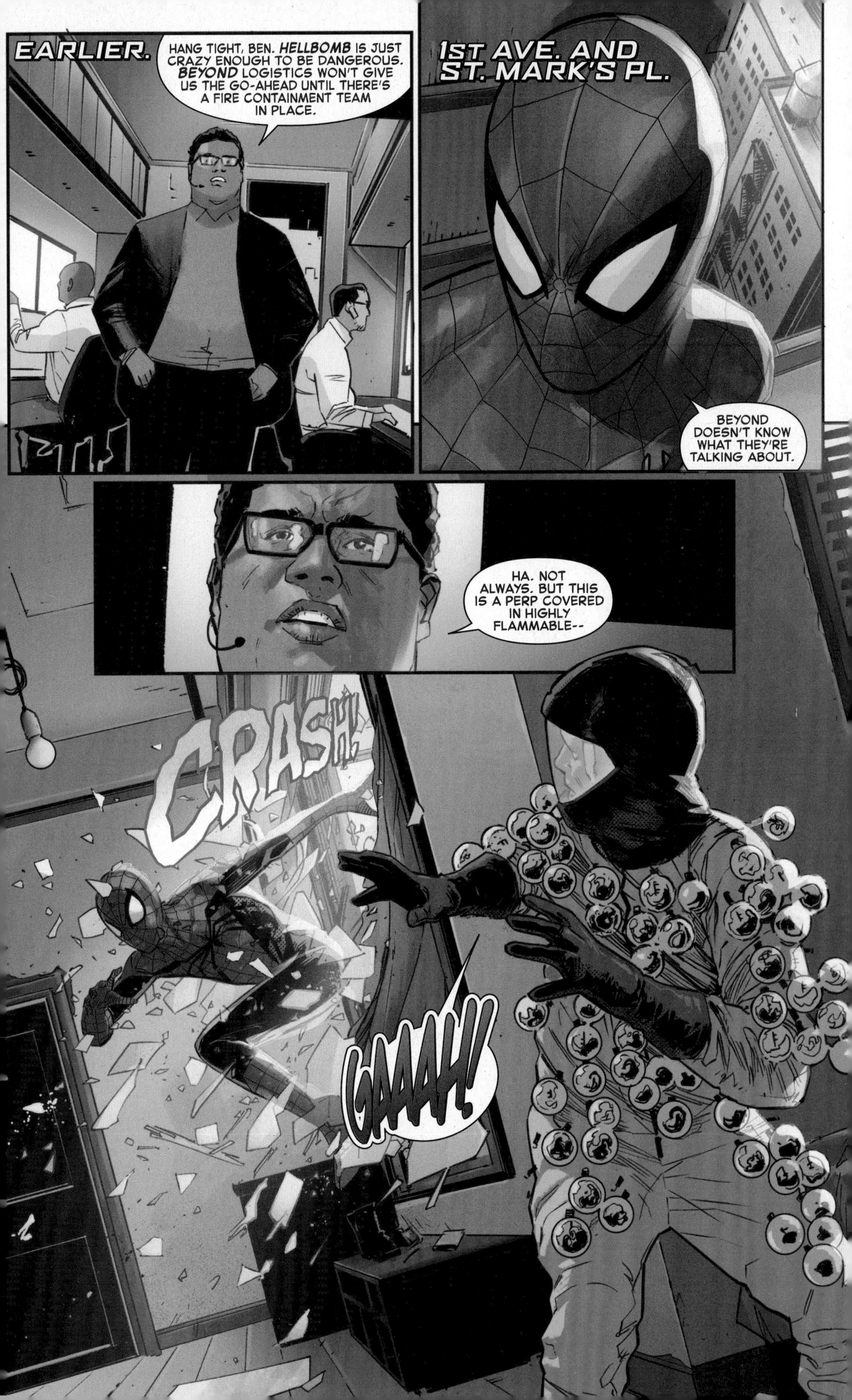

EARLIER.
HANG TIGHT, BEN. HELLBOMB IS JUST CRAZY ENOUGH TO BE DANGEROUS. BEYOND LOGISTICS WON'T GIVE US THE GO-AHEAD UNTIL THERE'S A FIRE CONTAINMENT TEAM IN PLACE.
1st AVE. AND ST. MARK'S PL.
BEYOND DOESN'T KNOW WHAT THEY'RE TALKING ABOUT.
HA. NOT ALWAYS. BUT THIS IS A PERP COVERED IN HIGHLY FLAMMABLE--
CRASH!
GAAAH!

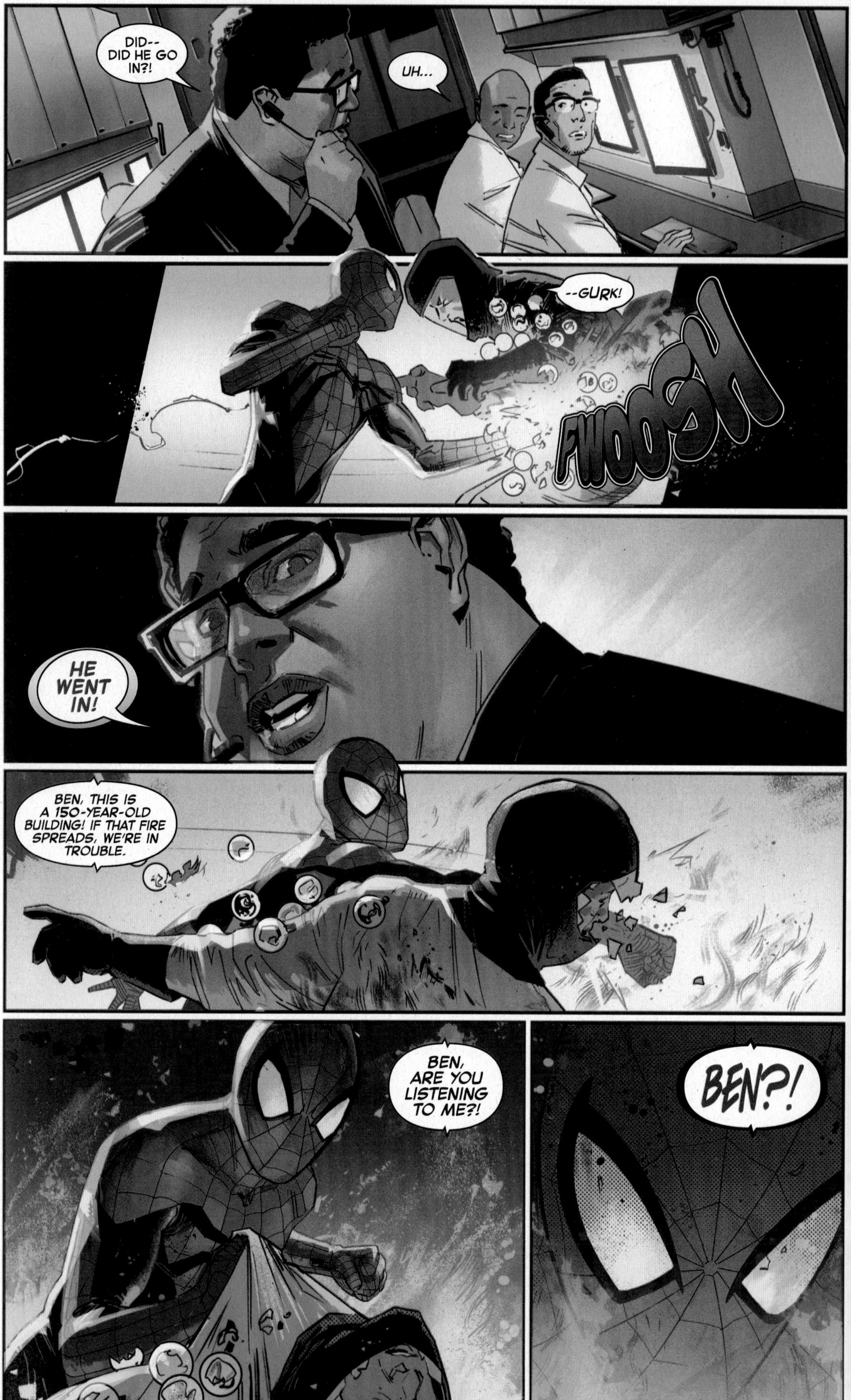
DID-- DID HE GO IN?!
UH...
--GURK!
FWOOSH
HE WENT IN!
BEN, THIS IS A 150-YEAR-OLD BUILDING! IF THAT FIRE SPREADS, WE'RE IN TROUBLE.
BEN, ARE YOU LISTENING TO ME?!
BEN?!

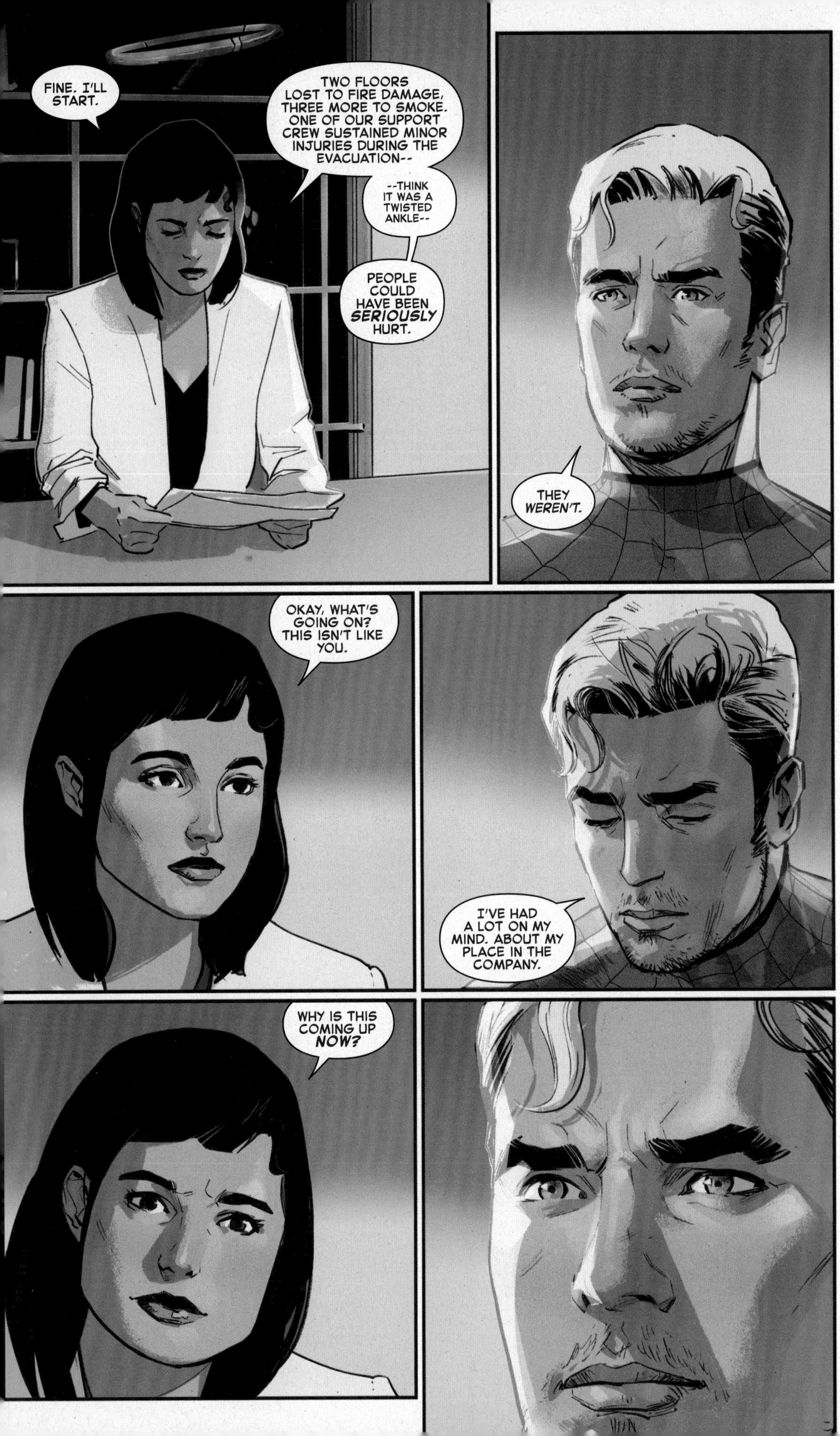
FINE. I'LL START.
TWO FLOORS LOST TO FIRE DAMAGE, THREE MORE TO SMOKE. ONE OF OUR SUPPORT CREW SUSTAINED MINOR INJURIES DURING THE EVACUATION--
--THINK IT WAS A TWISTED ANKLE--
PEOPLE COULD HAVE BEEN SERIOUSLY HURT.
THEY WEREN'T.
OKAY, WHAT'S GOING ON? THIS ISN'T LIKE YOU.
I'VE HAD A LOT ON MY MIND. ABOUT MY PLACE IN THE COMPANY.
WHY IS THIS COMING UP NOW?

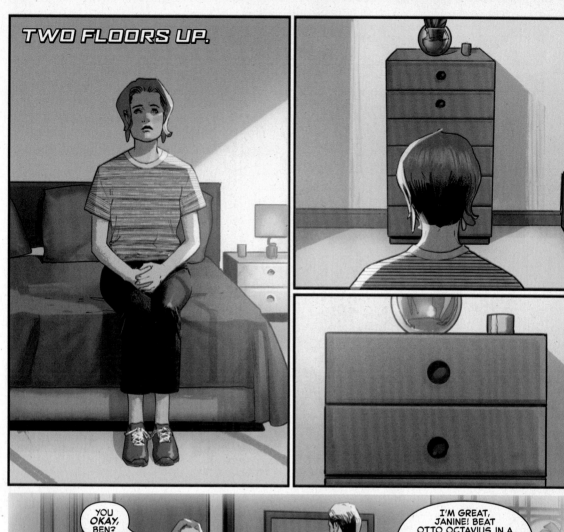

YOU OKAY, BEN?

I'M GREAT, JANINE! BEAT OTTO OCTAVIUS IN A ONE-ON-ONE. THE DRIVE HE STOLE WAS DESTROYED IN THE PROCESS, BUT AT LEAST IT WON'T FALL INTO THE WRONG HANDS.

HEY, DO YOU MIND CLEANING MY MASK?

UH, SURE?

IT GOT REAL DIRTY.

DON'T LOSE THAT.

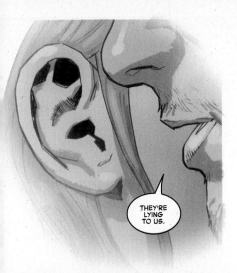

THEY'RE LYING TO US.

ANYWAY, LONG DAY. GONNA TAKE THE WORLD'S LONGEST SHOWER.

"WE CAN'T JUST SIT HERE IN SILENCE."

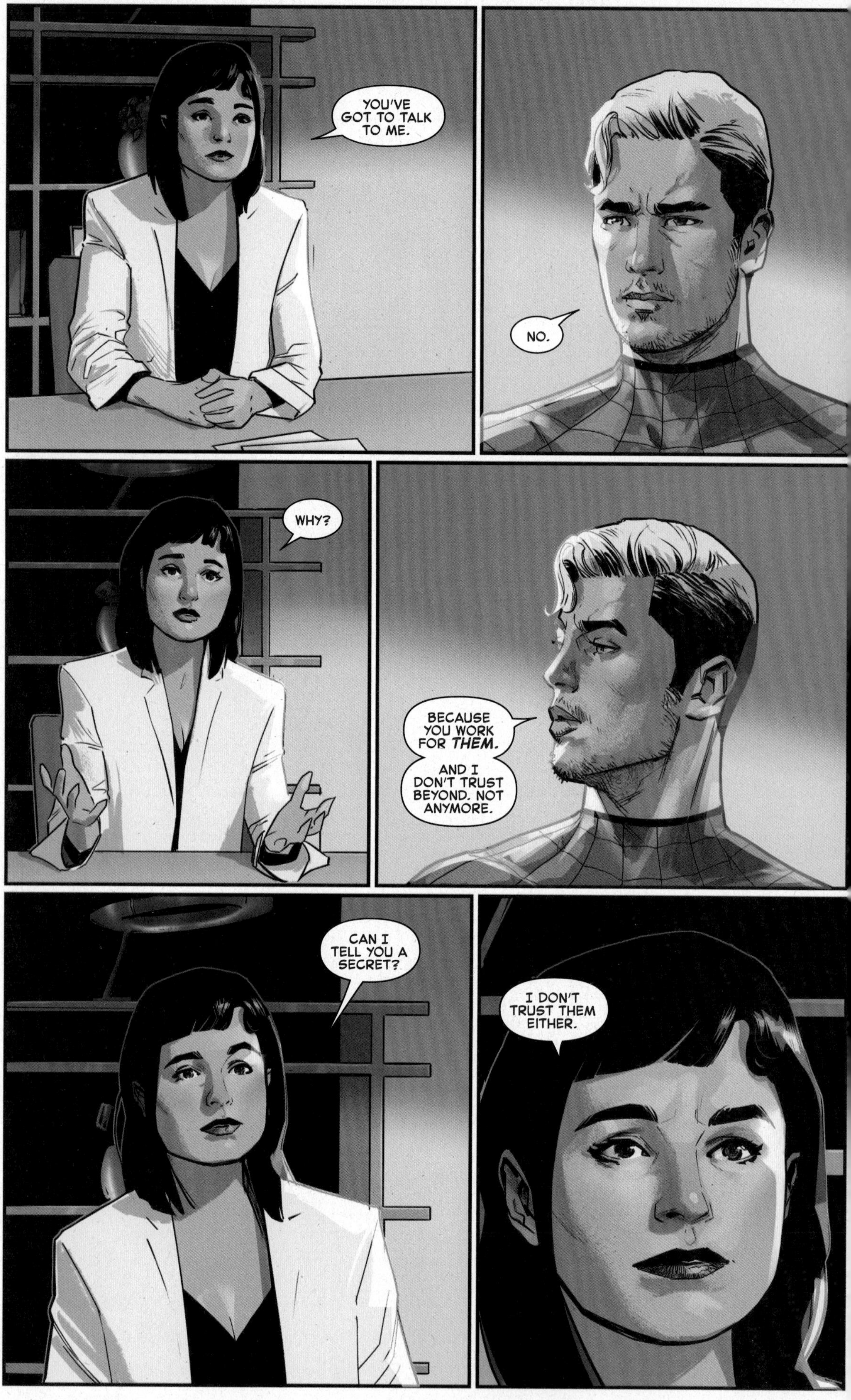
YOU'VE GOT TO TALK TO ME.
NO.
WHY?
BECAUSE YOU WORK FOR *THEM.*
AND I DON'T TRUST BEYOND. NOT ANYMORE.
CAN I TELL YOU A SECRET?
I DON'T TRUST THEM EITHER.

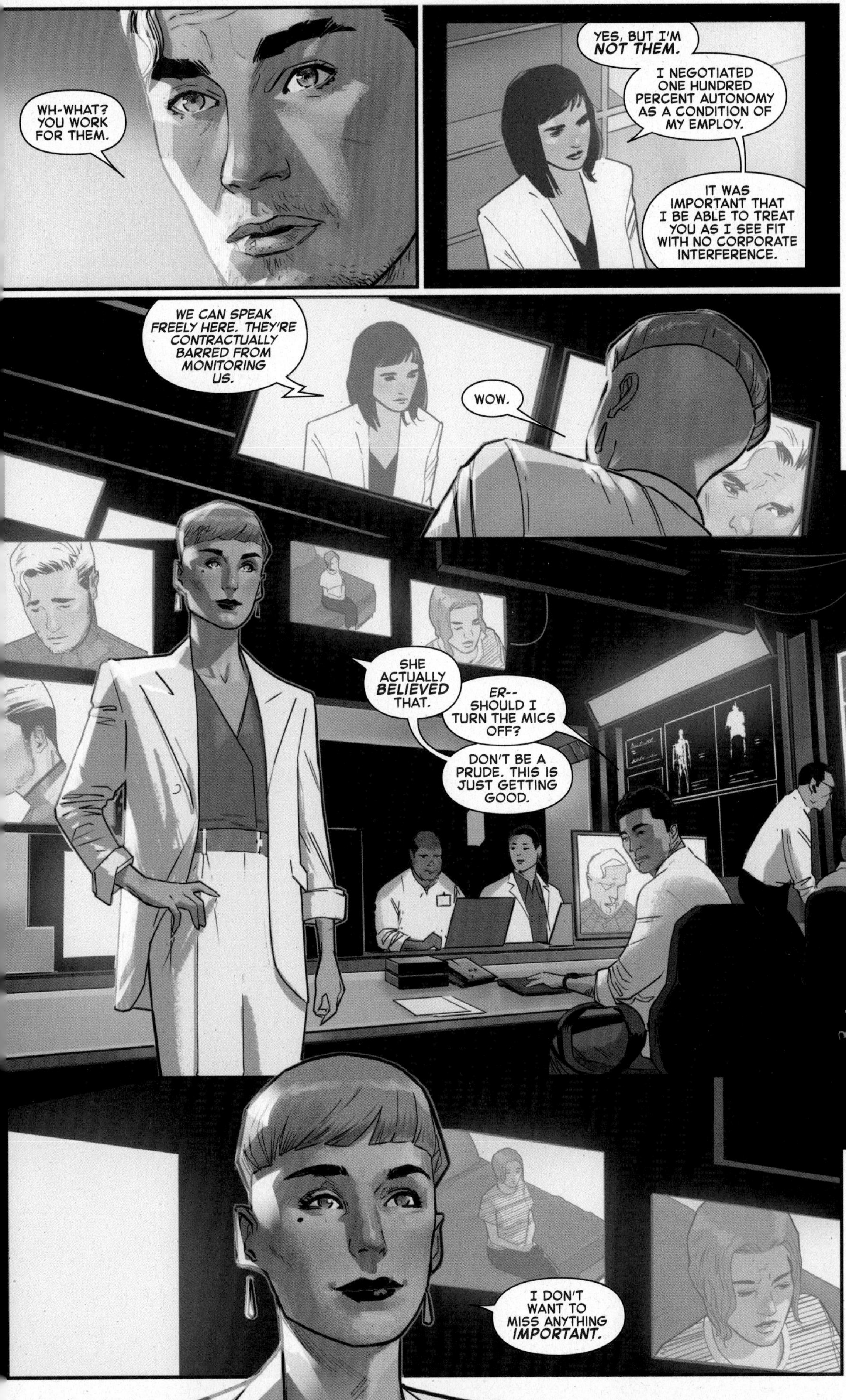
WH-WHAT? YOU WORK FOR THEM.
YES, BUT I'M NOT THEM.
I NEGOTIATED ONE HUNDRED PERCENT AUTONOMY AS A CONDITION OF MY EMPLOY.
IT WAS IMPORTANT THAT I BE ABLE TO TREAT YOU AS I SEE FIT WITH NO CORPORATE INTERFERENCE.
WE CAN SPEAK FREELY HERE. THEY'RE CONTRACTUALLY BARRED FROM MONITORING US.
WOW.
SHE ACTUALLY BELIEVED THAT.
ER-- SHOULD I TURN THE MICS OFF?
DON'T BE A PRUDE. THIS IS JUST GETTING GOOD.
I DON'T WANT TO MISS ANYTHING IMPORTANT.

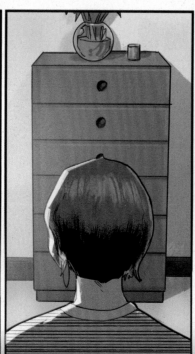

"IT'S COME TO MY ATTENTION YOU'D LIKE PRIVILEGES TO LEAVE THE APARTMENT UNSUPERVISED."

I'M SHOCKED I HAVE TO REMIND YOU THAT YOU WERE *EXTRICATED* FROM A *CORRECTIONAL INSTITUTION.*

IT WOULDN'T BE SAFE FOR EITHER OF US IF YOU WERE ALLOWED TO PRANCE DOWN OUR HALLS UNCHAPERONED. I KNOW THIS IS DISAPPOINTING...

"...BUT YOU'LL HAVE TO TRUST THAT *BEYOND* KNOWS BEST."

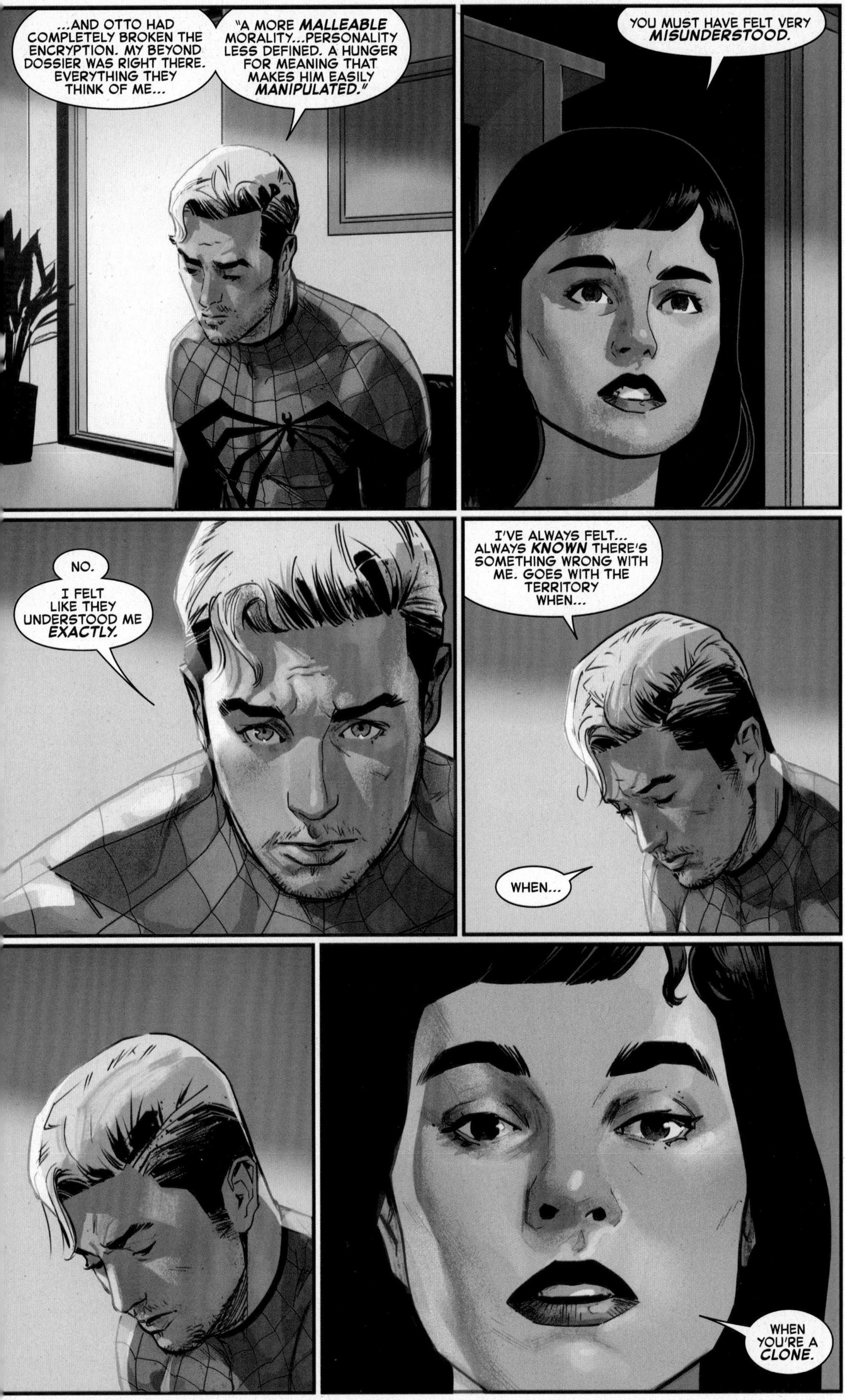
...AND OTTO HAD COMPLETELY BROKEN THE ENCRYPTION. MY BEYOND DOSSIER WAS RIGHT THERE. EVERYTHING THEY THINK OF ME...
"A MORE MALLEABLE MORALITY...PERSONALITY LESS DEFINED. A HUNGER FOR MEANING THAT MAKES HIM EASILY MANIPULATED."
YOU MUST HAVE FELT VERY MISUNDERSTOOD.
NO.
I FELT LIKE THEY UNDERSTOOD ME EXACTLY.
I'VE ALWAYS FELT... ALWAYS KNOWN THERE'S SOMETHING WRONG WITH ME. GOES WITH THE TERRITORY WHEN...
WHEN...
WHEN YOU'RE A CLONE.

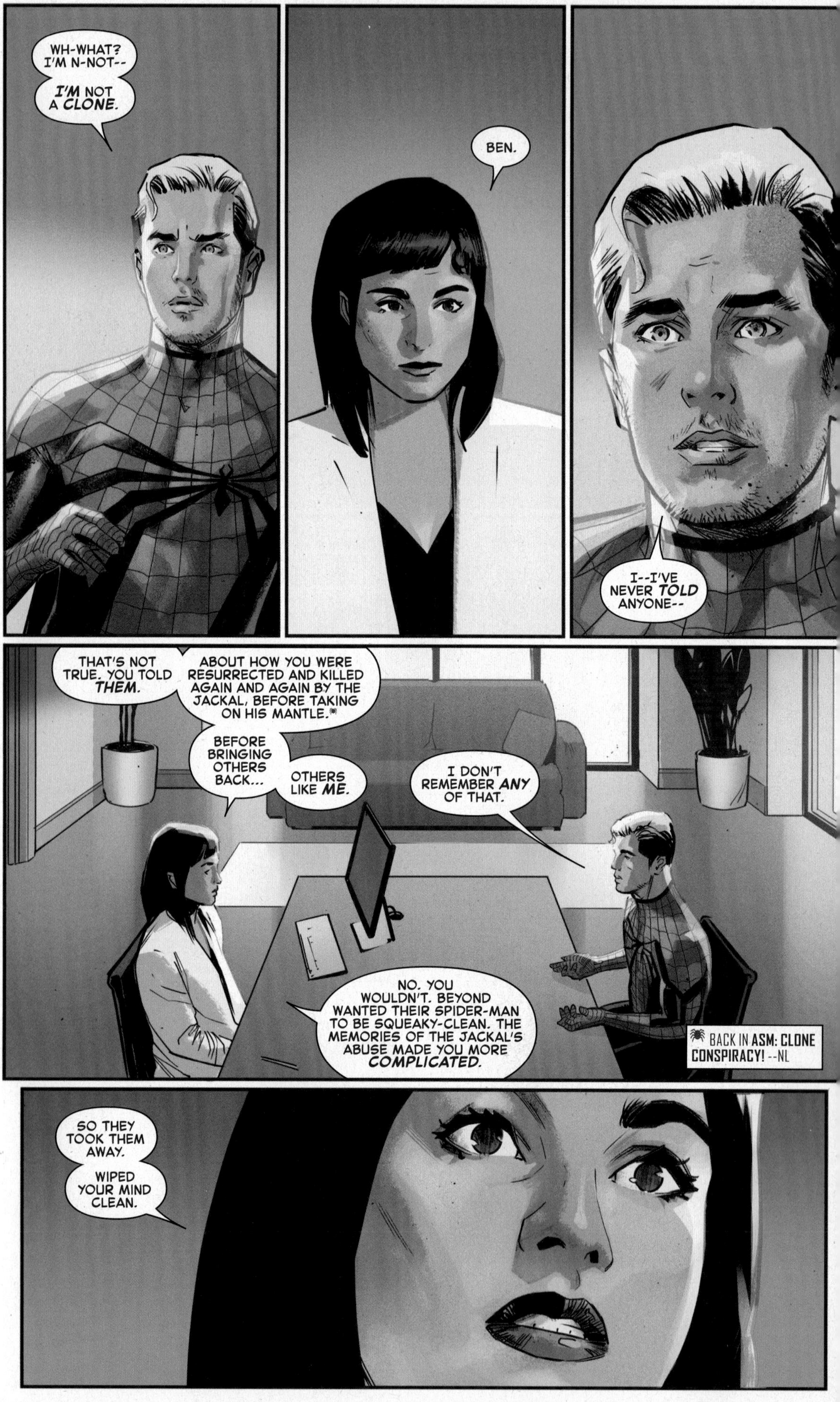
WH-WHAT? I'M N-NOT--
I'M NOT A CLONE.
BEN.
I--I'VE NEVER TOLD ANYONE--
THAT'S NOT TRUE. YOU TOLD THEM.
ABOUT HOW YOU WERE RESURRECTED AND KILLED AGAIN AND AGAIN BY THE JACKAL, BEFORE TAKING ON HIS MANTLE.*
BEFORE BRINGING OTHERS BACK...
OTHERS LIKE ME.
I DON'T REMEMBER ANY OF THAT.
NO. YOU WOULDN'T. BEYOND WANTED THEIR SPIDER-MAN TO BE SQUEAKY-CLEAN. THE MEMORIES OF THE JACKAL'S ABUSE MADE YOU MORE COMPLICATED.
*BACK IN ASM: CLONE CONSPIRACY! --NL
SO THEY TOOK THEM AWAY.
WIPED YOUR MIND CLEAN.

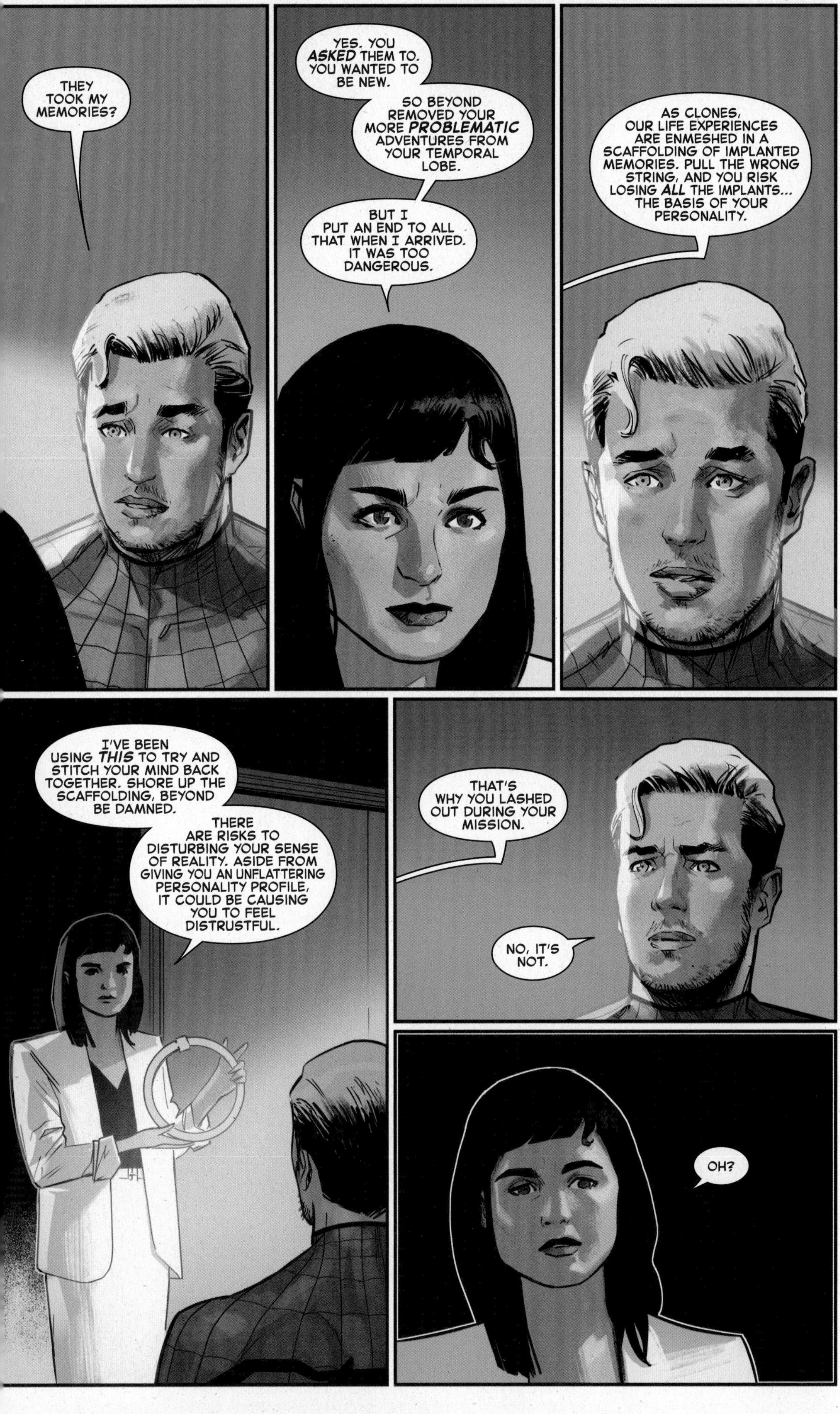
THEY TOOK MY MEMORIES?
YES. YOU ASKED THEM TO. YOU WANTED TO BE NEW.
SO BEYOND REMOVED YOUR MORE PROBLEMATIC ADVENTURES FROM YOUR TEMPORAL LOBE.
BUT I PUT AN END TO ALL THAT WHEN I ARRIVED. IT WAS TOO DANGEROUS.
AS CLONES, OUR LIFE EXPERIENCES ARE ENMESHED IN A SCAFFOLDING OF IMPLANTED MEMORIES. PULL THE WRONG STRING, AND YOU RISK LOSING ALL THE IMPLANTS... THE BASIS OF YOUR PERSONALITY.
I'VE BEEN USING THIS TO TRY AND STITCH YOUR MIND BACK TOGETHER. SHORE UP THE SCAFFOLDING, BEYOND BE DAMNED.
THERE ARE RISKS TO DISTURBING YOUR SENSE OF REALITY. ASIDE FROM GIVING YOU AN UNFLATTERING PERSONALITY PROFILE, IT COULD BE CAUSING YOU TO FEEL DISTRUSTFUL.
THAT'S WHY YOU LASHED OUT DURING YOUR MISSION.
NO, IT'S NOT.
OH?

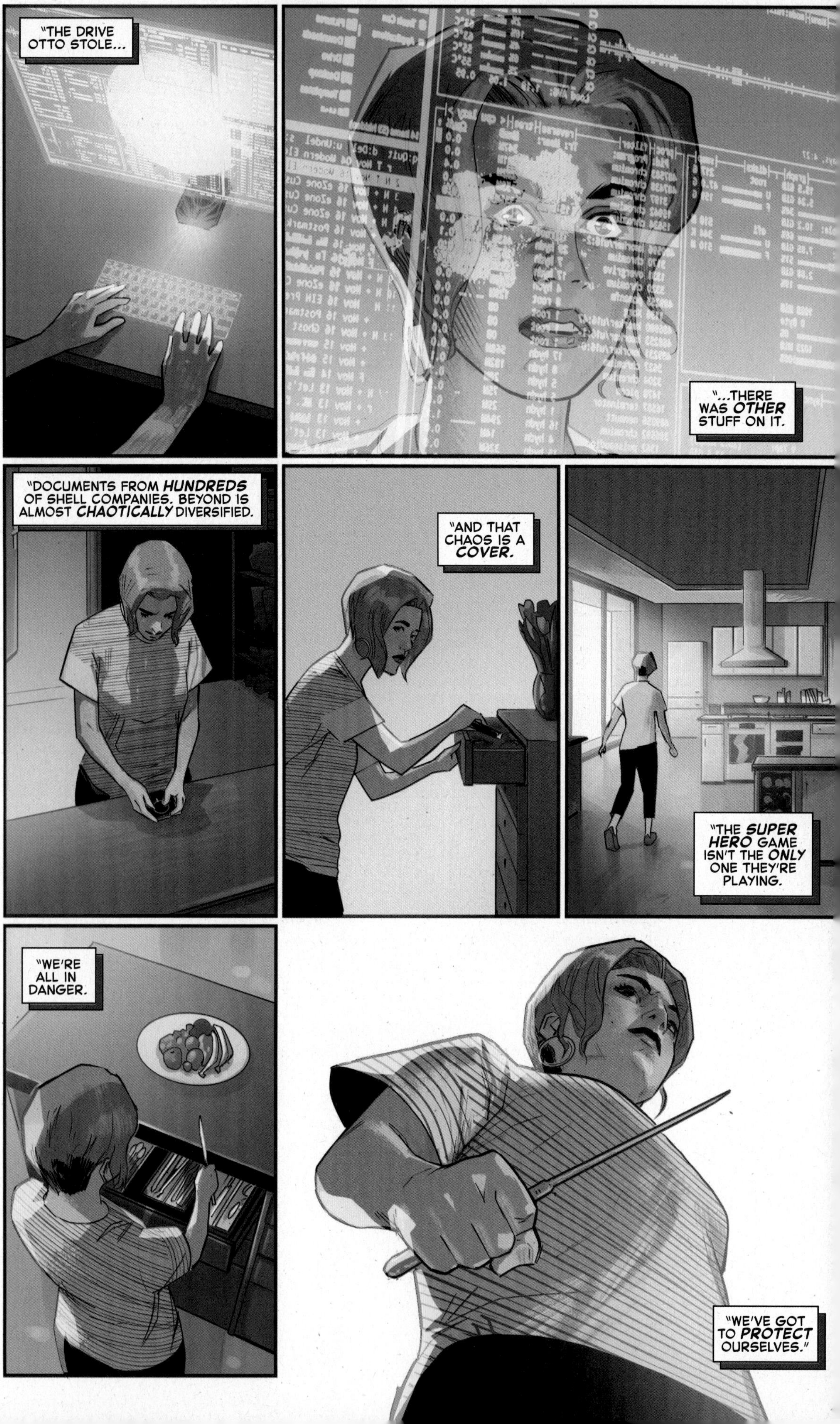
"THE DRIVE OTTO STOLE...
"...THERE WAS OTHER STUFF ON IT.
"DOCUMENTS FROM HUNDREDS OF SHELL COMPANIES. BEYOND IS ALMOST CHAOTICALLY DIVERSIFIED.
"AND THAT CHAOS IS A COVER.
"THE SUPER HERO GAME ISN'T THE ONLY ONE THEY'RE PLAYING.
"WE'RE ALL IN DANGER.
"WE'VE GOT TO PROTECT OURSELVES."

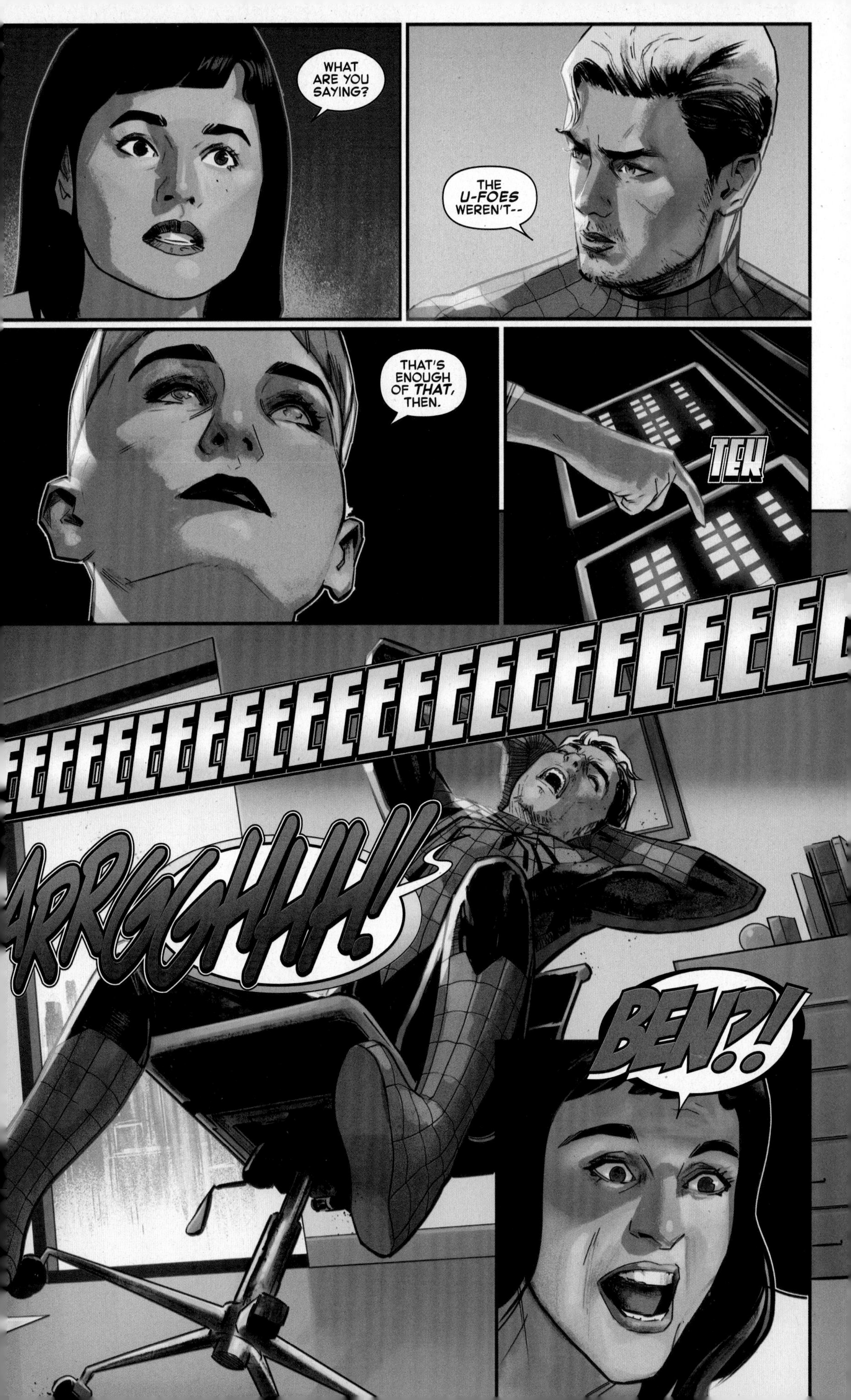
WHAT ARE YOU SAYING?
THE U-FOES WEREN'T--
THAT'S ENOUGH OF THAT, THEN.
TEK
EEEEEEEEEEEEEEEEEEEEEEEEEEEEE
ARRGGHHH!!
BEN?!

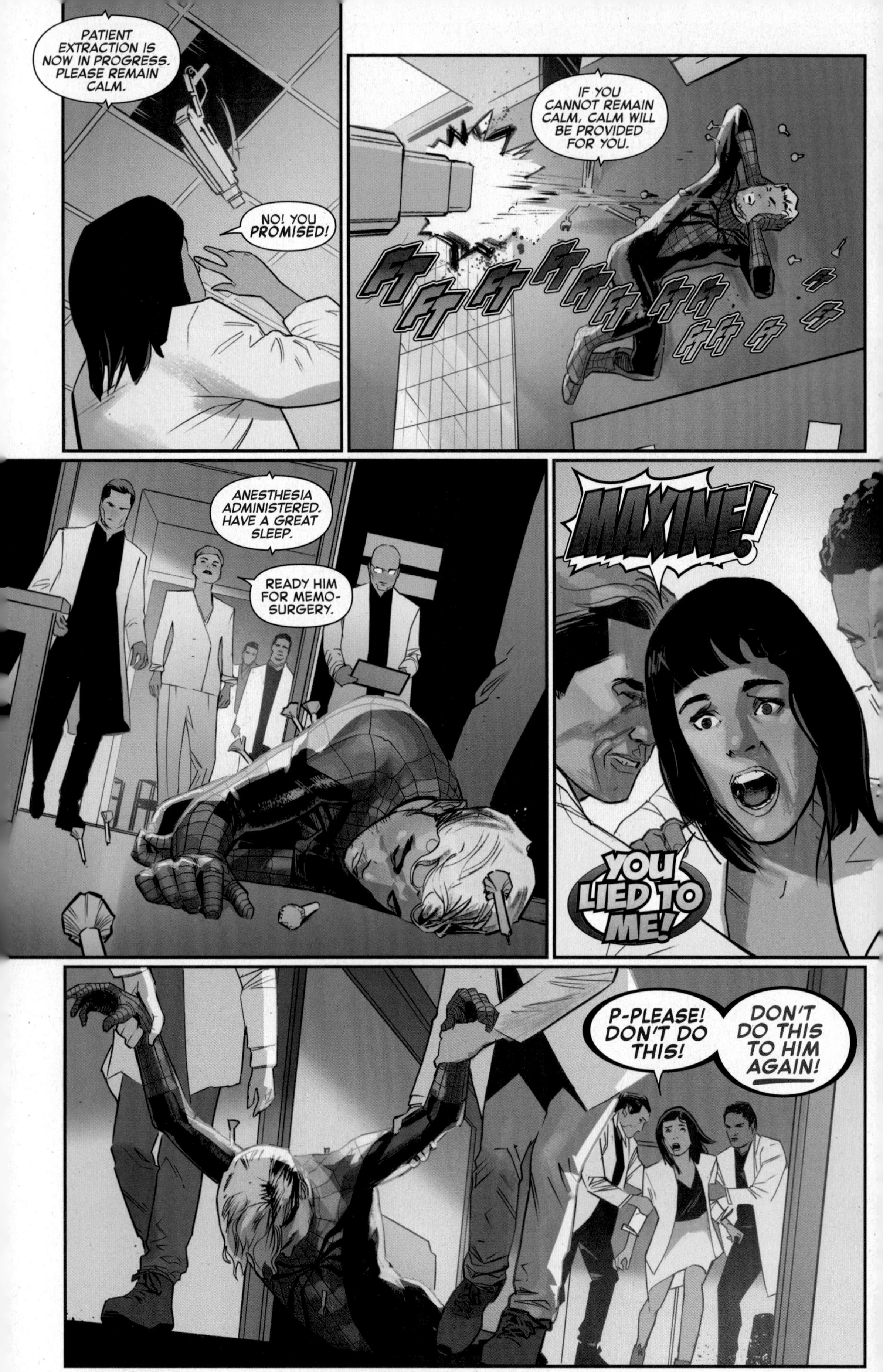
PATIENT EXTRACTION IS NOW IN PROGRESS. PLEASE REMAIN CALM.
NO! YOU PROMISED!
IF YOU CANNOT REMAIN CALM, CALM WILL BE PROVIDED FOR YOU.
FT FT FT FT FT FT FT FT FT FT FT FT FT FT FT FT
ANESTHESIA ADMINISTERED. HAVE A GREAT SLEEP.
READY HIM FOR MEMO-SURGERY.
MAXINE!
YOU LIED TO ME!
P-PLEASE! DON'T DO THIS!
DON'T DO THIS TO HIM AGAIN!

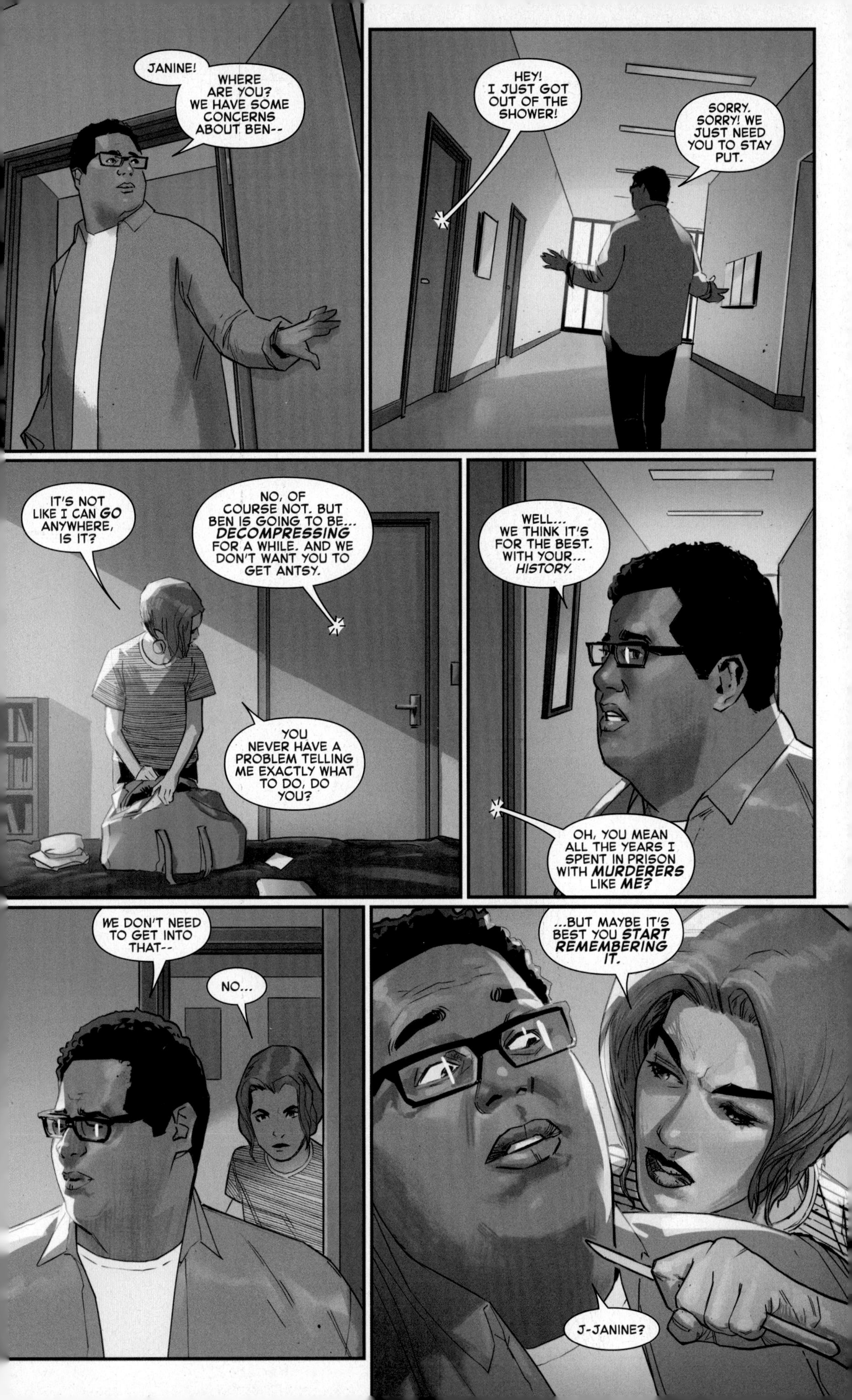
JANINE!
WHERE ARE YOU? WE HAVE SOME CONCERNS ABOUT BEN--
HEY! I JUST GOT OUT OF THE SHOWER!
SORRY. SORRY! WE JUST NEED YOU TO STAY PUT.
IT'S NOT LIKE I CAN GO ANYWHERE, IS IT?
NO, OF COURSE NOT. BUT BEN IS GOING TO BE... DECOMPRESSING FOR A WHILE. AND WE DON'T WANT YOU TO GET ANTSY.
YOU NEVER HAVE A PROBLEM TELLING ME EXACTLY WHAT TO DO, DO YOU?
WELL... WE THINK IT'S FOR THE BEST. WITH YOUR... HISTORY.
OH, YOU MEAN ALL THE YEARS I SPENT IN PRISON WITH MURDERERS LIKE ME?
WE DON'T NEED TO GET INTO THAT--
NO...
...BUT MAYBE IT'S BEST YOU START REMEMBERING IT.
J-JANINE?

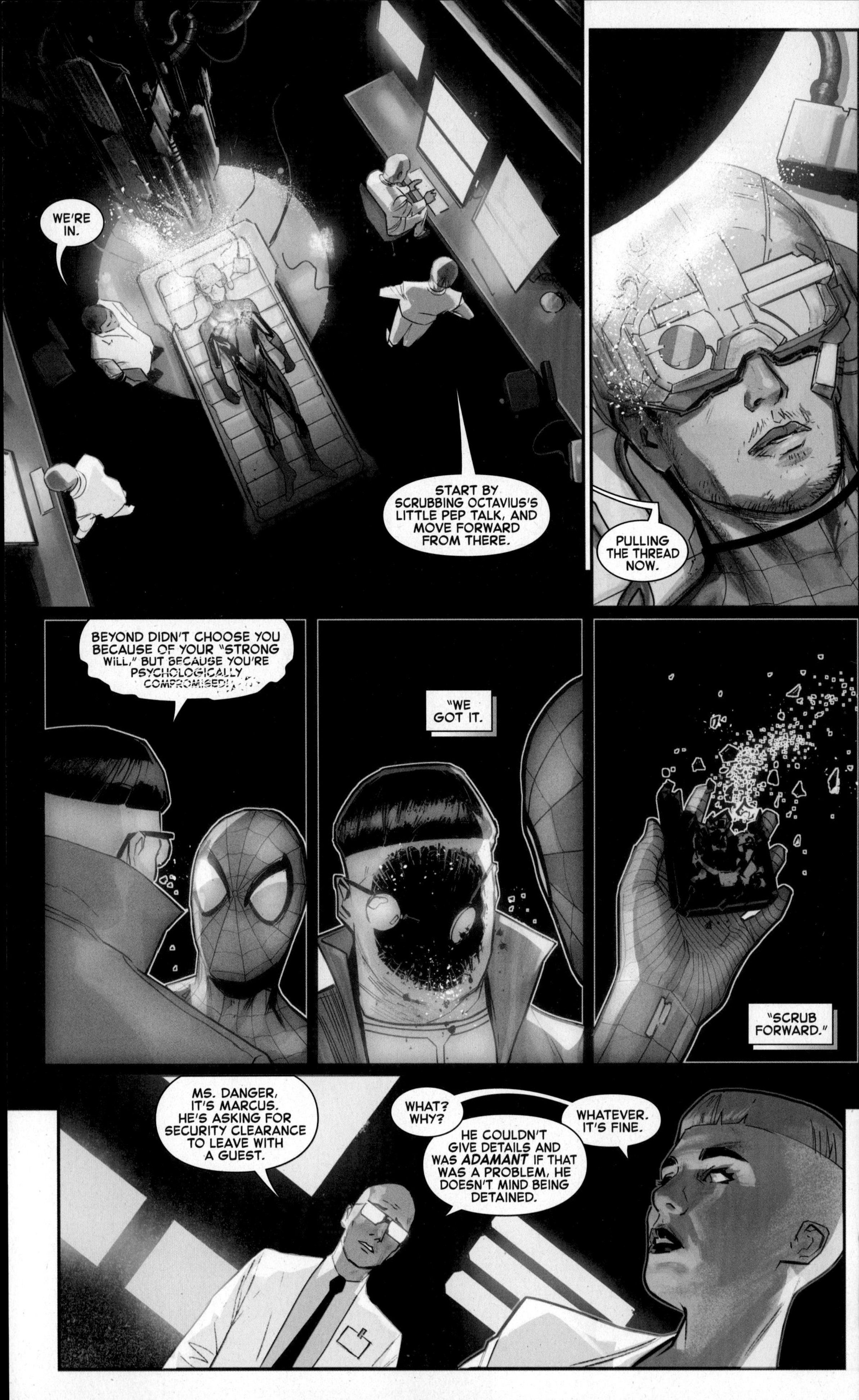
WE'RE IN.
START BY SCRUBBING OCTAVIUS'S LITTLE PEP TALK, AND MOVE FORWARD FROM THERE.
PULLING THE THREAD NOW.
BEYOND DIDN'T CHOOSE YOU BECAUSE OF YOUR "STRONG WILL," BUT BECAUSE YOU'RE PSYCHOLOGICALLY COMPROMISED!
"WE GOT IT.
"SCRUB FORWARD."
MS. DANGER, IT'S MARCUS. HE'S ASKING FOR SECURITY CLEARANCE TO LEAVE WITH A GUEST.
WHAT? WHY?
HE COULDN'T GIVE DETAILS AND WAS *ADAMANT* IF THAT WAS A PROBLEM, HE DOESN'T MIND BEING DETAINED.
WHATEVER. IT'S FINE.

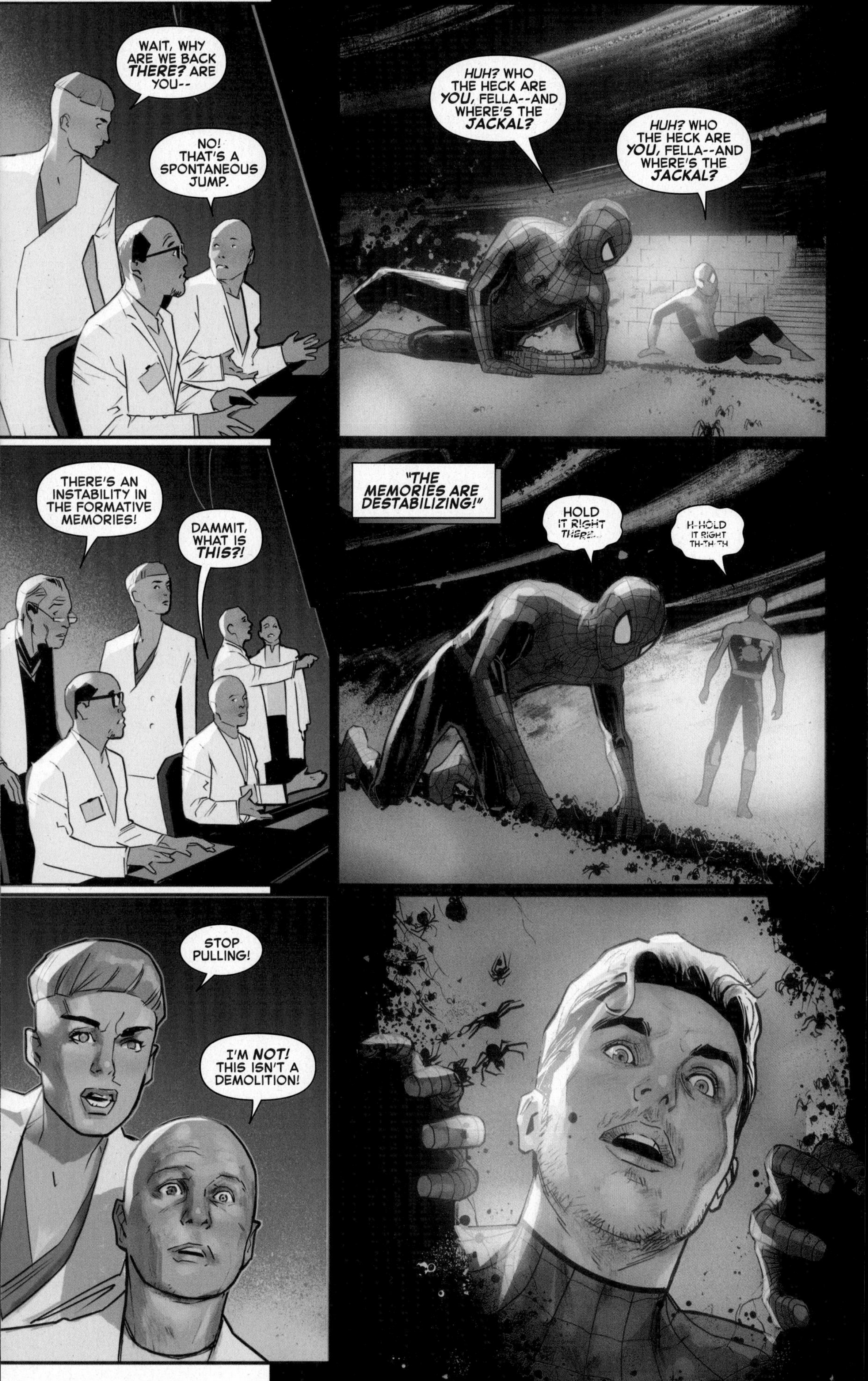
WAIT, WHY ARE WE BACK THERE? ARE YOU--
NO! THAT'S A SPONTANEOUS JUMP.
HUH? WHO THE HECK ARE YOU, FELLA--AND WHERE'S THE JACKAL?
HUH? WHO THE HECK ARE YOU, FELLA--AND WHERE'S THE JACKAL?
THERE'S AN INSTABILITY IN THE FORMATIVE MEMORIES!
DAMMIT, WHAT IS THIS?!
"THE MEMORIES ARE DESTABILIZING!"
HOLD IT RIGHT THERE...
H-HOLD IT RIGHT TH-TH-TH
STOP PULLING!
I'M NOT! THIS ISN'T A DEMOLITION!

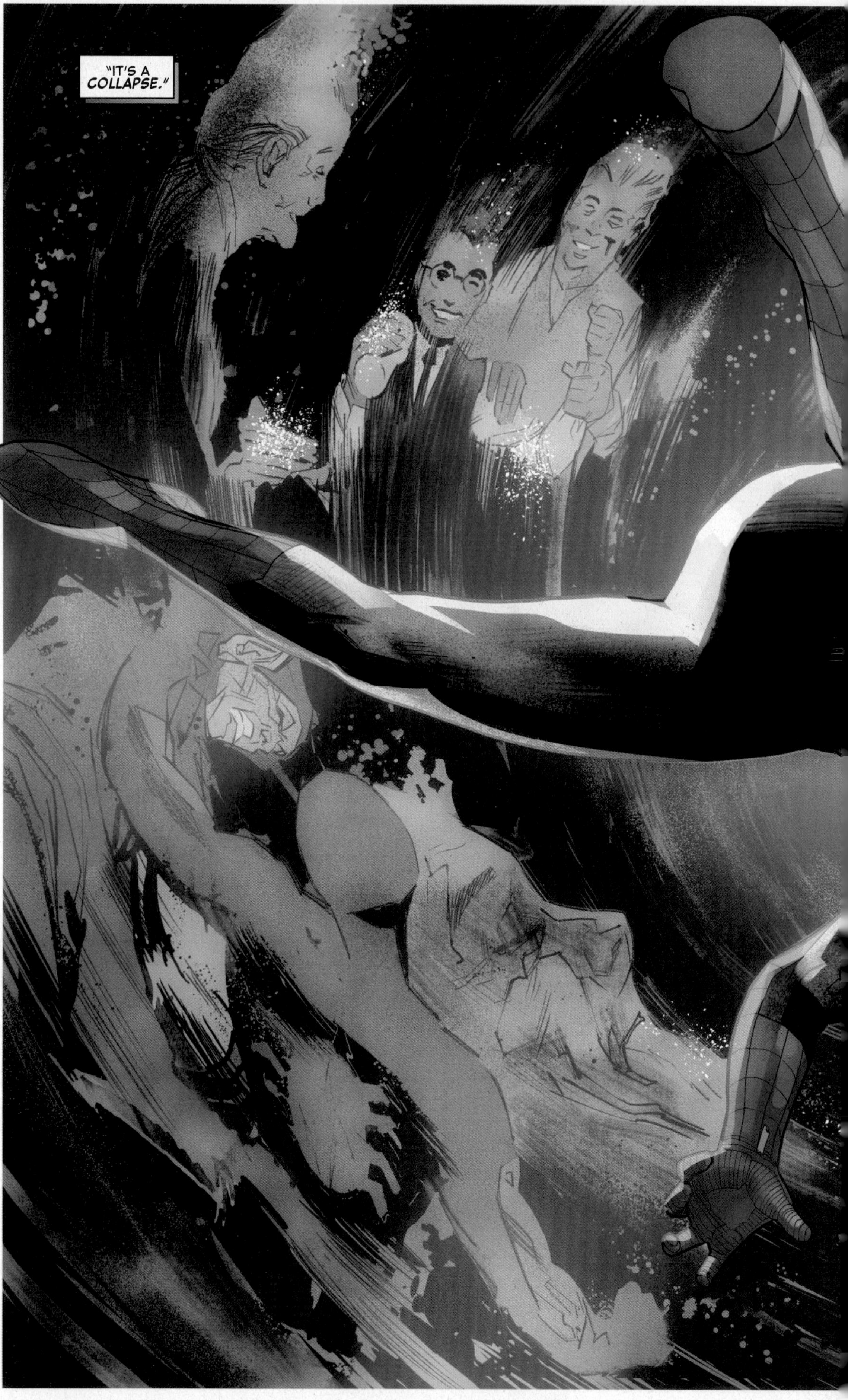
"IT'S A COLLAPSE."

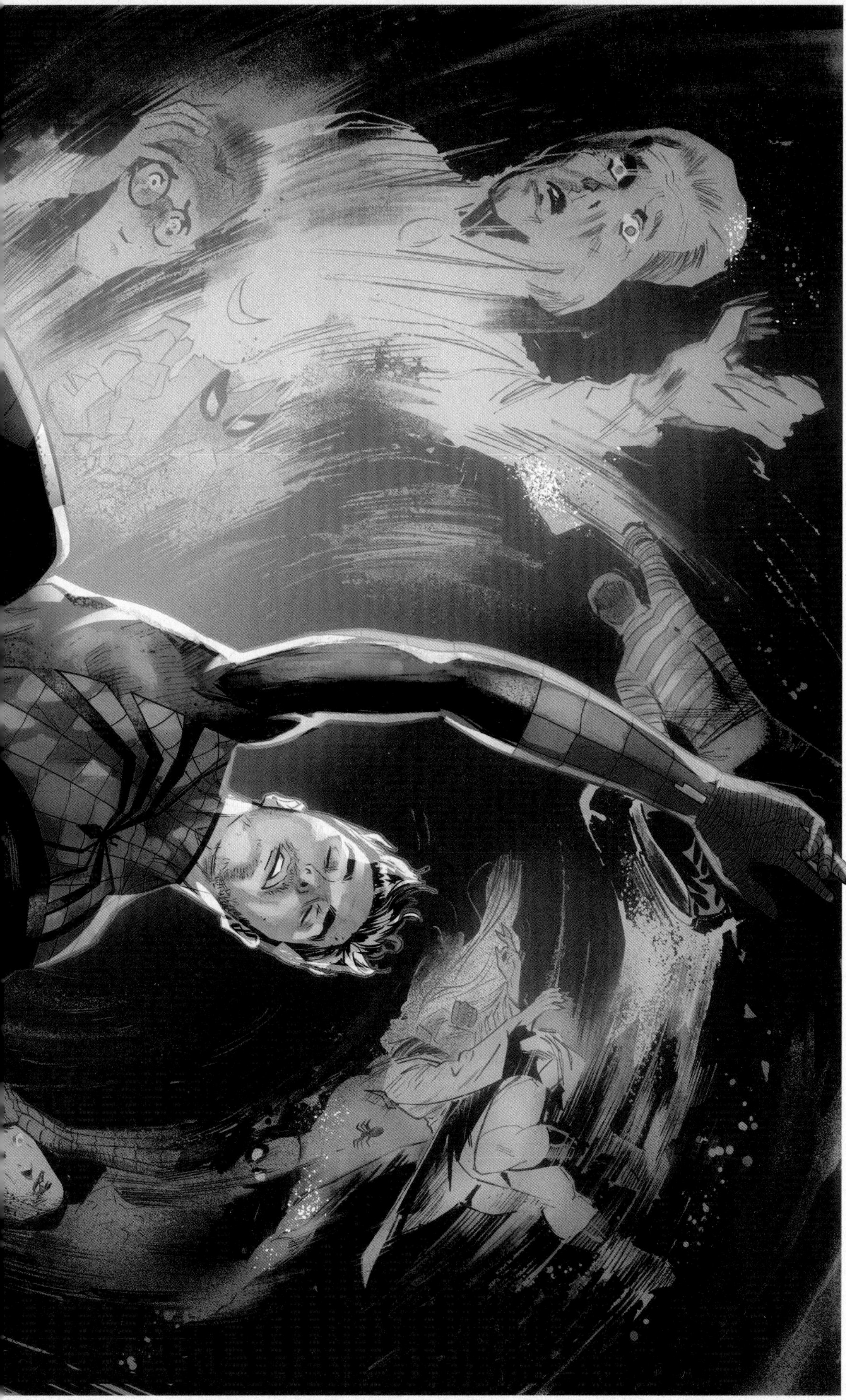

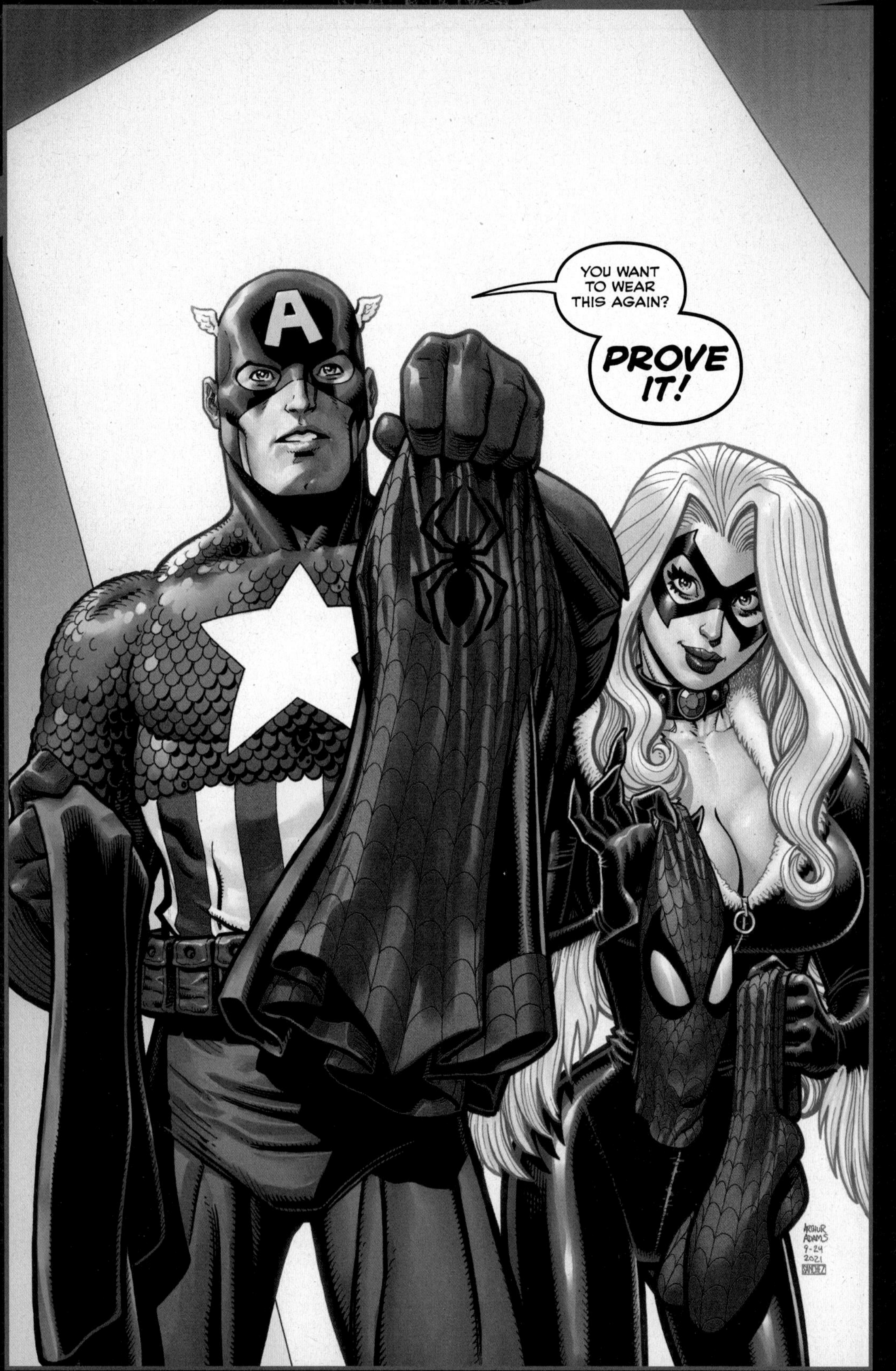
YOU WANT TO WEAR THIS AGAIN?
PROVE IT!
ARTHUR ADAMS 9-24 2021
SANCHEZ

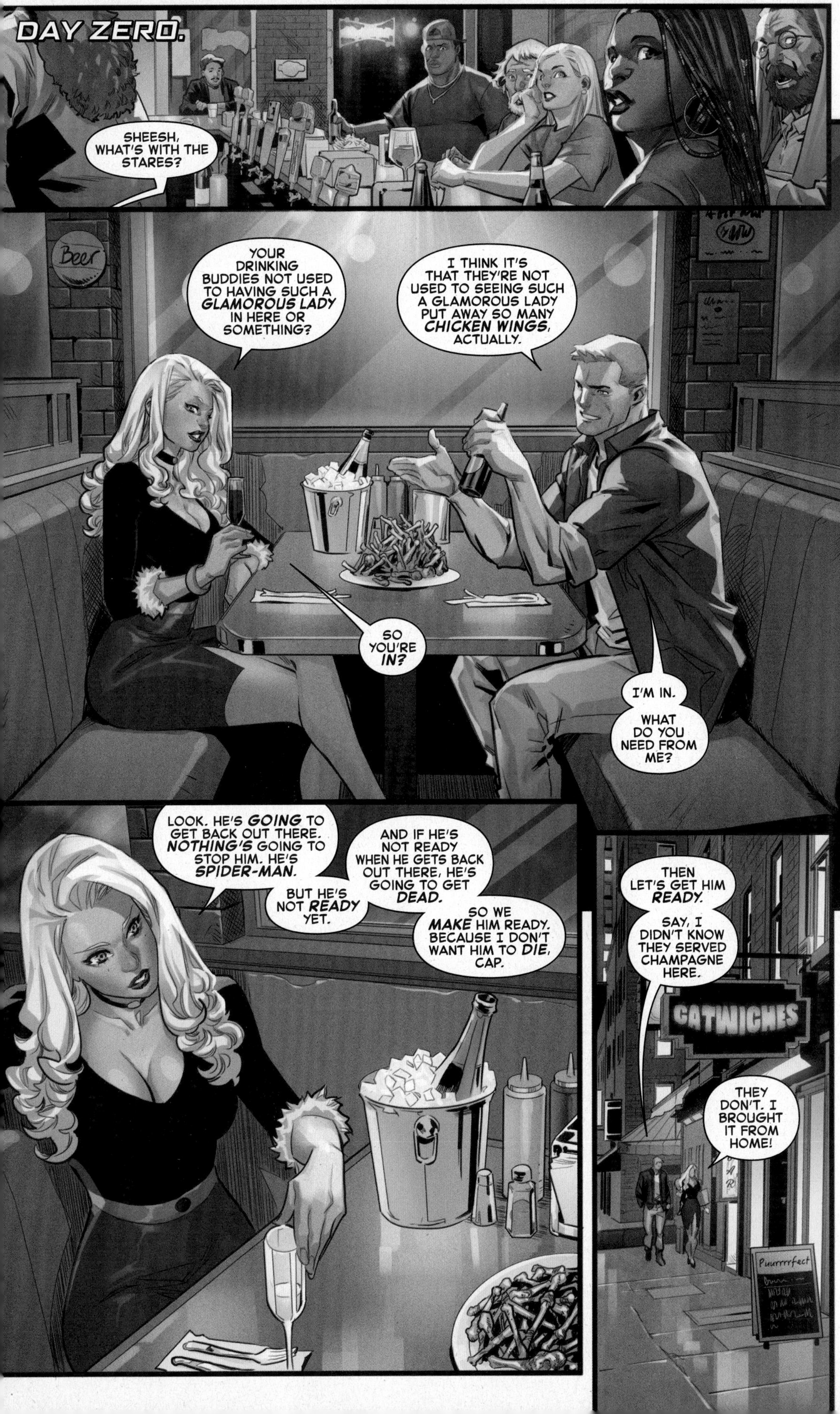

DAY ZERO.
SHEESH, WHAT'S WITH THE STARES?
YOUR DRINKING BUDDIES NOT USED TO HAVING SUCH A GLAMOROUS LADY IN HERE OR SOMETHING?
I THINK IT'S THAT THEY'RE NOT USED TO SEEING SUCH A GLAMOROUS LADY PUT AWAY SO MANY CHICKEN WINGS, ACTUALLY.
Beer
SO YOU'RE IN?
I'M IN.
WHAT DO YOU NEED FROM ME?
LOOK. HE'S GOING TO GET BACK OUT THERE. NOTHING'S GOING TO STOP HIM. HE'S SPIDER-MAN.
BUT HE'S NOT READY YET.
AND IF HE'S NOT READY WHEN HE GETS BACK OUT THERE, HE'S GOING TO GET DEAD.
SO WE MAKE HIM READY. BECAUSE I DON'T WANT HIM TO DIE, CAP.
THEN LET'S GET HIM READY.
SAY, I DIDN'T KNOW THEY SERVED CHAMPAGNE HERE.
CATWICHES
THEY DON'T. I BROUGHT IT FROM HOME!
Puurrrrfect

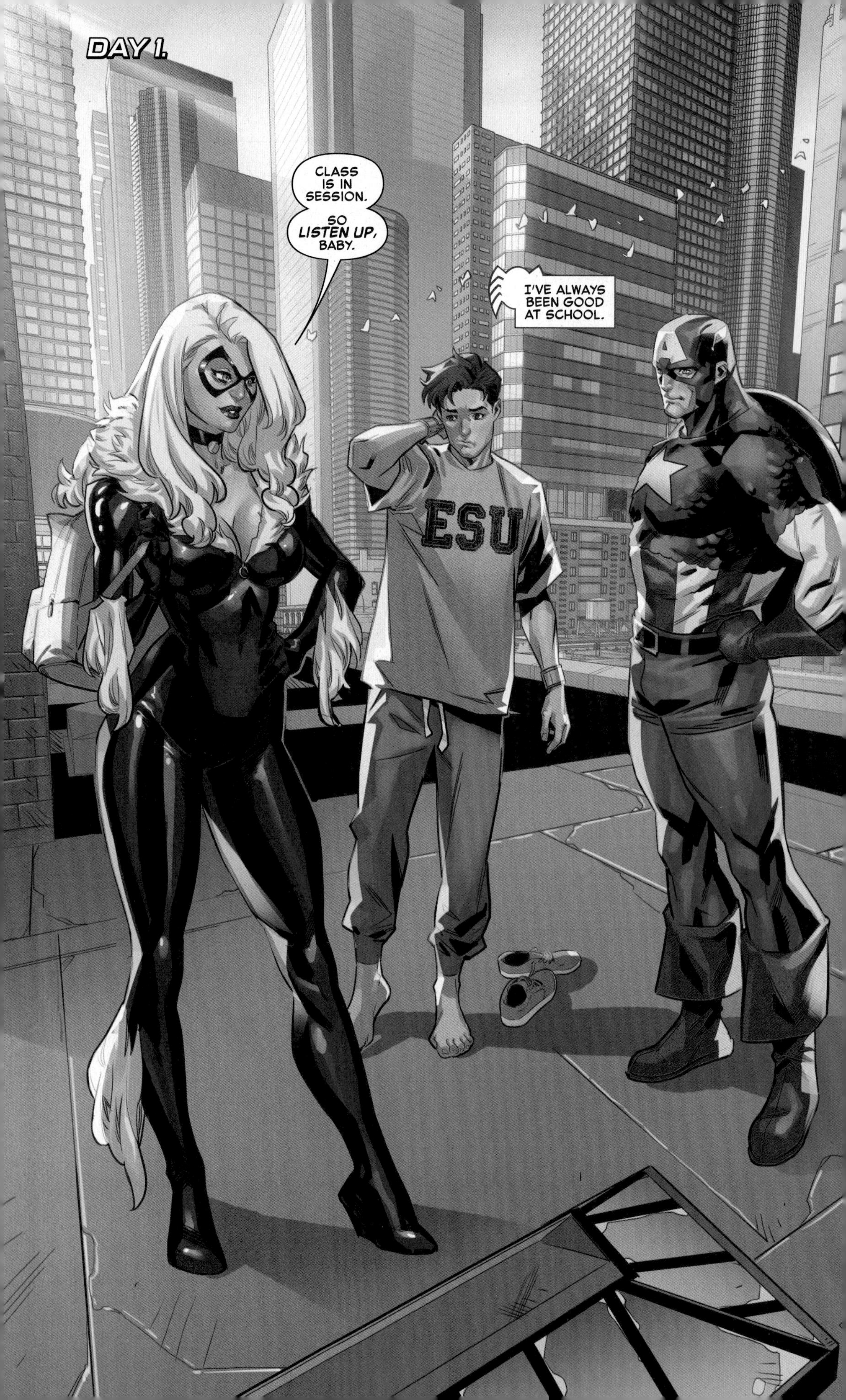

DAY 1.
CLASS IS IN SESSION.
SO LISTEN UP, BABY.
I'VE ALWAYS BEEN GOOD AT SCHOOL.

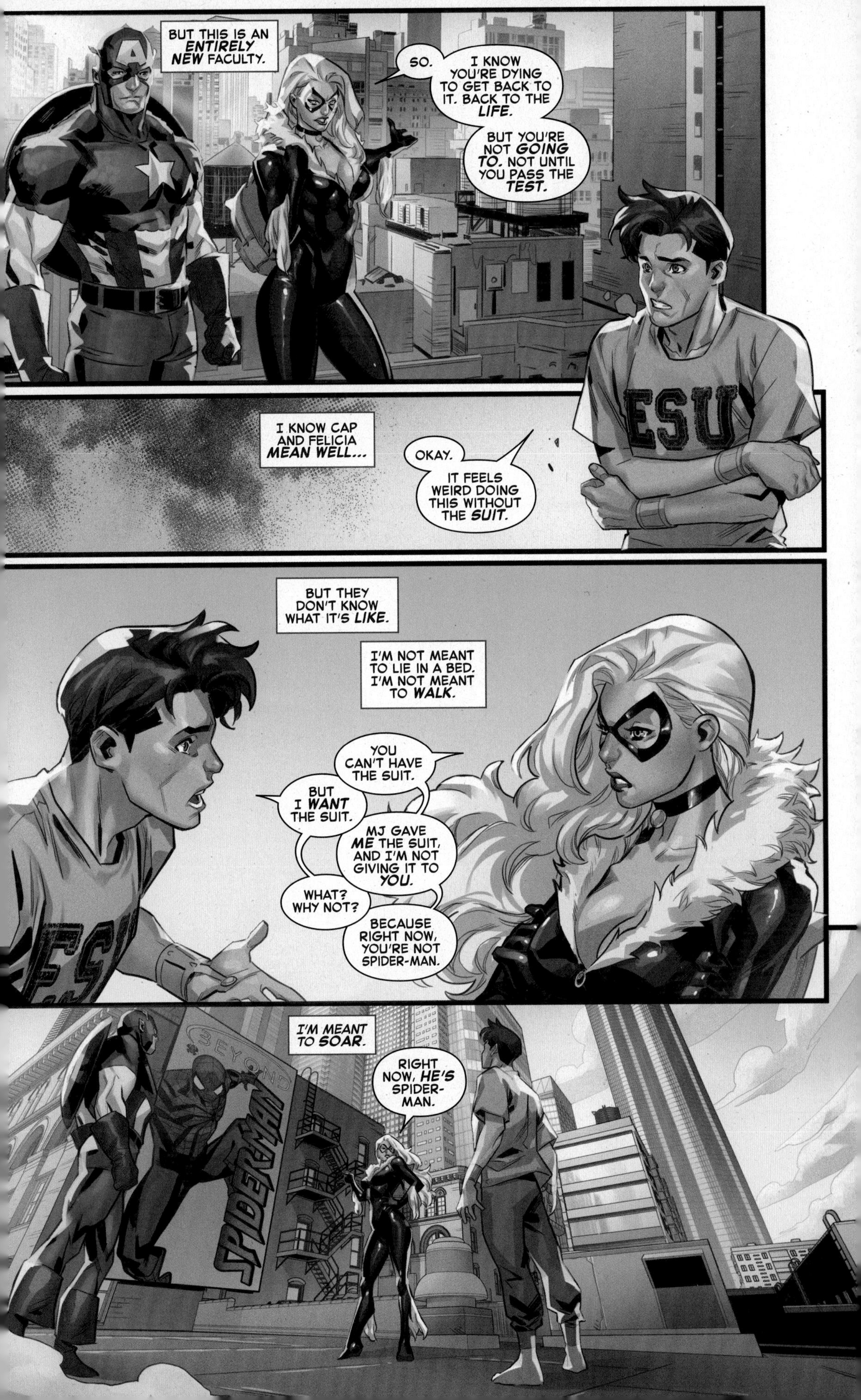
BUT THIS IS AN ENTIRELY NEW FACULTY.
SO.
I KNOW YOU'RE DYING TO GET BACK TO IT. BACK TO THE LIFE.
BUT YOU'RE NOT GOING TO. NOT UNTIL YOU PASS THE TEST.
I KNOW CAP AND FELICIA MEAN WELL...
OKAY.
IT FEELS WEIRD DOING THIS WITHOUT THE SUIT.
ESU
BUT THEY DON'T KNOW WHAT IT'S LIKE.
I'M NOT MEANT TO LIE IN A BED. I'M NOT MEANT TO WALK.
YOU CAN'T HAVE THE SUIT.
BUT I WANT THE SUIT.
MJ GAVE ME THE SUIT, AND I'M NOT GIVING IT TO YOU.
WHAT? WHY NOT?
BECAUSE RIGHT NOW, YOU'RE NOT SPIDER-MAN.
I'M MEANT TO SOAR.
RIGHT NOW, HE'S SPIDER-MAN.
BEYOND
SPIDER-MAN

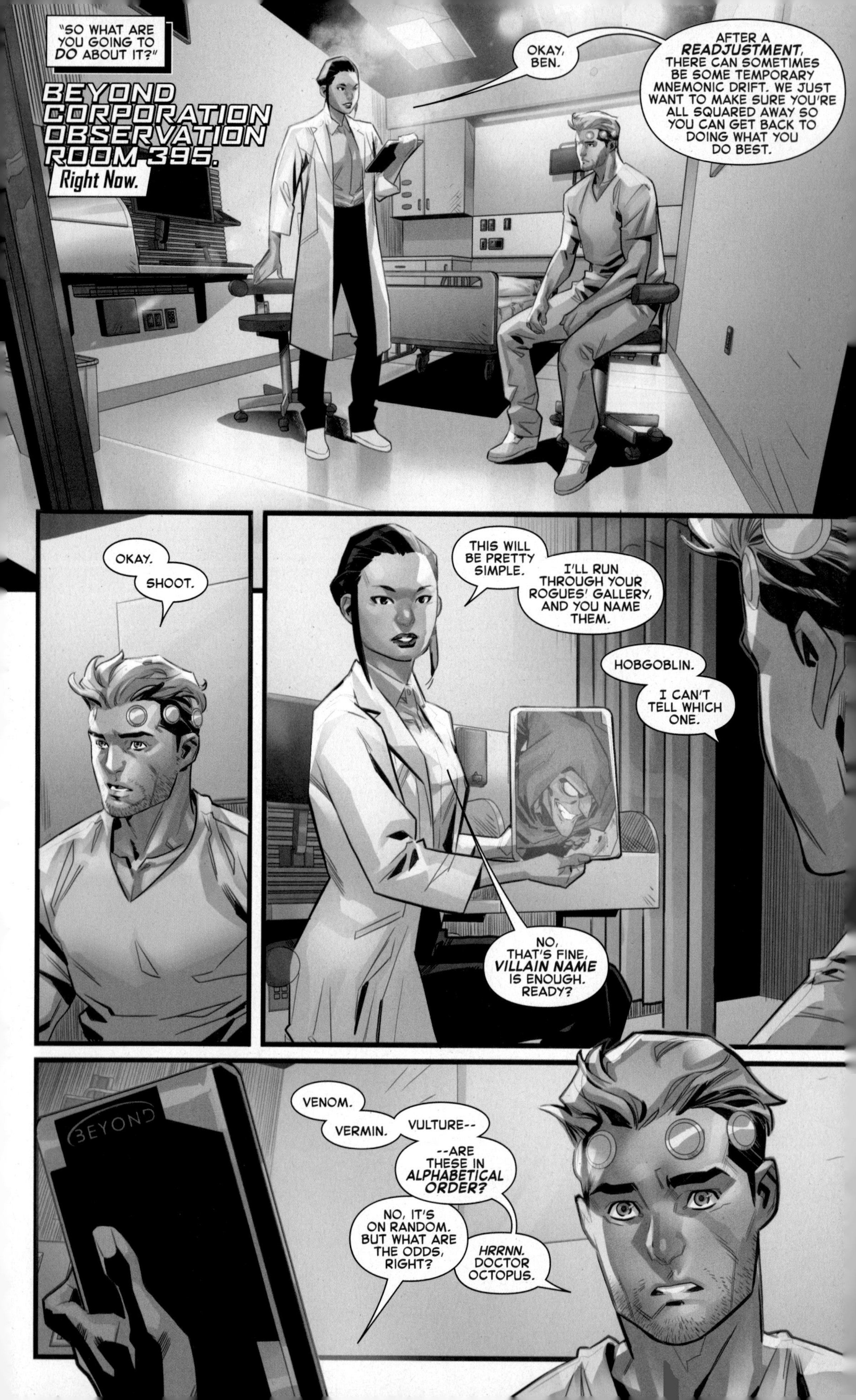
"SO WHAT ARE YOU GOING TO DO ABOUT IT?"
BEYOND CORPORATION OBSERVATION ROOM 395.
Right Now.
OKAY, BEN.
AFTER A READJUSTMENT, THERE CAN SOMETIMES BE SOME TEMPORARY MNEMONIC DRIFT. WE JUST WANT TO MAKE SURE YOU'RE ALL SQUARED AWAY SO YOU CAN GET BACK TO DOING WHAT YOU DO BEST.
OKAY.
SHOOT.
THIS WILL BE PRETTY SIMPLE.
I'LL RUN THROUGH YOUR ROGUES' GALLERY, AND YOU NAME THEM.
HOBGOBLIN.
I CAN'T TELL WHICH ONE.
NO, THAT'S FINE, VILLAIN NAME IS ENOUGH. READY?
BEYOND
VENOM.
VERMIN.
VULTURE--
--ARE THESE IN ALPHABETICAL ORDER?
NO, IT'S ON RANDOM. BUT WHAT ARE THE ODDS, RIGHT?
HRRNN. DOCTOR OCTOPUS.

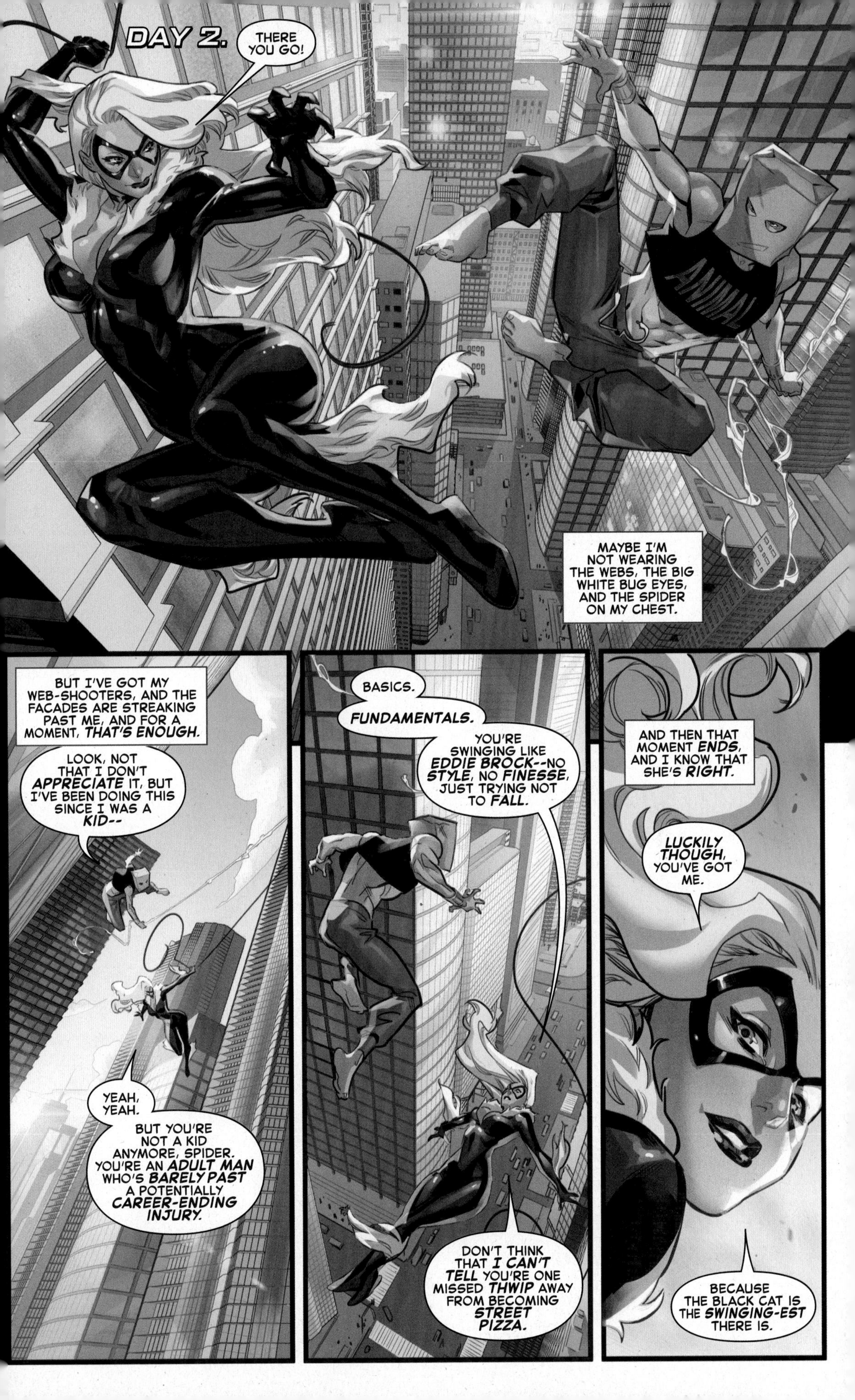
DAY 2.
THERE YOU GO!
MAYBE I'M NOT WEARING THE WEBS, THE BIG WHITE BUG EYES, AND THE SPIDER ON MY CHEST.
BUT I'VE GOT MY WEB-SHOOTERS, AND THE FACADES ARE STREAKING PAST ME, AND FOR A MOMENT, THAT'S ENOUGH.
LOOK, NOT THAT I DON'T APPRECIATE IT, BUT I'VE BEEN DOING THIS SINCE I WAS A KID--
YEAH, YEAH.
BUT YOU'RE NOT A KID ANYMORE, SPIDER. YOU'RE AN ADULT MAN WHO'S BARELY PAST A POTENTIALLY CAREER-ENDING INJURY.
BASICS.
FUNDAMENTALS.
YOU'RE SWINGING LIKE EDDIE BROCK--NO STYLE, NO FINESSE, JUST TRYING NOT TO FALL.
DON'T THINK THAT I CAN'T TELL YOU'RE ONE MISSED THWIP AWAY FROM BECOMING STREET PIZZA.
AND THEN THAT MOMENT ENDS, AND I KNOW THAT SHE'S RIGHT.
LUCKILY THOUGH, YOU'VE GOT ME.
BECAUSE THE BLACK CAT IS THE SWINGING-EST THERE IS.

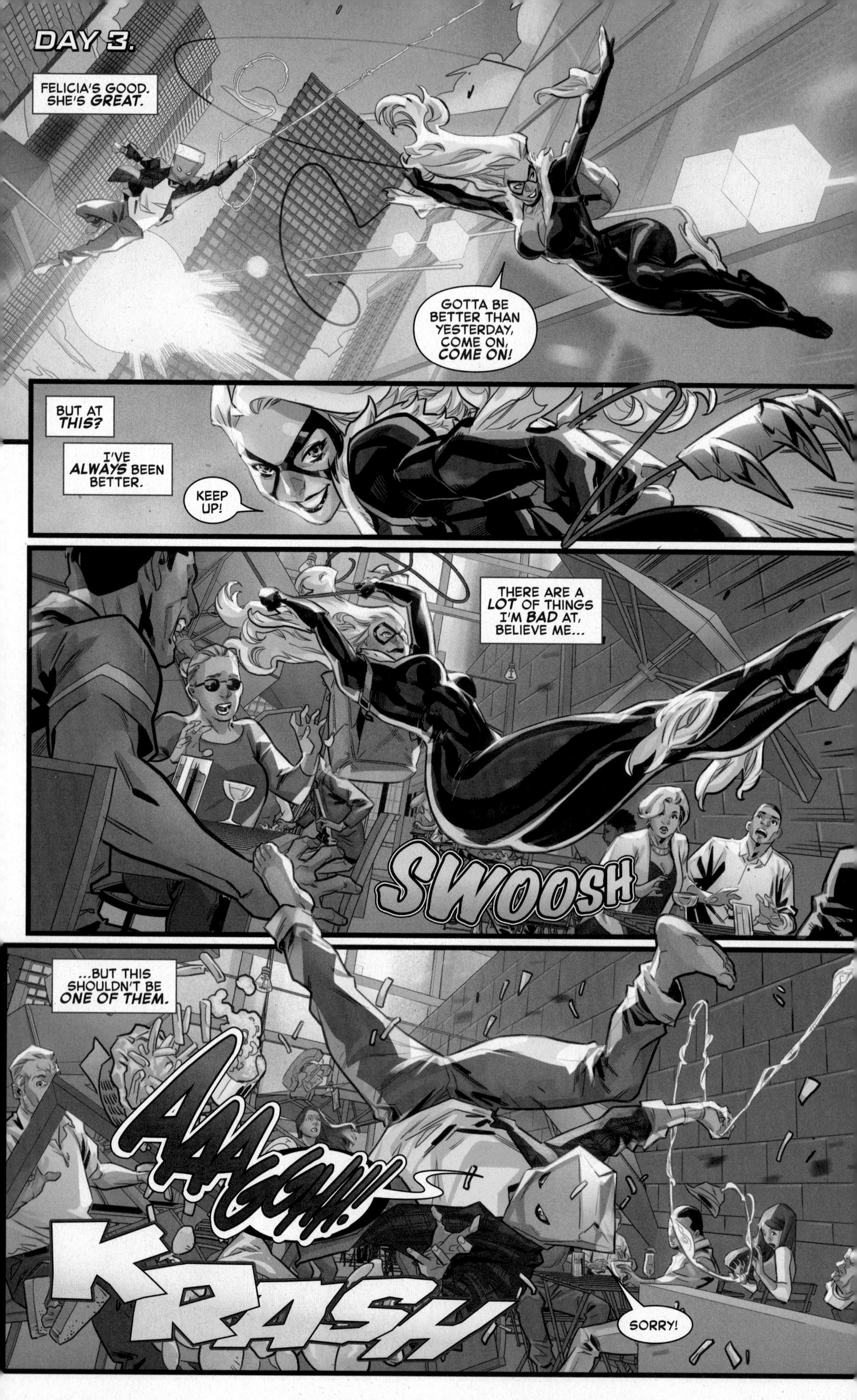
DAY 3.
FELICIA'S GOOD. SHE'S GREAT.
GOTTA BE BETTER THAN YESTERDAY, COME ON, COME ON!
BUT AT THIS?
I'VE ALWAYS BEEN BETTER.
KEEP UP!
THERE ARE A LOT OF THINGS I'M BAD AT, BELIEVE ME...
SWOOSH
...BUT THIS SHOULDN'T BE ONE OF THEM.
AAAGGH!!
KRASH
SORRY!

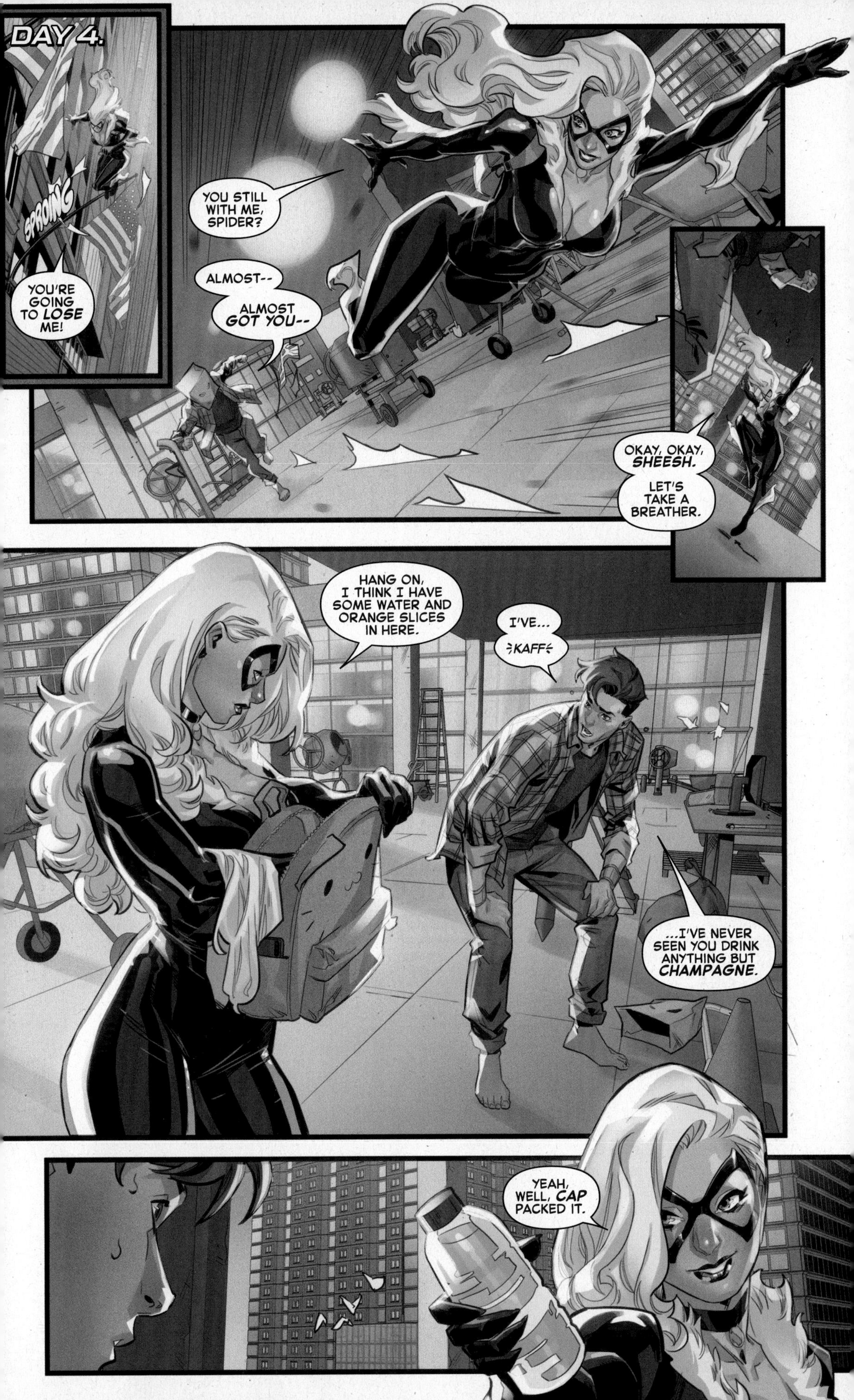
DAY 4.
SPROING
YOU'RE GOING TO LOSE ME!
YOU STILL WITH ME, SPIDER?
ALMOST--
ALMOST GOT YOU--
OKAY, OKAY, SHEESH.
LET'S TAKE A BREATHER.
HANG ON, I THINK I HAVE SOME WATER AND ORANGE SLICES IN HERE.
I'VE...
KAFF
...I'VE NEVER SEEN YOU DRINK ANYTHING BUT CHAMPAGNE.
YEAH, WELL, CAP PACKED IT.

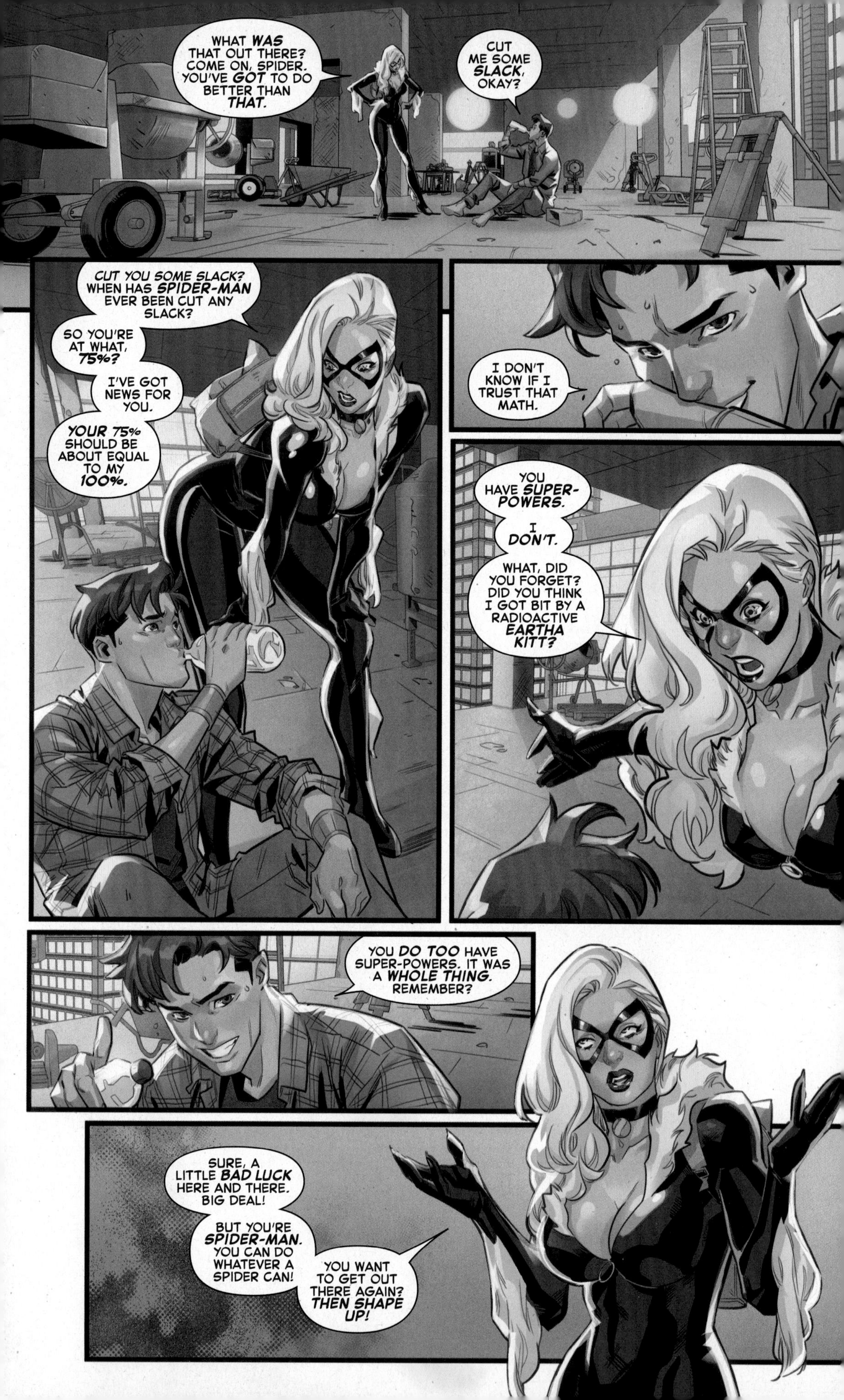
WHAT WAS THAT OUT THERE? COME ON, SPIDER. YOU'VE GOT TO DO BETTER THAN THAT.
CUT ME SOME SLACK, OKAY?
CUT YOU SOME SLACK? WHEN HAS SPIDER-MAN EVER BEEN CUT ANY SLACK?
SO YOU'RE AT WHAT, 75%?
I'VE GOT NEWS FOR YOU.
YOUR 75% SHOULD BE ABOUT EQUAL TO MY 100%.
I DON'T KNOW IF I TRUST THAT MATH.
YOU HAVE SUPER-POWERS.
I DON'T.
WHAT, DID YOU FORGET? DID YOU THINK I GOT BIT BY A RADIOACTIVE EARTHA KITT?
YOU DO TOO HAVE SUPER-POWERS. IT WAS A WHOLE THING. REMEMBER?
SURE, A LITTLE BAD LUCK HERE AND THERE. BIG DEAL!
BUT YOU'RE SPIDER-MAN. YOU CAN DO WHATEVER A SPIDER CAN!
YOU WANT TO GET OUT THERE AGAIN? THEN SHAPE UP!

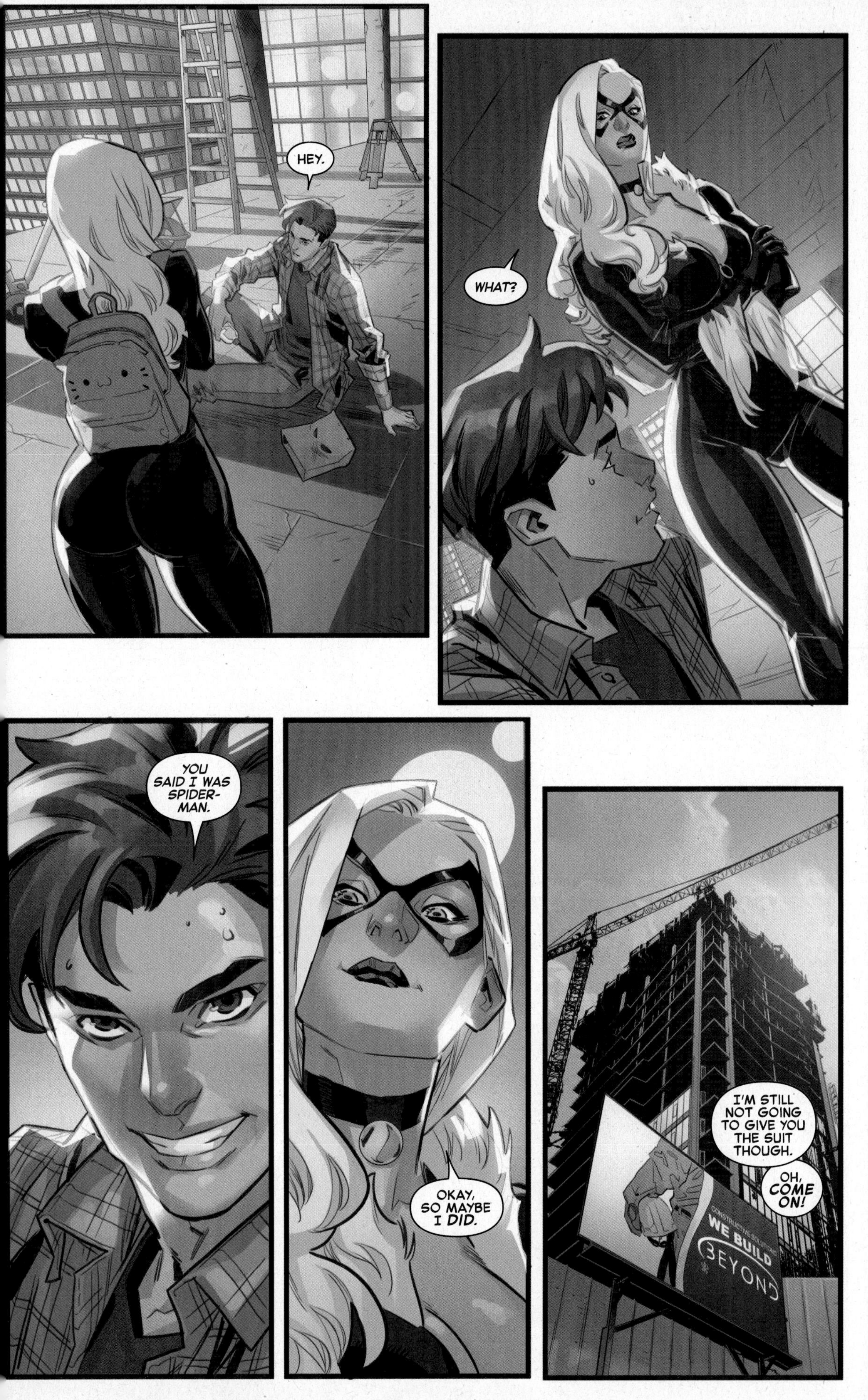
HEY.
WHAT?
YOU SAID I WAS SPIDER-MAN.
OKAY, SO MAYBE I *DID*.
I'M STILL NOT GOING TO GIVE YOU THE SUIT THOUGH.
OH, *COME ON!*
CONSTRUCTIVE SOLUTIONS
WE BUILD
BEYOND

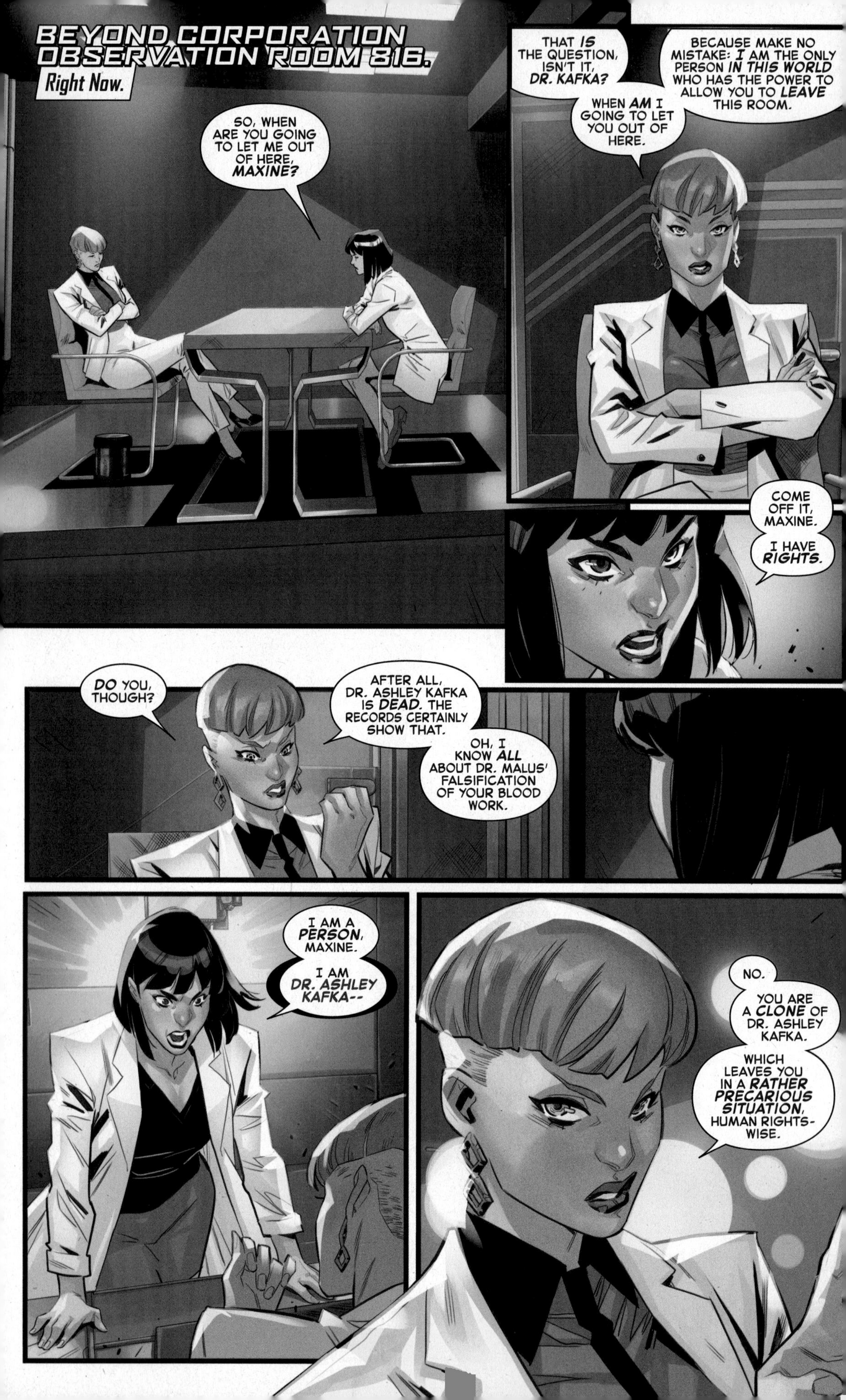
BEYOND CORPORATION OBSERVATION ROOM 816.
Right Now.
SO, WHEN ARE YOU GOING TO LET ME OUT OF HERE, MAXINE?
THAT IS THE QUESTION, ISN'T IT, DR. KAFKA?
WHEN AM I GOING TO LET YOU OUT OF HERE.
BECAUSE MAKE NO MISTAKE: I AM THE ONLY PERSON IN THIS WORLD WHO HAS THE POWER TO ALLOW YOU TO LEAVE THIS ROOM.
COME OFF IT, MAXINE.
I HAVE RIGHTS.
DO YOU, THOUGH?
AFTER ALL, DR. ASHLEY KAFKA IS DEAD. THE RECORDS CERTAINLY SHOW THAT.
OH, I KNOW ALL ABOUT DR. MALUS' FALSIFICATION OF YOUR BLOOD WORK.
I AM A PERSON, MAXINE.
I AM DR. ASHLEY KAFKA--
NO.
YOU ARE A CLONE OF DR. ASHLEY KAFKA.
WHICH LEAVES YOU IN A RATHER PRECARIOUS SITUATION, HUMAN RIGHTS-WISE.

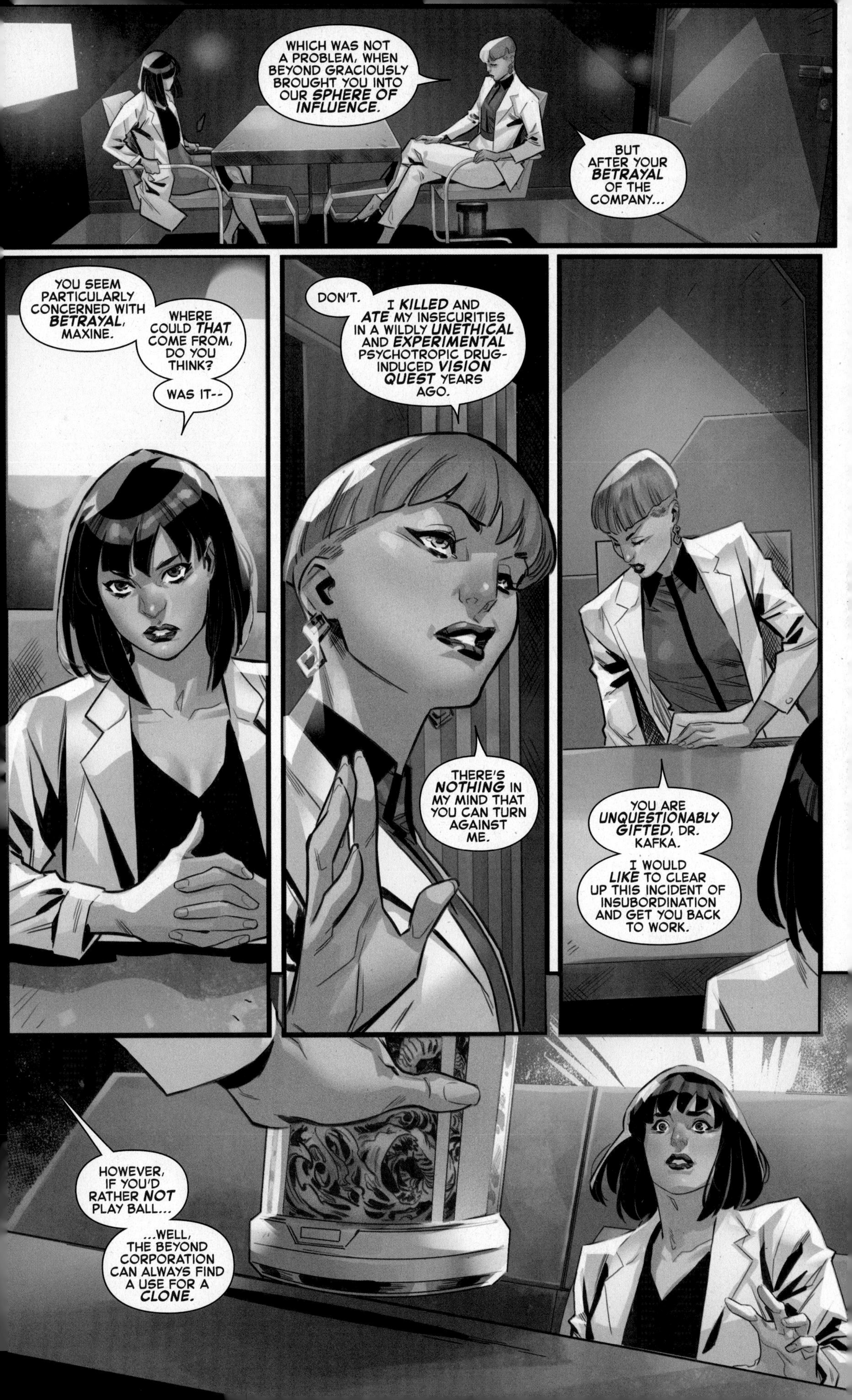
WHICH WAS NOT A PROBLEM, WHEN BEYOND GRACIOUSLY BROUGHT YOU INTO OUR SPHERE OF INFLUENCE.
BUT AFTER YOUR BETRAYAL OF THE COMPANY...
YOU SEEM PARTICULARLY CONCERNED WITH BETRAYAL, MAXINE.
WHERE COULD THAT COME FROM, DO YOU THINK?
WAS IT--
DON'T.
I KILLED AND ATE MY INSECURITIES IN A WILDLY UNETHICAL AND EXPERIMENTAL PSYCHOTROPIC DRUG-INDUCED VISION QUEST YEARS AGO.
THERE'S NOTHING IN MY MIND THAT YOU CAN TURN AGAINST ME.
YOU ARE UNQUESTIONABLY GIFTED, DR. KAFKA.
I WOULD LIKE TO CLEAR UP THIS INCIDENT OF INSUBORDINATION AND GET YOU BACK TO WORK.
HOWEVER, IF YOU'D RATHER NOT PLAY BALL...
...WELL, THE BEYOND CORPORATION CAN ALWAYS FIND A USE FOR A CLONE.

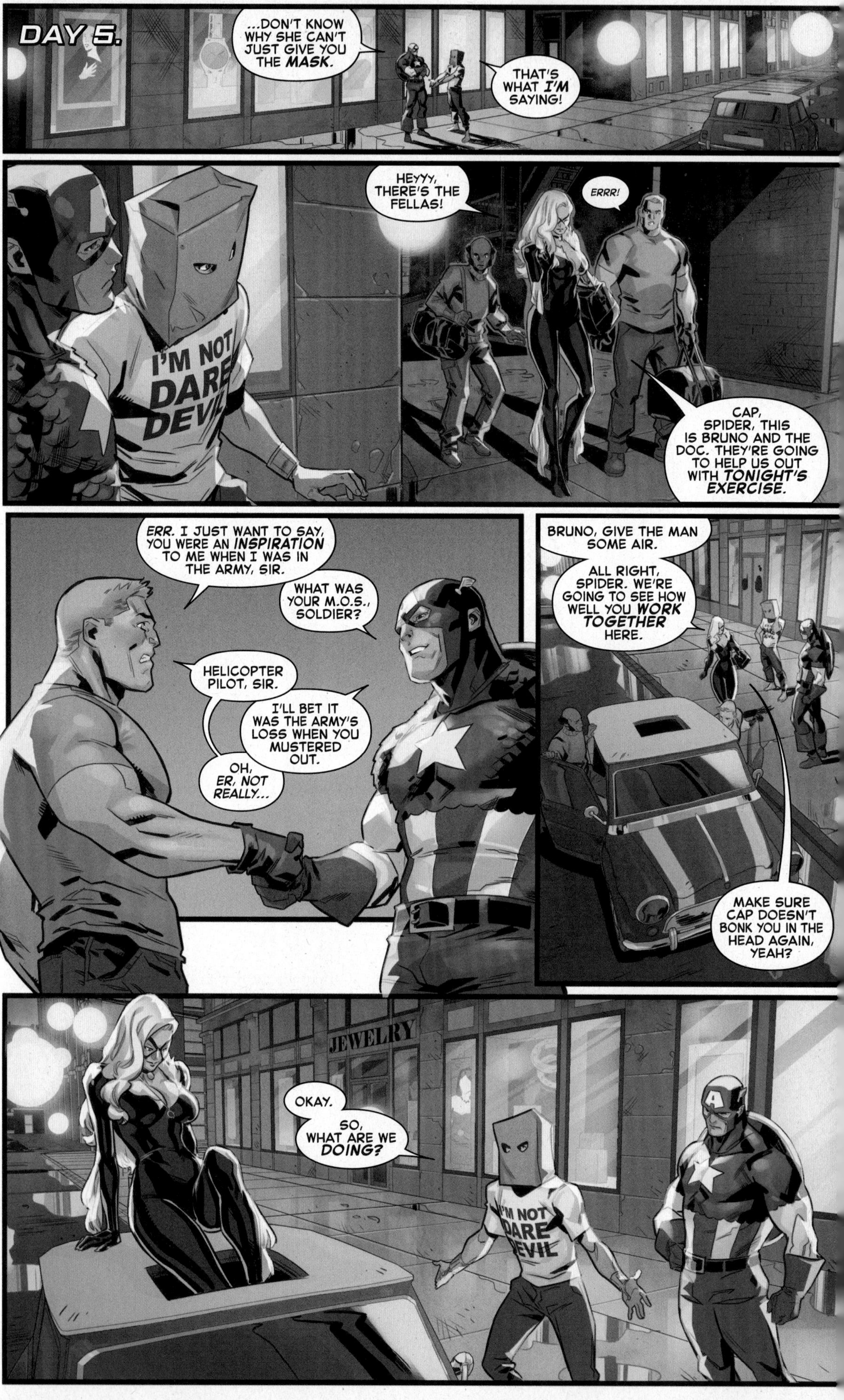
DAY 5.
...DON'T KNOW WHY SHE CAN'T JUST GIVE YOU THE MASK.
THAT'S WHAT I'M SAYING!
HEYYY, THERE'S THE FELLAS!
ERRR!
CAP, SPIDER, THIS IS BRUNO AND THE DOC. THEY'RE GOING TO HELP US OUT WITH TONIGHT'S EXERCISE.
I'M NOT DARE DEVIL
ERR. I JUST WANT TO SAY, YOU WERE AN INSPIRATION TO ME WHEN I WAS IN THE ARMY, SIR.
WHAT WAS YOUR M.O.S., SOLDIER?
HELICOPTER PILOT, SIR.
I'LL BET IT WAS THE ARMY'S LOSS WHEN YOU MUSTERED OUT.
OH, ER, NOT REALLY...
BRUNO, GIVE THE MAN SOME AIR.
ALL RIGHT, SPIDER. WE'RE GOING TO SEE HOW WELL YOU WORK TOGETHER HERE.
MAKE SURE CAP DOESN'T BONK YOU IN THE HEAD AGAIN, YEAH?
JEWELRY
OKAY.
SO, WHAT ARE WE DOING?
I'M NOT DARE DEVIL

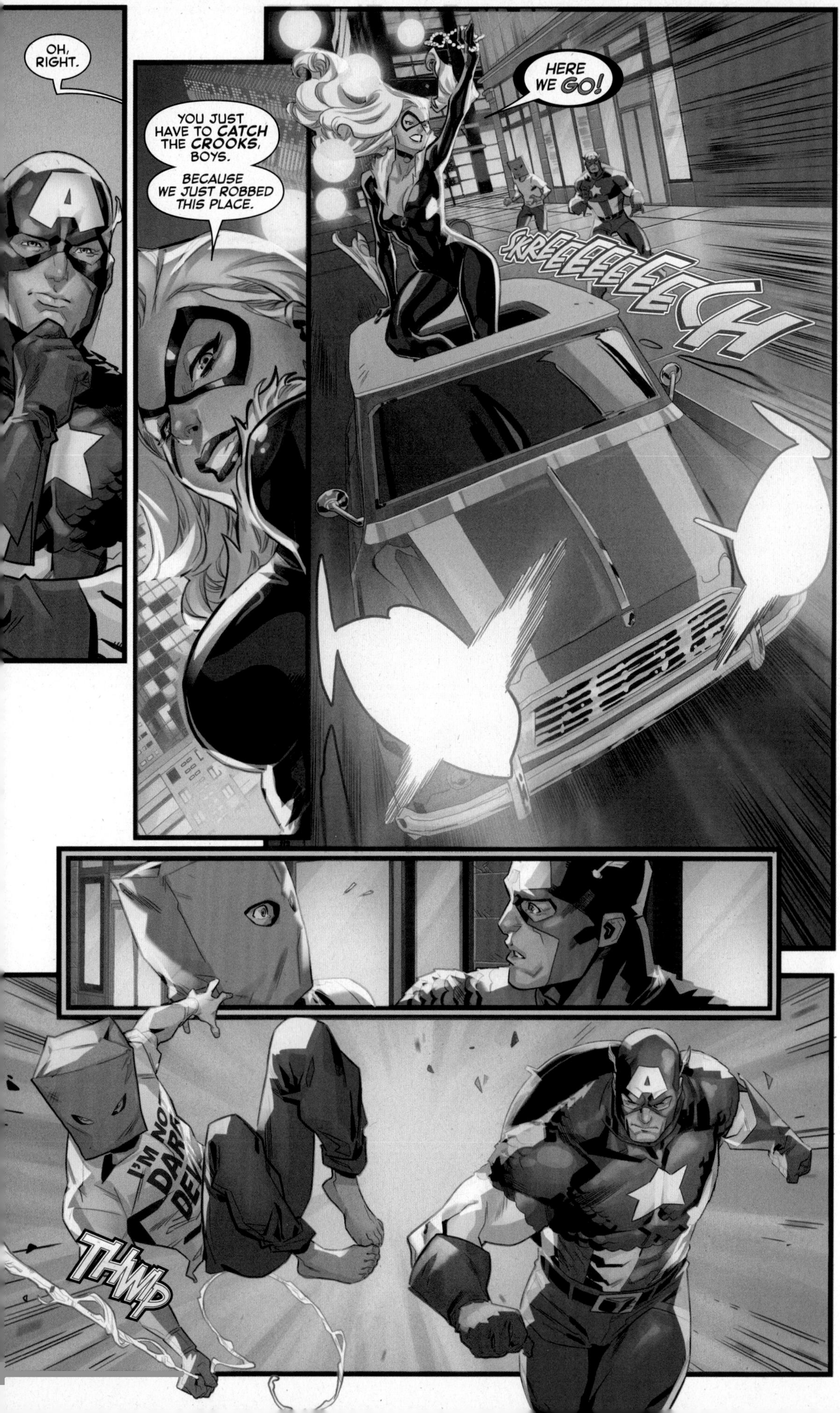
OH, RIGHT.
YOU JUST HAVE TO CATCH THE CROOKS, BOYS.
BECAUSE WE JUST ROBBED THIS PLACE.
HERE WE GO!
SKREEEEEEEECH
I'M NOT DARE DEV
THWIP

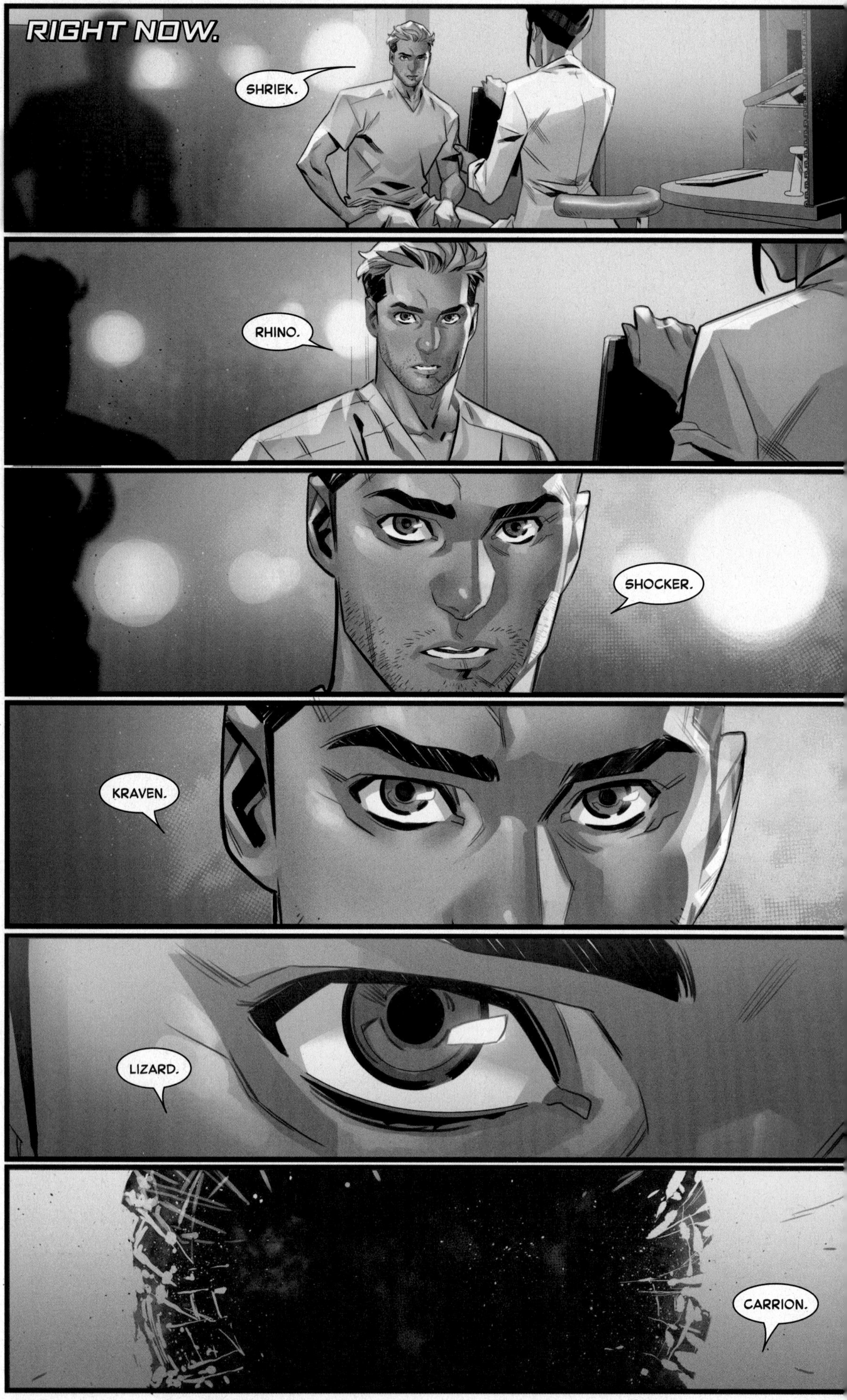
RIGHT NOW.
SHRIEK.
RHINO.
SHOCKER.
KRAVEN.
LIZARD.
CARRION.

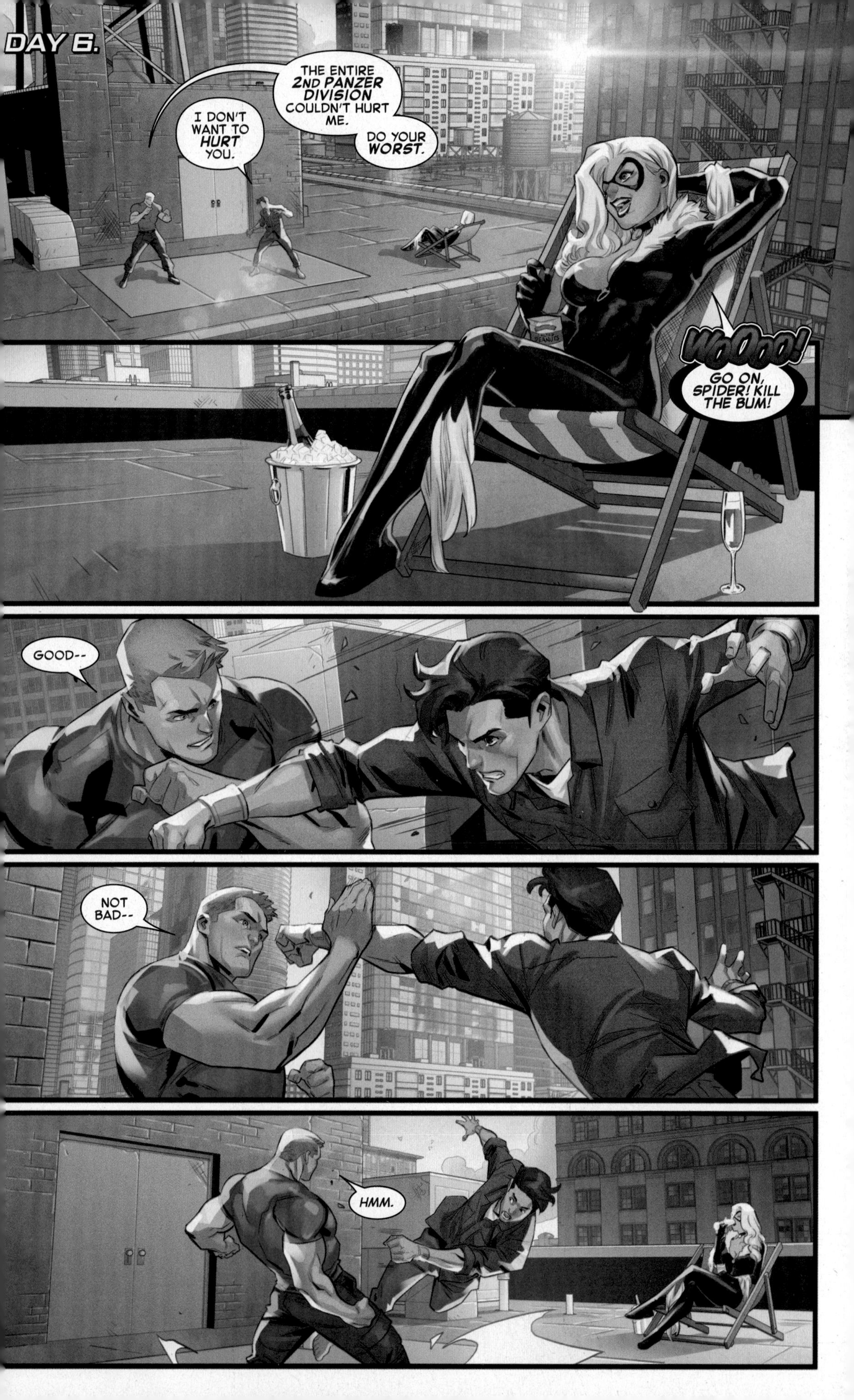
DAY 6.
I DON'T WANT TO HURT YOU.
THE ENTIRE 2nd PANZER DIVISION COULDN'T HURT ME.
DO YOUR WORST.
WOOOOO!
GO ON, SPIDER! KILL THE BUM!
GOOD--
NOT BAD--
HMM.

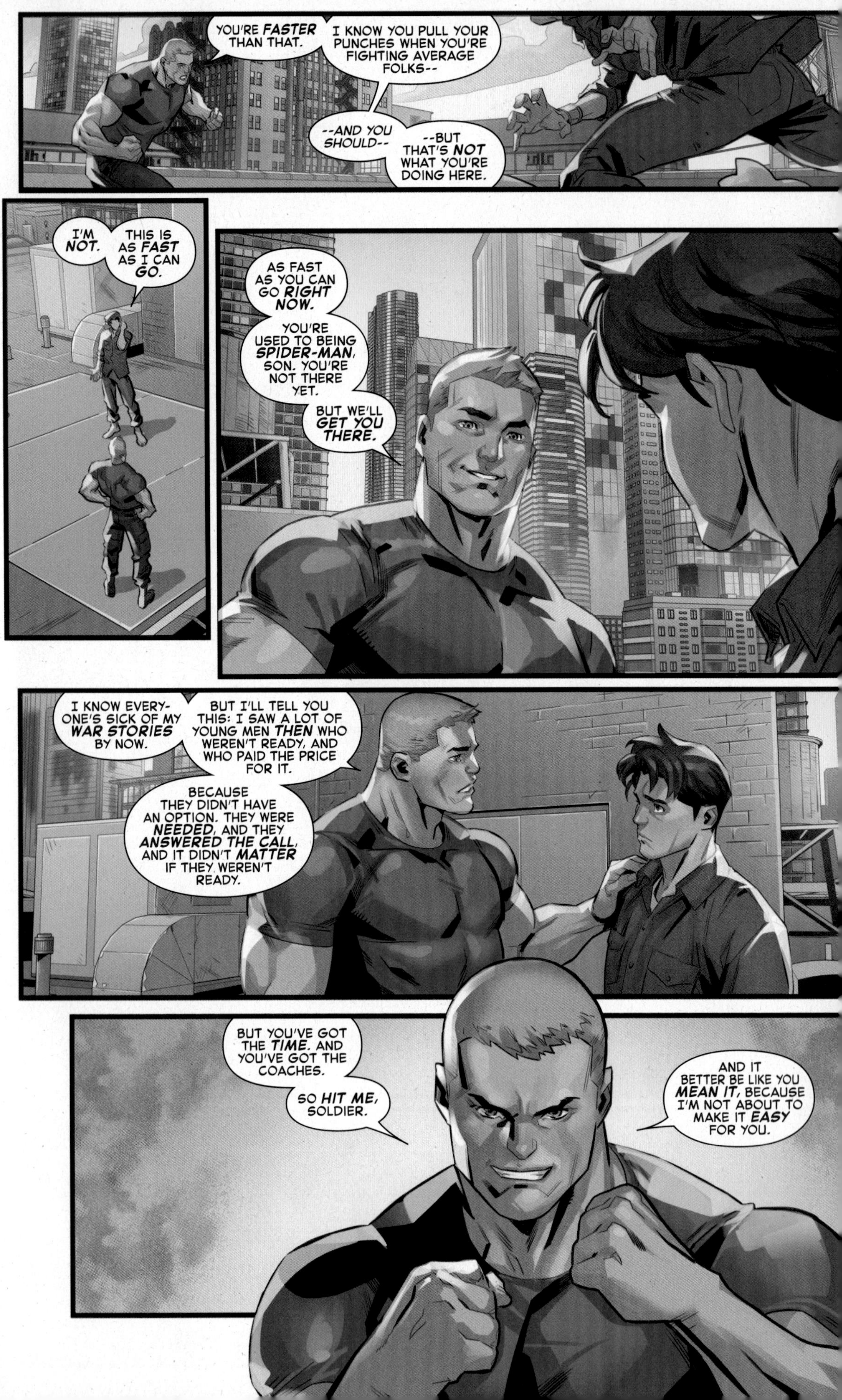
YOU'RE FASTER THAN THAT.
I KNOW YOU PULL YOUR PUNCHES WHEN YOU'RE FIGHTING AVERAGE FOLKS--
--AND YOU SHOULD--
--BUT THAT'S NOT WHAT YOU'RE DOING HERE.
I'M NOT.
THIS IS AS FAST AS I CAN GO.
AS FAST AS YOU CAN GO RIGHT NOW.
YOU'RE USED TO BEING SPIDER-MAN, SON. YOU'RE NOT THERE YET.
BUT WE'LL GET YOU THERE.
I KNOW EVERY-ONE'S SICK OF MY WAR STORIES BY NOW.
BUT I'LL TELL YOU THIS: I SAW A LOT OF YOUNG MEN THEN WHO WEREN'T READY, AND WHO PAID THE PRICE FOR IT.
BECAUSE THEY DIDN'T HAVE AN OPTION. THEY WERE NEEDED, AND THEY ANSWERED THE CALL, AND IT DIDN'T MATTER IF THEY WEREN'T READY.
BUT YOU'VE GOT THE TIME. AND YOU'VE GOT THE COACHES.
SO HIT ME, SOLDIER.
AND IT BETTER BE LIKE YOU MEAN IT, BECAUSE I'M NOT ABOUT TO MAKE IT EASY FOR YOU.

THAT SHOULD DO IT! I'LL JUST TAKE *THESE* BACK...

THAT'S IT! YOU'RE CLEARED FOR THE FIELD.

YOU MUST BE RARING TO GO, I'LL BET.

LIKE YOU SAID THE OTHER DAY, "WITH GREAT POWER, THERE MUST ALSO COME..."

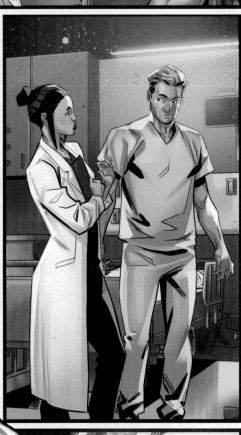

I DON'T GET IT.

WITH GREAT POWER THERE MUST ALSO COME *WHAT?*

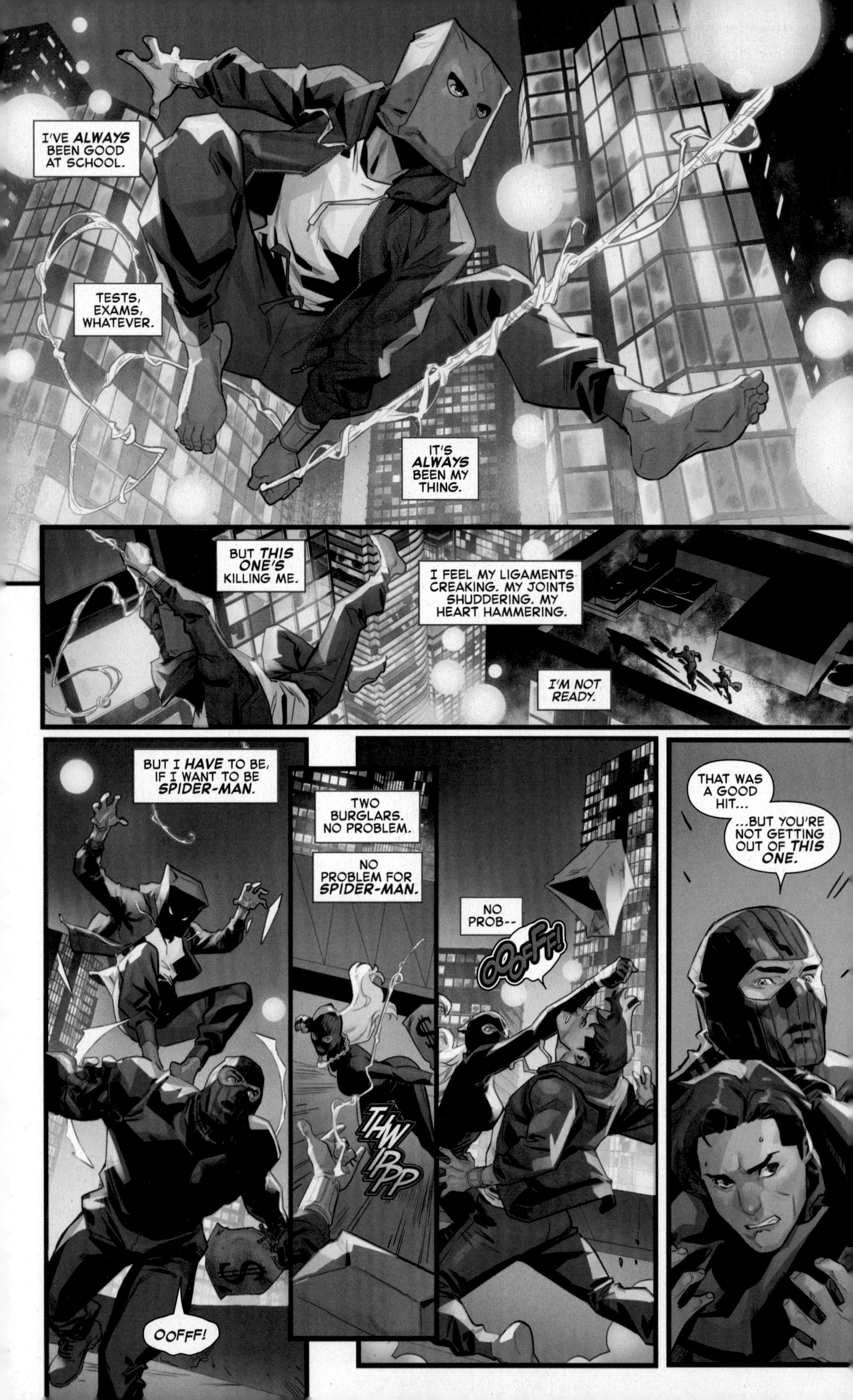
I'VE ALWAYS BEEN GOOD AT SCHOOL.
TESTS, EXAMS, WHATEVER.
IT'S ALWAYS BEEN MY THING.
BUT THIS ONE'S KILLING ME.
I FEEL MY LIGAMENTS CREAKING. MY JOINTS SHUDDERING. MY HEART HAMMERING.
I'M NOT READY.
BUT I HAVE TO BE, IF I WANT TO BE SPIDER-MAN.
OOFFF!
TWO BURGLARS. NO PROBLEM.
NO PROBLEM FOR SPIDER-MAN.
THWIPPP
NO PROB--
OOOFFF!
THAT WAS A GOOD HIT...
...BUT YOU'RE NOT GETTING OUT OF THIS ONE.

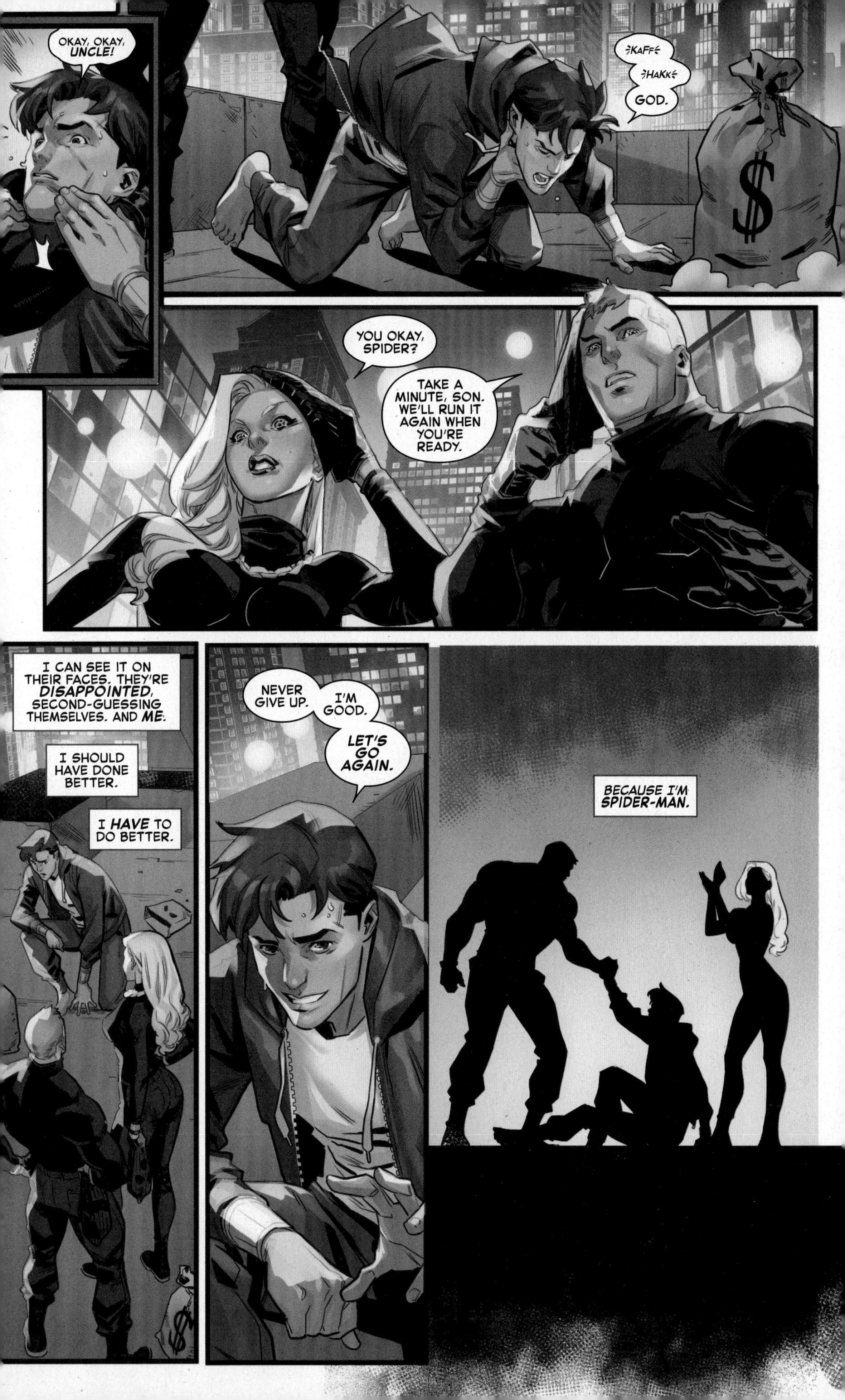
OKAY, OKAY, UNCLE!
KAFF
HAKK
GOD.
YOU OKAY, SPIDER?
TAKE A MINUTE, SON. WE'LL RUN IT AGAIN WHEN YOU'RE READY.
I CAN SEE IT ON THEIR FACES. THEY'RE DISAPPOINTED, SECOND-GUESSING THEMSELVES. AND ME.
I SHOULD HAVE DONE BETTER.
I HAVE TO DO BETTER.
NEVER GIVE UP.
I'M GOOD.
LET'S GO AGAIN.
BECAUSE I'M SPIDER-MAN.

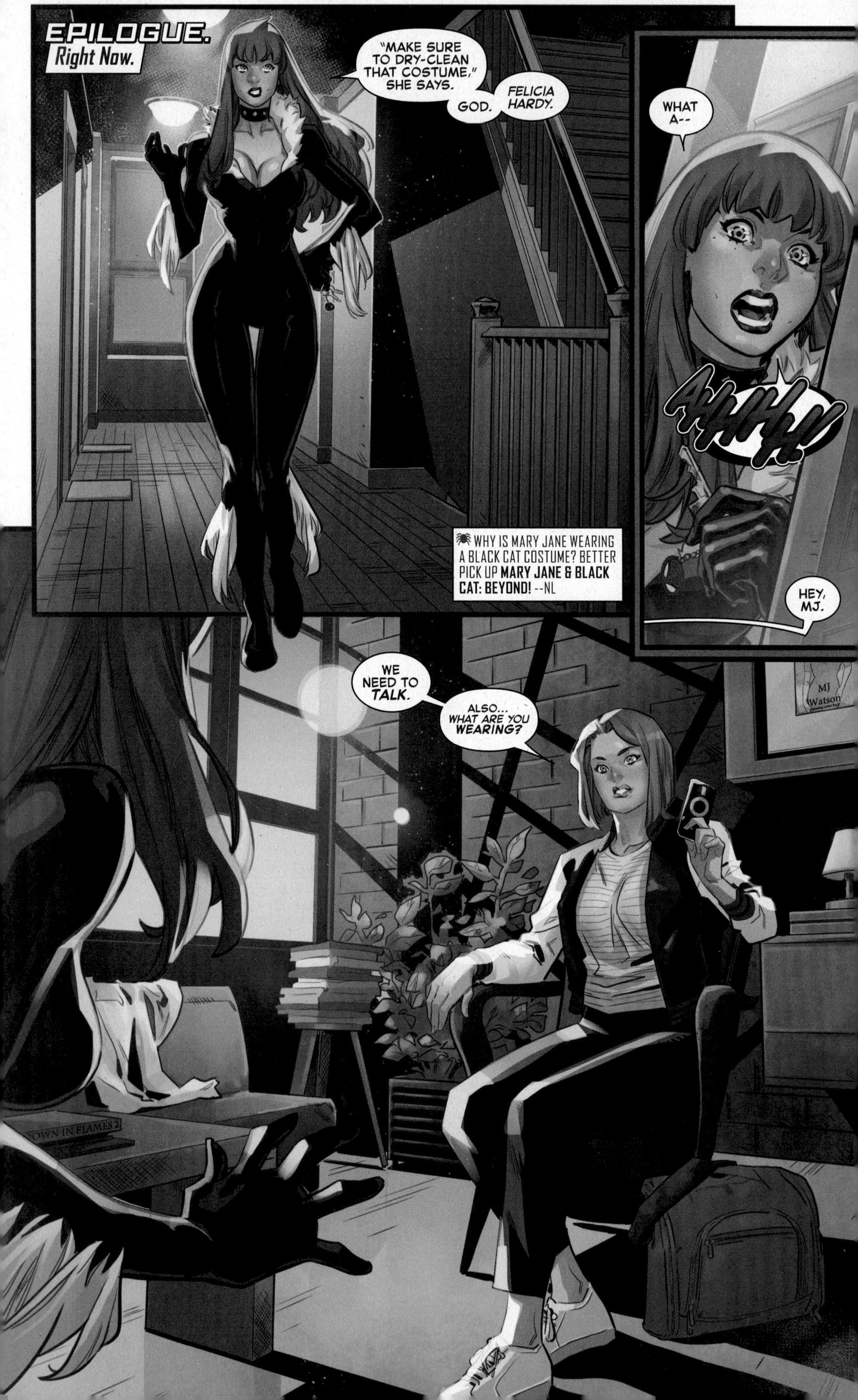
EPILOGUE.
Right Now.
"MAKE SURE TO DRY-CLEAN THAT COSTUME," SHE SAYS.
GOD.
FELICIA HARDY.
WHAT A--
AHHHH!
HEY, MJ.
WHY IS MARY JANE WEARING A BLACK CAT COSTUME? BETTER PICK UP MARY JANE & BLACK CAT: BEYOND! --NL
WE NEED TO TALK.
ALSO... WHAT ARE YOU WEARING?
MJ Watson
DOWN IN FLAMES 2

MARY JANE & BLACK CAT: BEYOND VARIANT BY
PEACH MOMOKO

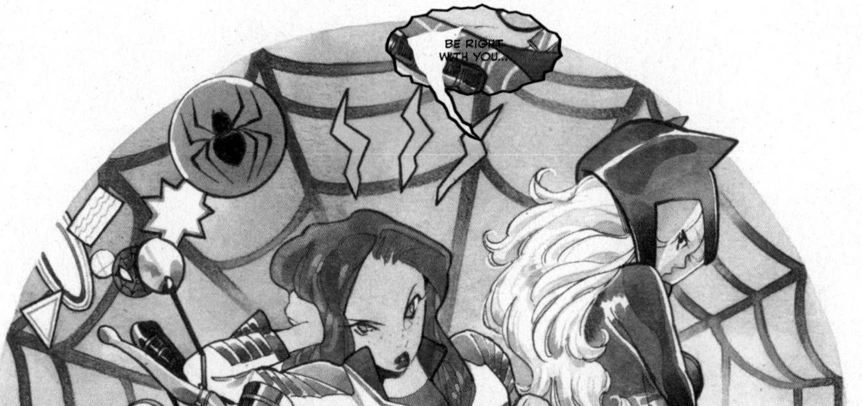
BE RIGHT WITH YOU...

BEYOND CORPORATION MARY JANE & BLACK CAT: BEYOND

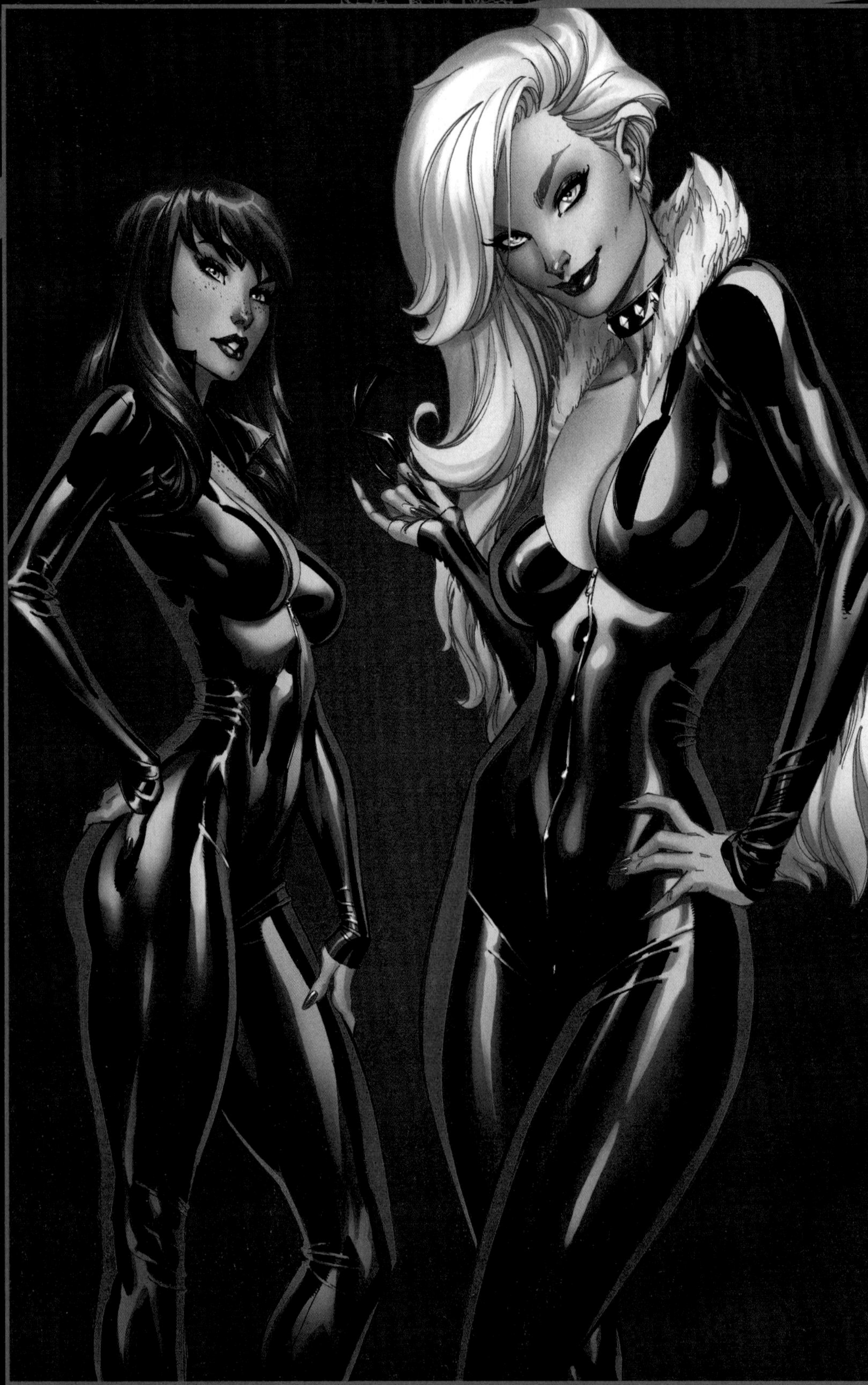

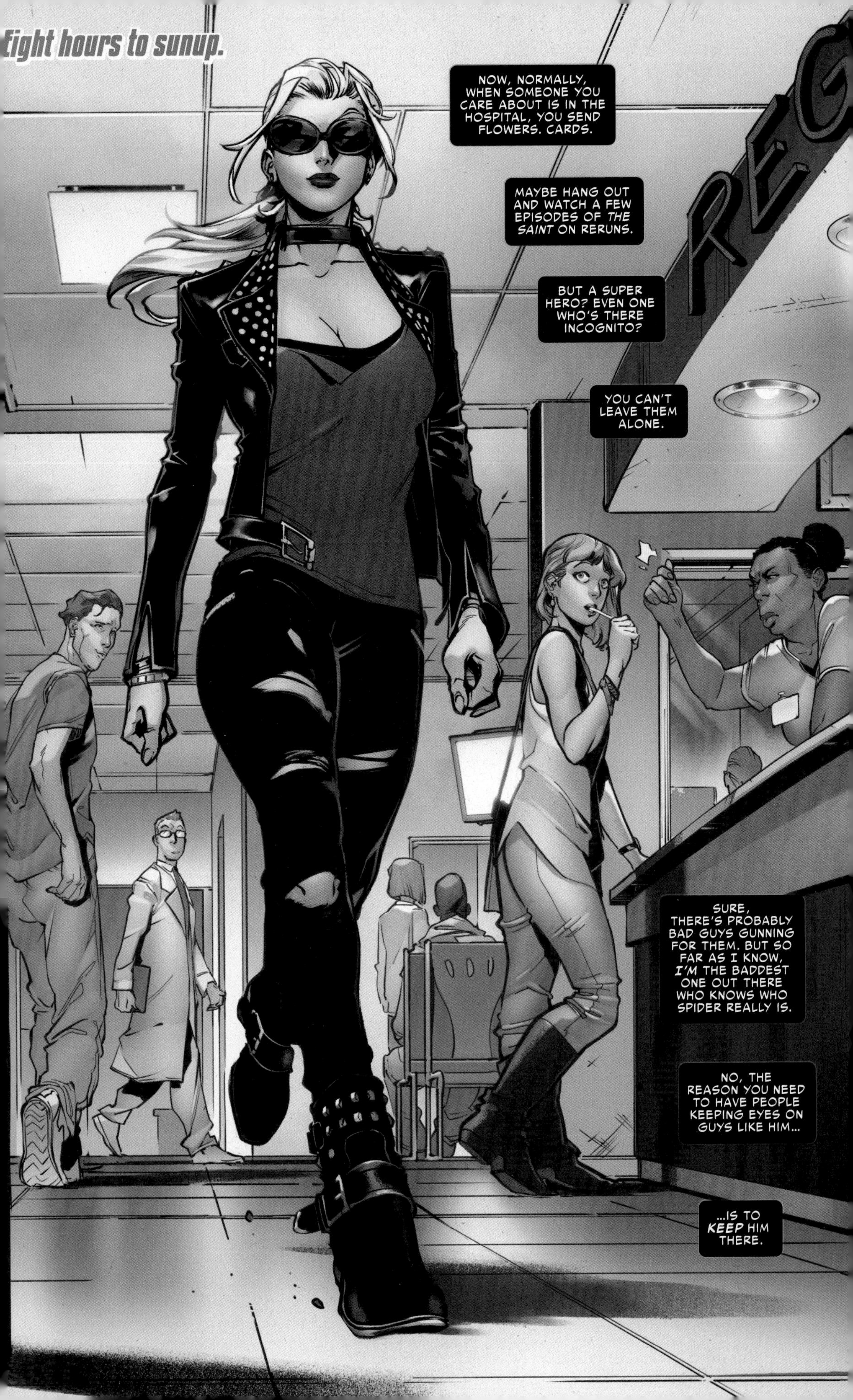
Eight hours to sunup.
NOW, NORMALLY, WHEN SOMEONE YOU CARE ABOUT IS IN THE HOSPITAL, YOU SEND FLOWERS. CARDS.
MAYBE HANG OUT AND WATCH A FEW EPISODES OF *THE SAINT* ON RERUNS.
BUT A SUPER HERO? EVEN ONE WHO'S THERE INCOGNITO?
YOU CAN'T LEAVE THEM ALONE.
SURE, THERE'S PROBABLY BAD GUYS GUNNING FOR THEM. BUT SO FAR AS I KNOW, *I'M* THE BADDEST ONE OUT THERE WHO KNOWS WHO SPIDER REALLY IS.
NO, THE REASON YOU NEED TO HAVE PEOPLE KEEPING EYES ON GUYS LIKE HIM...
...IS TO *KEEP* HIM THERE.

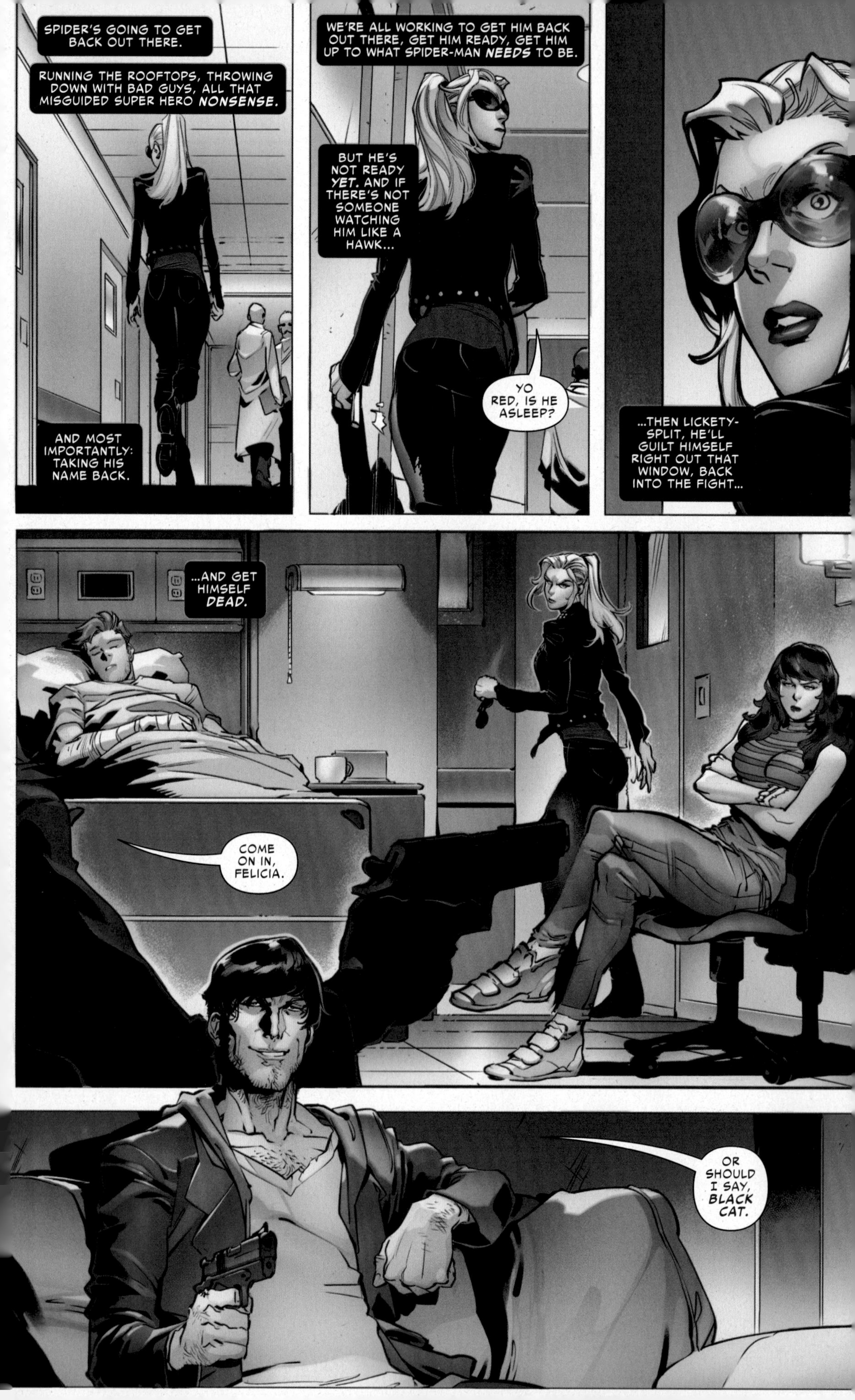
SPIDER'S GOING TO GET BACK OUT THERE.
RUNNING THE ROOFTOPS, THROWING DOWN WITH BAD GUYS, ALL THAT MISGUIDED SUPER HERO NONSENSE.
AND MOST IMPORTANTLY: TAKING HIS NAME BACK.
WE'RE ALL WORKING TO GET HIM BACK OUT THERE, GET HIM READY, GET HIM UP TO WHAT SPIDER-MAN NEEDS TO BE.
BUT HE'S NOT READY YET. AND IF THERE'S NOT SOMEONE WATCHING HIM LIKE A HAWK...
YO RED, IS HE ASLEEP?
...THEN LICKETY-SPLIT, HE'LL GUILT HIMSELF RIGHT OUT THAT WINDOW, BACK INTO THE FIGHT...
...AND GET HIMSELF DEAD.
COME ON IN, FELICIA.
OR SHOULD I SAY, BLACK CAT.

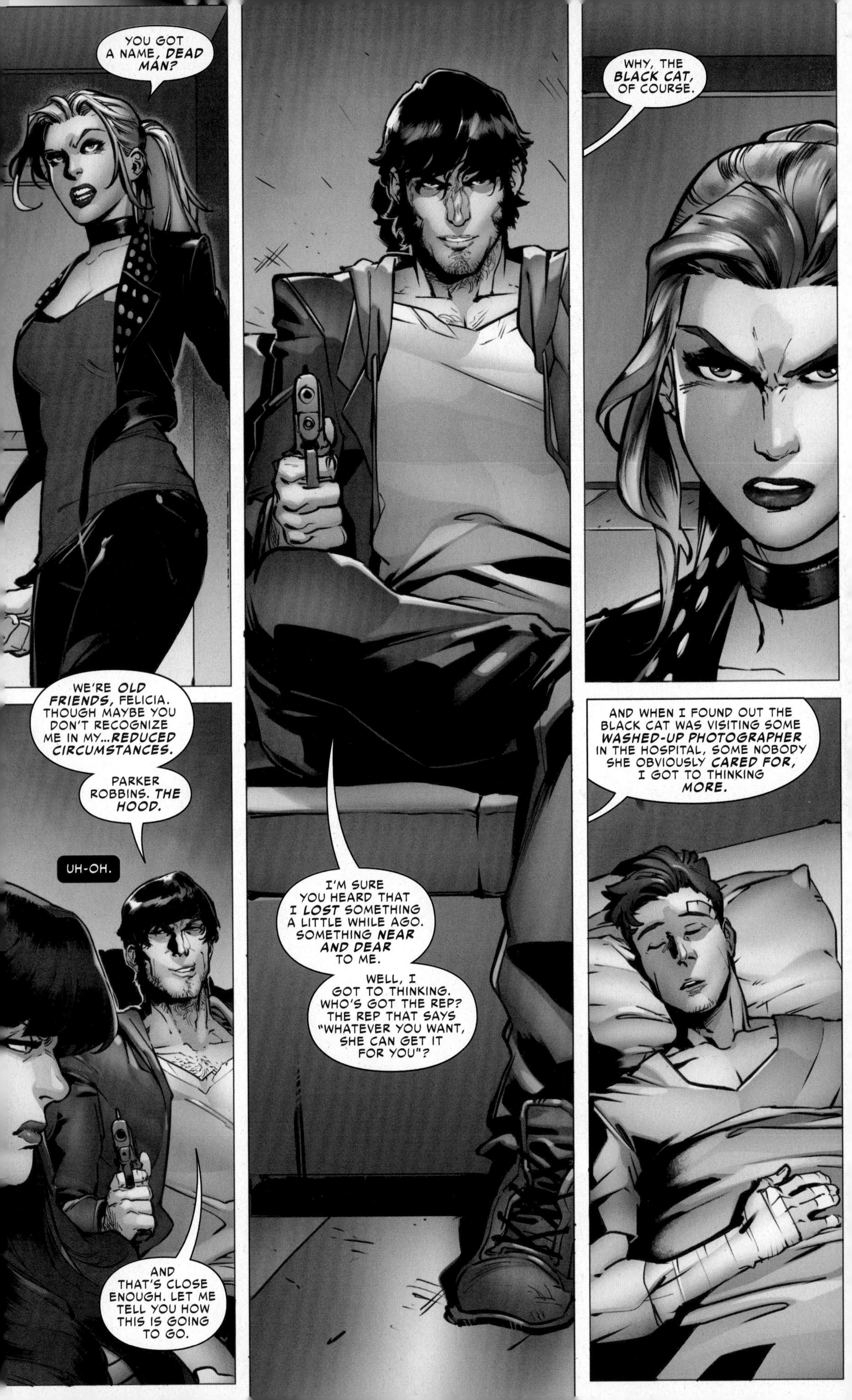
YOU GOT A NAME, DEAD MAN?
WHY, THE BLACK CAT, OF COURSE.
WE'RE OLD FRIENDS, FELICIA. THOUGH MAYBE YOU DON'T RECOGNIZE ME IN MY...REDUCED CIRCUMSTANCES.
PARKER ROBBINS. THE HOOD.
UH-OH.
AND THAT'S CLOSE ENOUGH. LET ME TELL YOU HOW THIS IS GOING TO GO.
I'M SURE YOU HEARD THAT I LOST SOMETHING A LITTLE WHILE AGO. SOMETHING NEAR AND DEAR TO ME.
WELL, I GOT TO THINKING. WHO'S GOT THE REP? THE REP THAT SAYS "WHATEVER YOU WANT, SHE CAN GET IT FOR YOU"?
AND WHEN I FOUND OUT THE BLACK CAT WAS VISITING SOME WASHED-UP PHOTOGRAPHER IN THE HOSPITAL, SOME NOBODY SHE OBVIOUSLY CARED FOR, I GOT TO THINKING MORE.

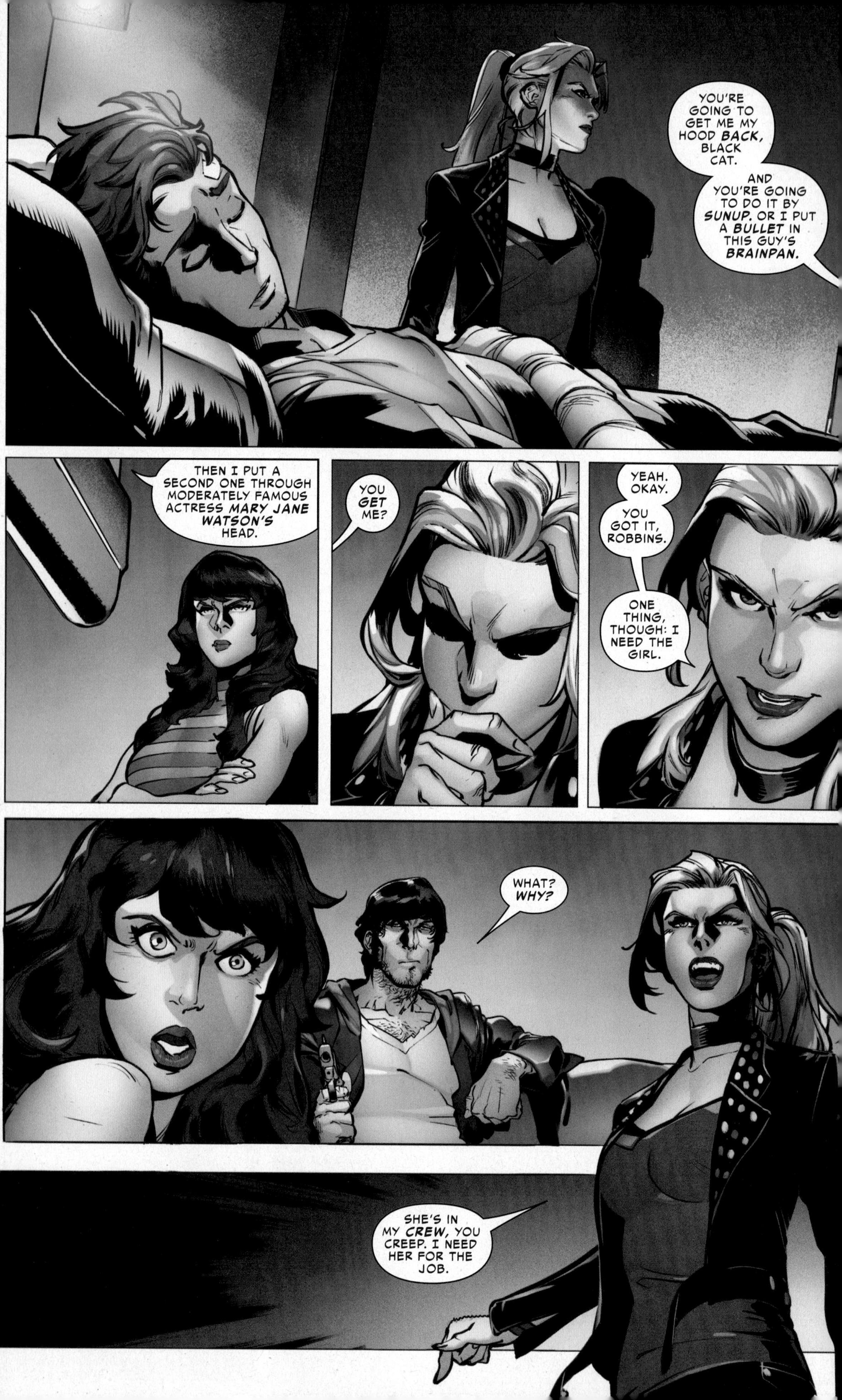
YOU'RE GOING TO GET ME MY HOOD BACK, BLACK CAT.
AND YOU'RE GOING TO DO IT BY SUNUP. OR I PUT A BULLET IN THIS GUY'S BRAINPAN.
THEN I PUT A SECOND ONE THROUGH MODERATELY FAMOUS ACTRESS MARY JANE WATSON'S HEAD.
YOU GET ME?
YEAH. OKAY.
YOU GOT IT, ROBBINS.
ONE THING, THOUGH: I NEED THE GIRL.
WHAT? WHY?
SHE'S IN MY CREW, YOU CREEP. I NEED HER FOR THE JOB.

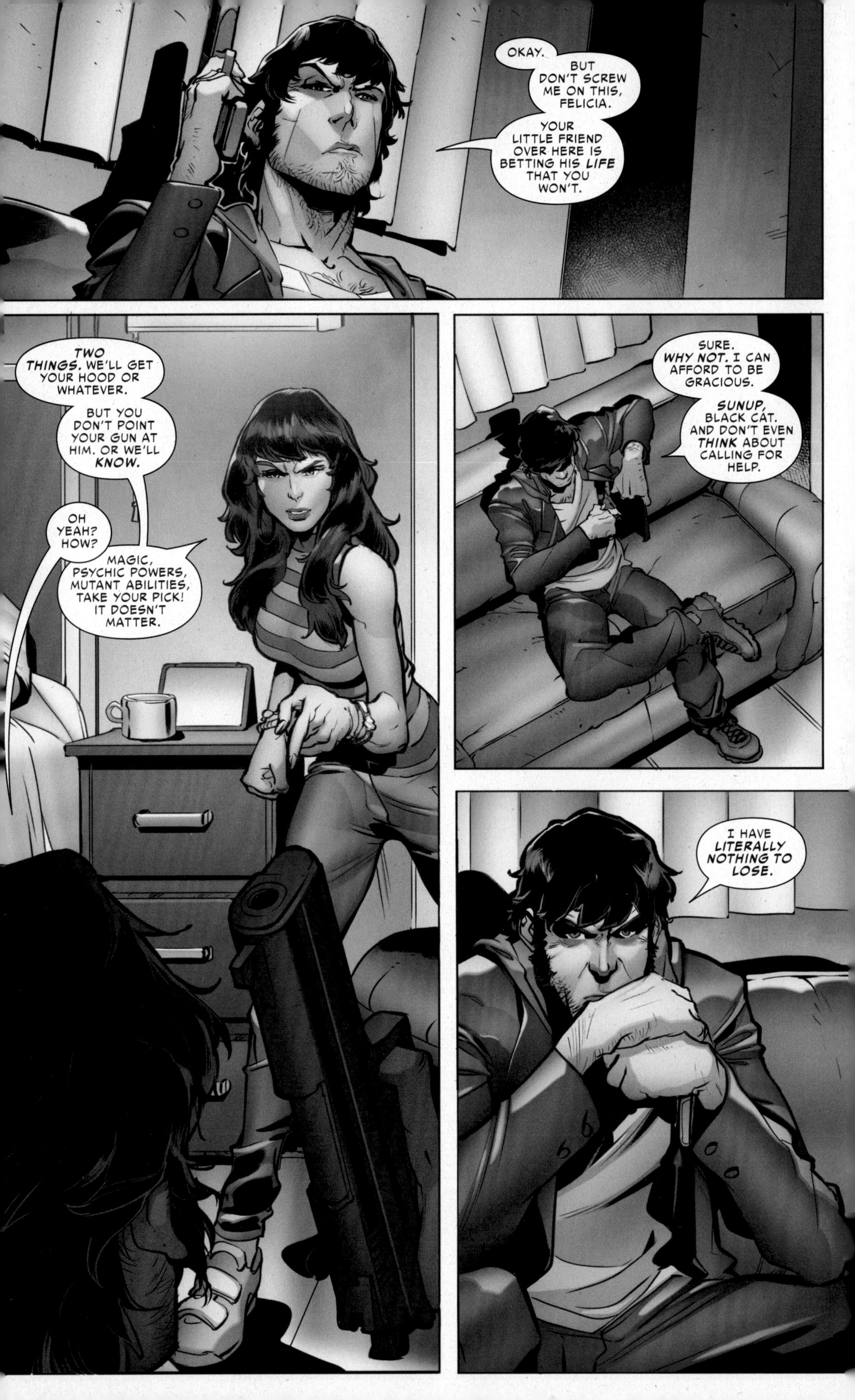
OKAY.
BUT DON'T SCREW ME ON THIS, FELICIA.
YOUR LITTLE FRIEND OVER HERE IS BETTING HIS *LIFE* THAT YOU WON'T.
TWO THINGS. WE'LL GET YOUR HOOD OR WHATEVER.
BUT YOU DON'T POINT YOUR GUN AT HIM. OR WE'LL *KNOW.*
OH YEAH? HOW?
MAGIC, PSYCHIC POWERS, MUTANT ABILITIES, TAKE YOUR PICK! IT DOESN'T MATTER.
SURE. *WHY NOT.* I CAN AFFORD TO BE GRACIOUS.
SUNUP, BLACK CAT. AND DON'T EVEN *THINK* ABOUT CALLING FOR HELP.
I HAVE *LITERALLY NOTHING TO LOSE.*

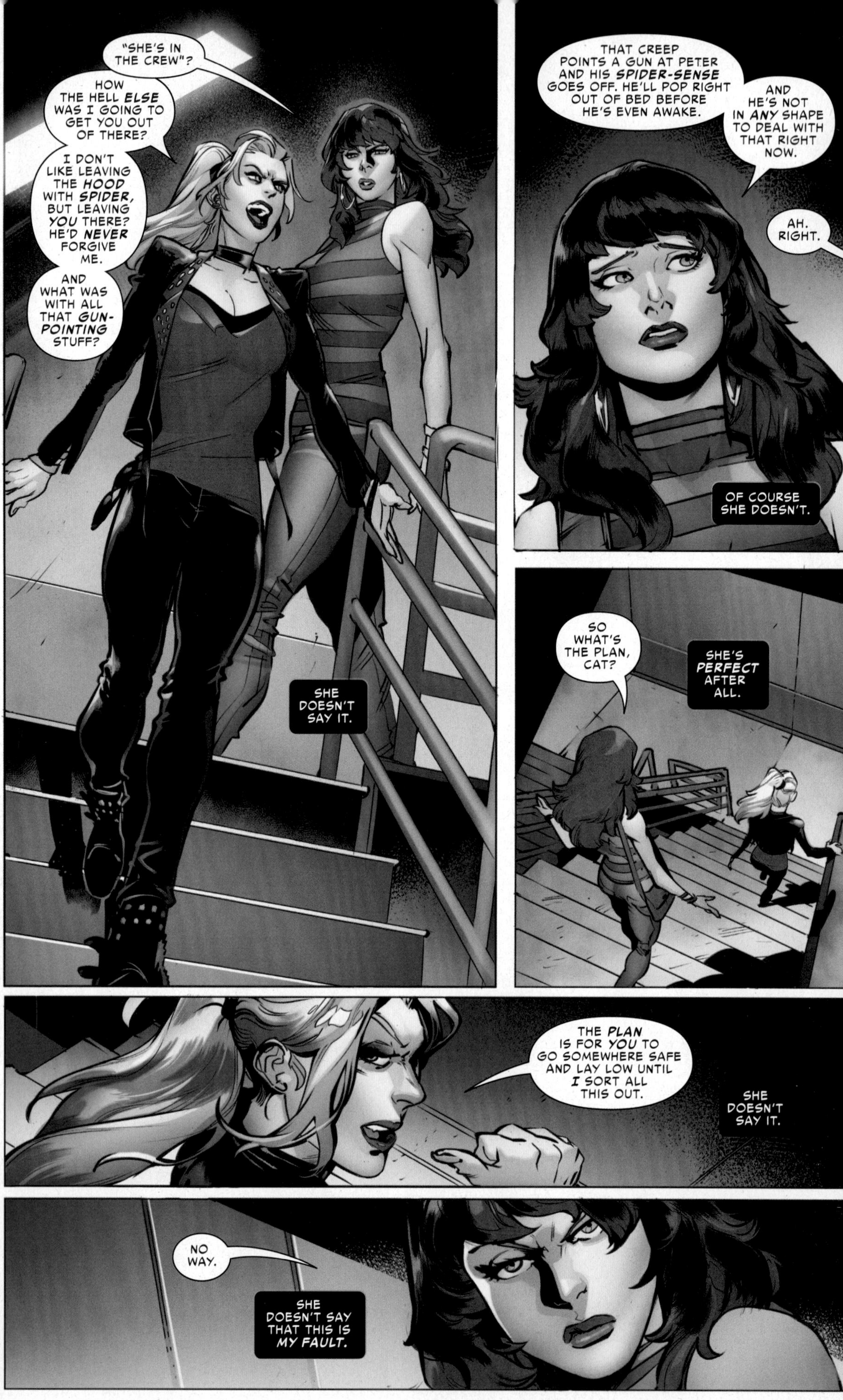
"SHE'S IN THE CREW"?
HOW THE HELL ELSE WAS I GOING TO GET YOU OUT OF THERE?
I DON'T LIKE LEAVING THE HOOD WITH SPIDER, BUT LEAVING YOU THERE? HE'D NEVER FORGIVE ME.
AND WHAT WAS WITH ALL THAT GUN-POINTING STUFF?
SHE DOESN'T SAY IT.
THAT CREEP POINTS A GUN AT PETER AND HIS SPIDER-SENSE GOES OFF. HE'LL POP RIGHT OUT OF BED BEFORE HE'S EVEN AWAKE.
AND HE'S NOT IN ANY SHAPE TO DEAL WITH THAT RIGHT NOW.
AH. RIGHT.
OF COURSE SHE DOESN'T.
SO WHAT'S THE PLAN, CAT?
SHE'S PERFECT AFTER ALL.
THE PLAN IS FOR YOU TO GO SOMEWHERE SAFE AND LAY LOW UNTIL I SORT ALL THIS OUT.
SHE DOESN'T SAY IT.
NO WAY.
SHE DOESN'T SAY THAT THIS IS MY FAULT.

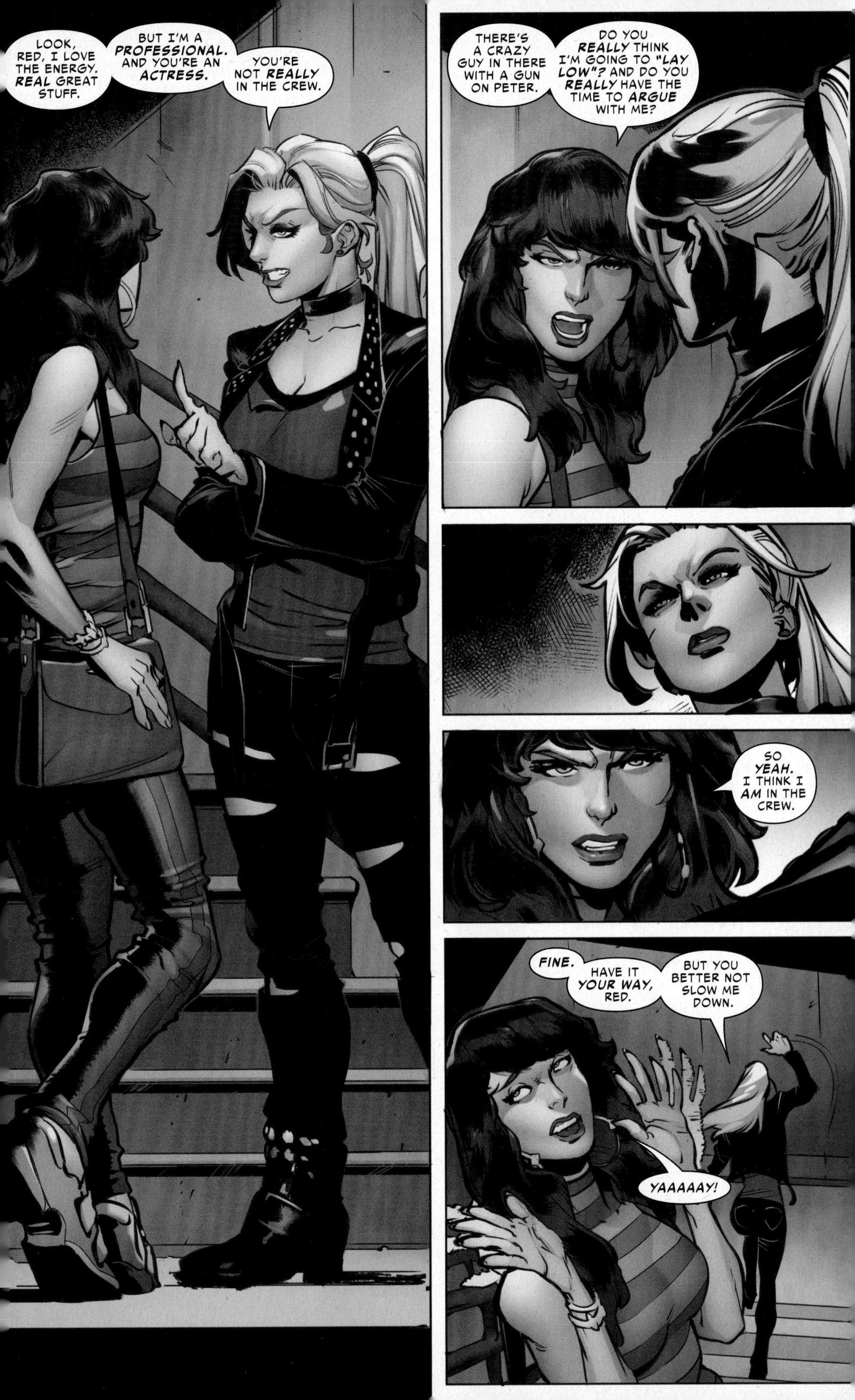
LOOK, RED, I LOVE THE ENERGY. REAL GREAT STUFF.
BUT I'M A PROFESSIONAL. AND YOU'RE AN ACTRESS.
YOU'RE NOT REALLY IN THE CREW.
THERE'S A CRAZY GUY IN THERE WITH A GUN ON PETER.
DO YOU REALLY THINK I'M GOING TO "LAY LOW"? AND DO YOU REALLY HAVE THE TIME TO ARGUE WITH ME?
SO YEAH. I THINK I AM IN THE CREW.
FINE.
HAVE IT YOUR WAY, RED.
BUT YOU BETTER NOT SLOW ME DOWN.
YAAAAAY!

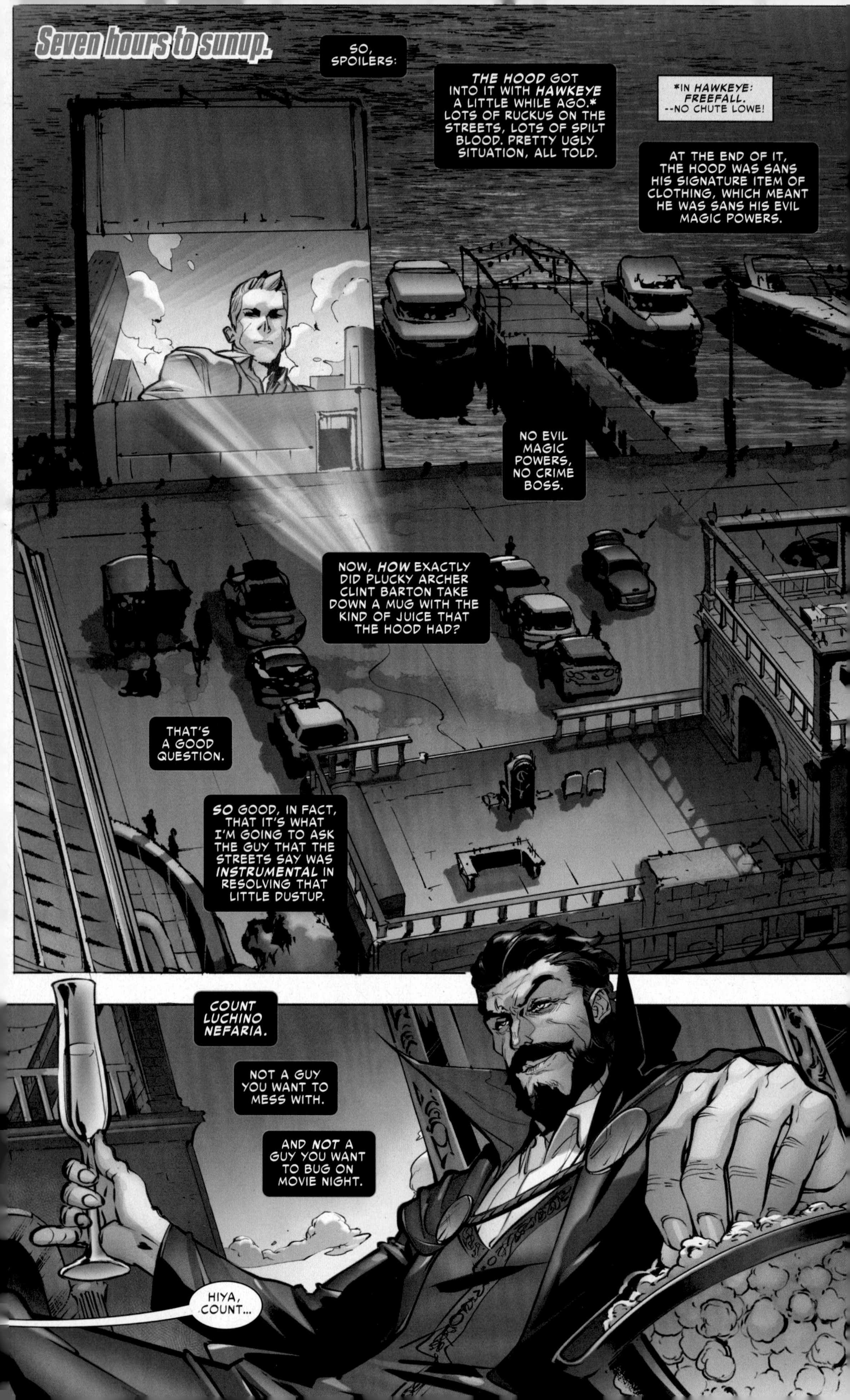
Seven hours to sunup.
SO, SPOILERS:
THE HOOD GOT INTO IT WITH HAWKEYE A LITTLE WHILE AGO.* LOTS OF RUCKUS ON THE STREETS, LOTS OF SPILT BLOOD. PRETTY UGLY SITUATION, ALL TOLD.
*IN HAWKEYE: FREEFALL. --NO CHUTE LOWE!
AT THE END OF IT, THE HOOD WAS SANS HIS SIGNATURE ITEM OF CLOTHING, WHICH MEANT HE WAS SANS HIS EVIL MAGIC POWERS.
NO EVIL MAGIC POWERS, NO CRIME BOSS.
NOW, HOW EXACTLY DID PLUCKY ARCHER CLINT BARTON TAKE DOWN A MUG WITH THE KIND OF JUICE THAT THE HOOD HAD?
THAT'S A GOOD QUESTION.
SO GOOD, IN FACT, THAT IT'S WHAT I'M GOING TO ASK THE GUY THAT THE STREETS SAY WAS INSTRUMENTAL IN RESOLVING THAT LITTLE DUSTUP.
COUNT LUCHINO NEFARIA.
NOT A GUY YOU WANT TO MESS WITH.
AND NOT A GUY YOU WANT TO BUG ON MOVIE NIGHT.
HIYA, COUNT...

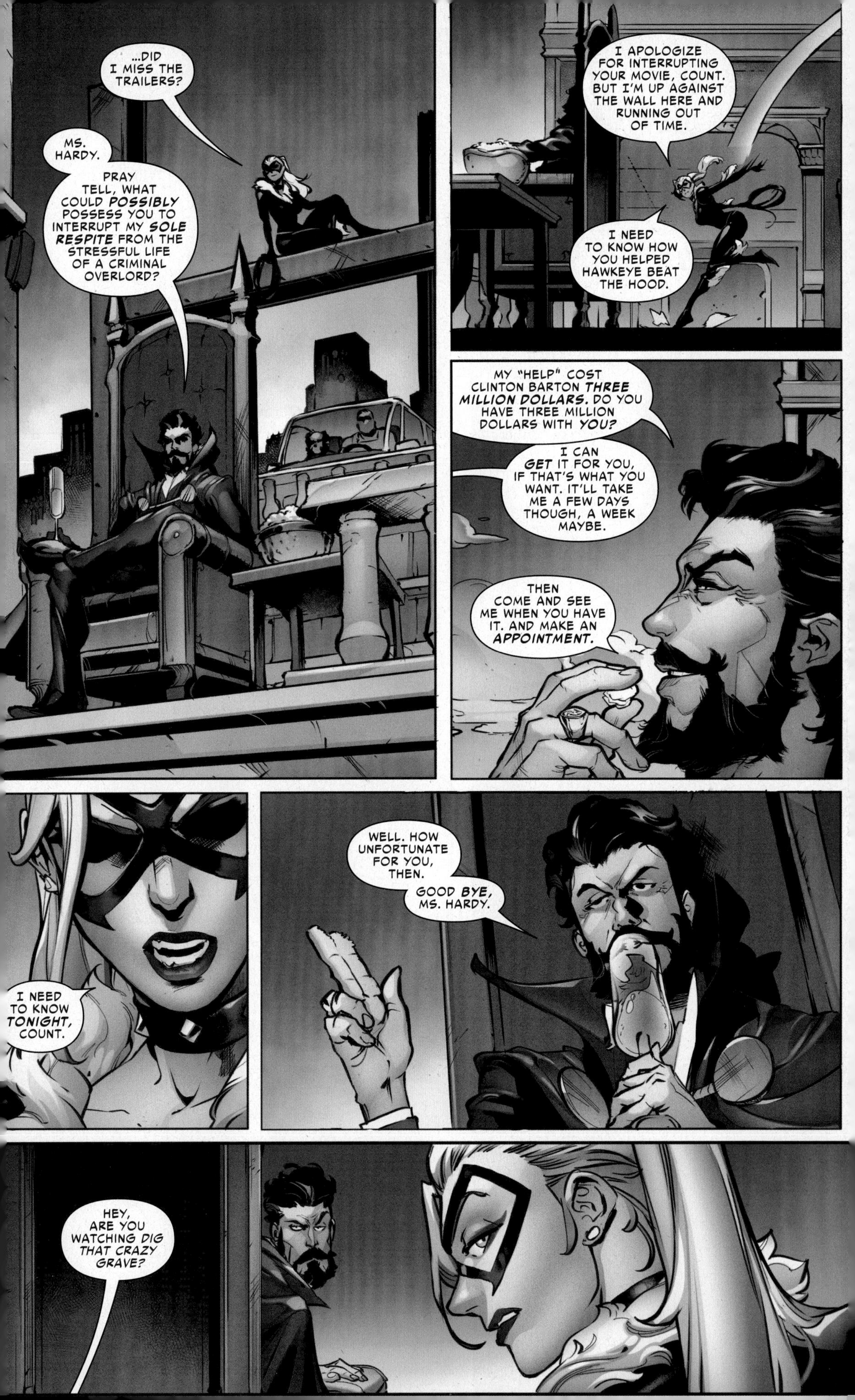

...DID I MISS THE TRAILERS?
MS. HARDY.
PRAY TELL, WHAT COULD POSSIBLY POSSESS YOU TO INTERRUPT MY SOLE RESPITE FROM THE STRESSFUL LIFE OF A CRIMINAL OVERLORD?
I APOLOGIZE FOR INTERRUPTING YOUR MOVIE, COUNT. BUT I'M UP AGAINST THE WALL HERE AND RUNNING OUT OF TIME.
I NEED TO KNOW HOW YOU HELPED HAWKEYE BEAT THE HOOD.
MY "HELP" COST CLINTON BARTON THREE MILLION DOLLARS. DO YOU HAVE THREE MILLION DOLLARS WITH YOU?
I CAN GET IT FOR YOU, IF THAT'S WHAT YOU WANT. IT'LL TAKE ME A FEW DAYS THOUGH, A WEEK MAYBE.
THEN COME AND SEE ME WHEN YOU HAVE IT. AND MAKE AN APPOINTMENT.
I NEED TO KNOW TONIGHT, COUNT.
WELL. HOW UNFORTUNATE FOR YOU, THEN.
GOOD BYE, MS. HARDY.
HEY, ARE YOU WATCHING DIG THAT CRAZY GRAVE?

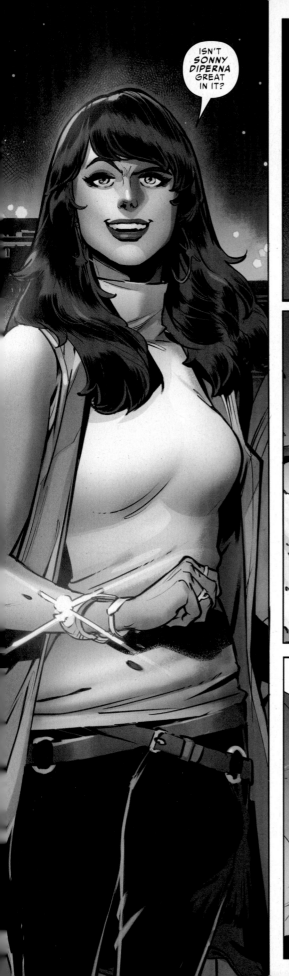

ISN'T SONNY DIPERNA GREAT IN IT?

IS THAT... MARY JANE WATSON?

OH BROTHER...

THE MARY JANE WATSON?

MS. WATSON. AN ABSOLUTE PLEASURE.

YOU WORKED WITH DIPERNA IN UP IN SMOKE, DOWN IN FLAMES! SAD ABOUT THE PREMIERE, BY THE WAY.*

*IT GOT INTERRUPTED IN SINISTER WAR #1! --IN-THE-KNOW KNICK!

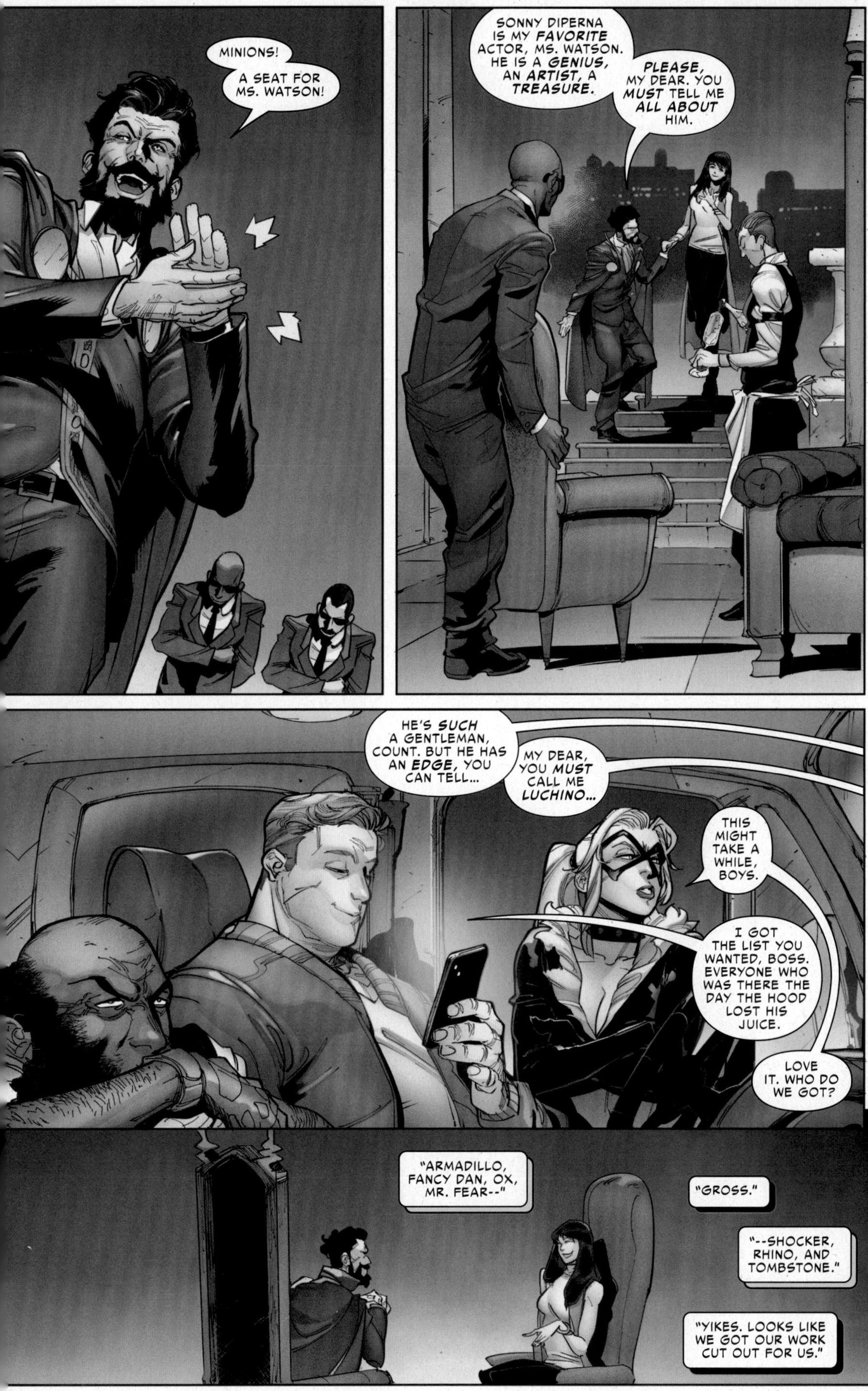
MINIONS!
A SEAT FOR MS. WATSON!
SONNY DIPERNA IS MY FAVORITE ACTOR, MS. WATSON. HE IS A GENIUS, AN ARTIST, A TREASURE.
PLEASE, MY DEAR. YOU MUST TELL ME ALL ABOUT HIM.
HE'S SUCH A GENTLEMAN, COUNT. BUT HE HAS AN EDGE, YOU CAN TELL...
MY DEAR, YOU MUST CALL ME LUCHINO...
THIS MIGHT TAKE A WHILE, BOYS.
I GOT THE LIST YOU WANTED, BOSS. EVERYONE WHO WAS THERE THE DAY THE HOOD LOST HIS JUICE.
LOVE IT. WHO DO WE GOT?
"ARMADILLO, FANCY DAN, OX, MR. FEAR--"
"GROSS."
"--SHOCKER, RHINO, AND TOMBSTONE."
"YIKES. LOOKS LIKE WE GOT OUR WORK CUT OUT FOR US."

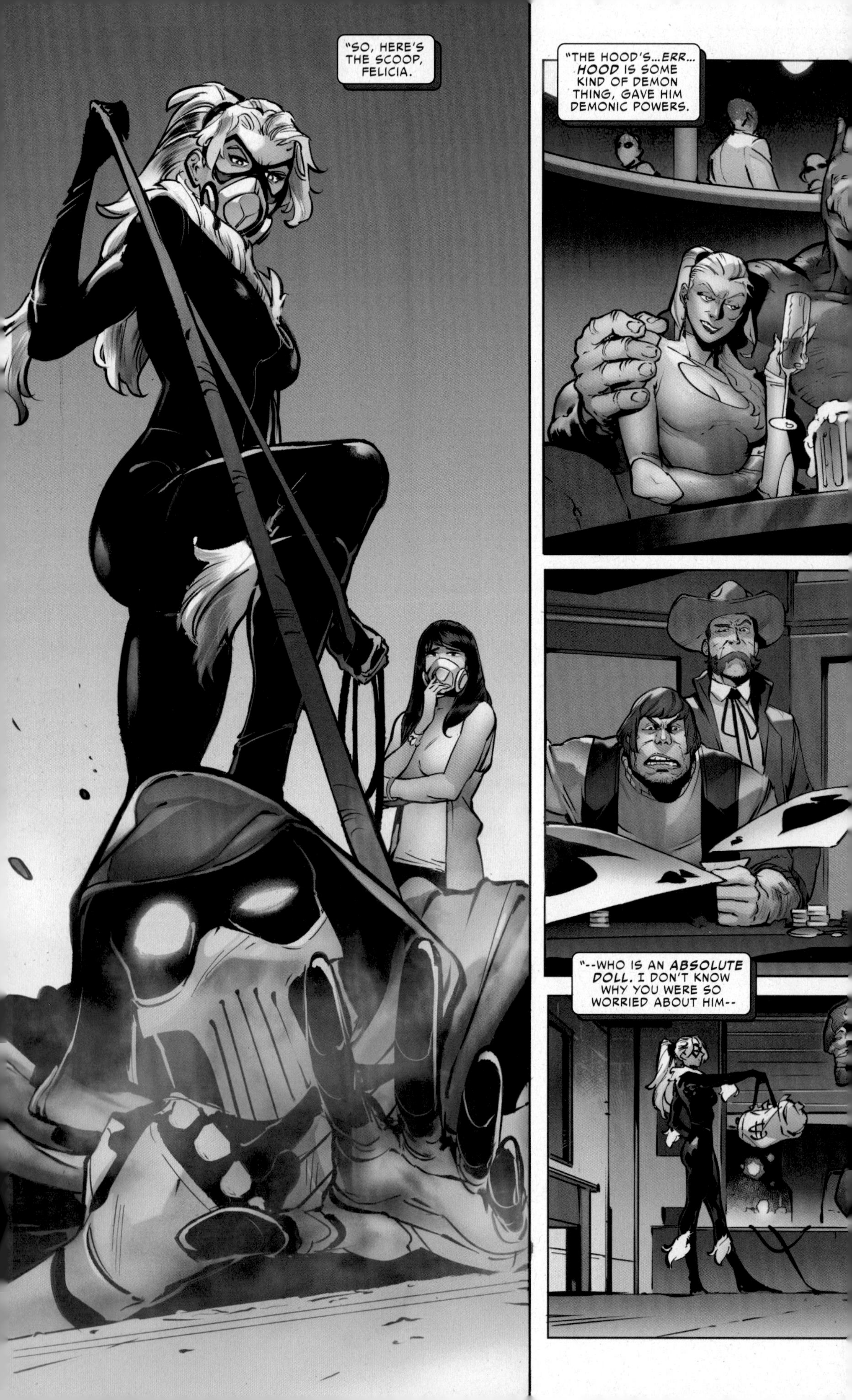
"SO, HERE'S THE SCOOP, FELICIA.
"THE HOOD'S...ERR... HOOD IS SOME KIND OF DEMON THING, GAVE HIM DEMONIC POWERS.
"--WHO IS AN ABSOLUTE DOLL. I DON'T KNOW WHY YOU WERE SO WORRIED ABOUT HIM--

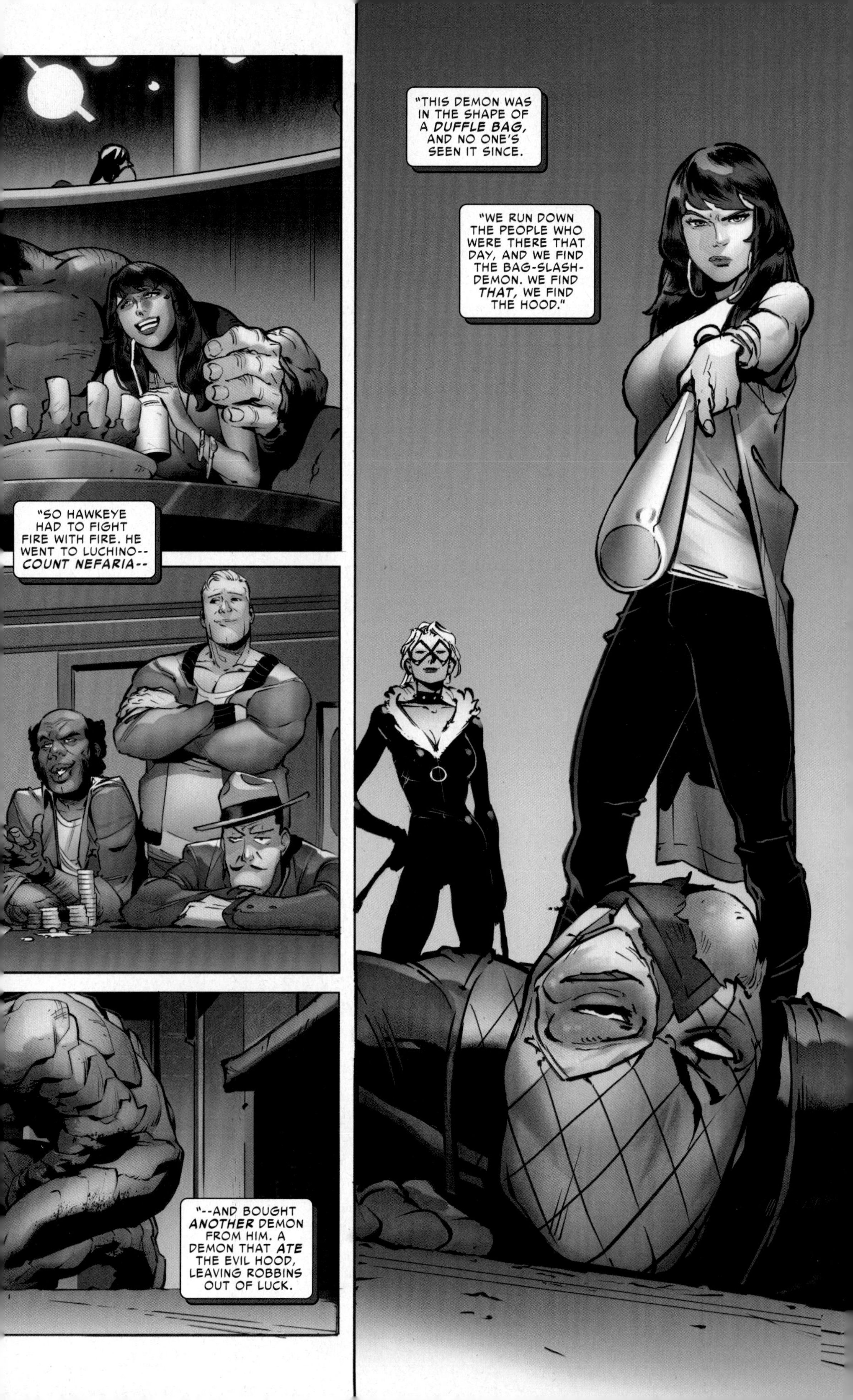
"SO HAWKEYE HAD TO FIGHT FIRE WITH FIRE. HE WENT TO LUCHINO-- COUNT NEFARIA--
"--AND BOUGHT ANOTHER DEMON FROM HIM. A DEMON THAT ATE THE EVIL HOOD, LEAVING ROBBINS OUT OF LUCK.
"THIS DEMON WAS IN THE SHAPE OF A DUFFLE BAG, AND NO ONE'S SEEN IT SINCE.
"WE RUN DOWN THE PEOPLE WHO WERE THERE THAT DAY, AND WE FIND THE BAG-SLASH-DEMON. WE FIND THAT, WE FIND THE HOOD."

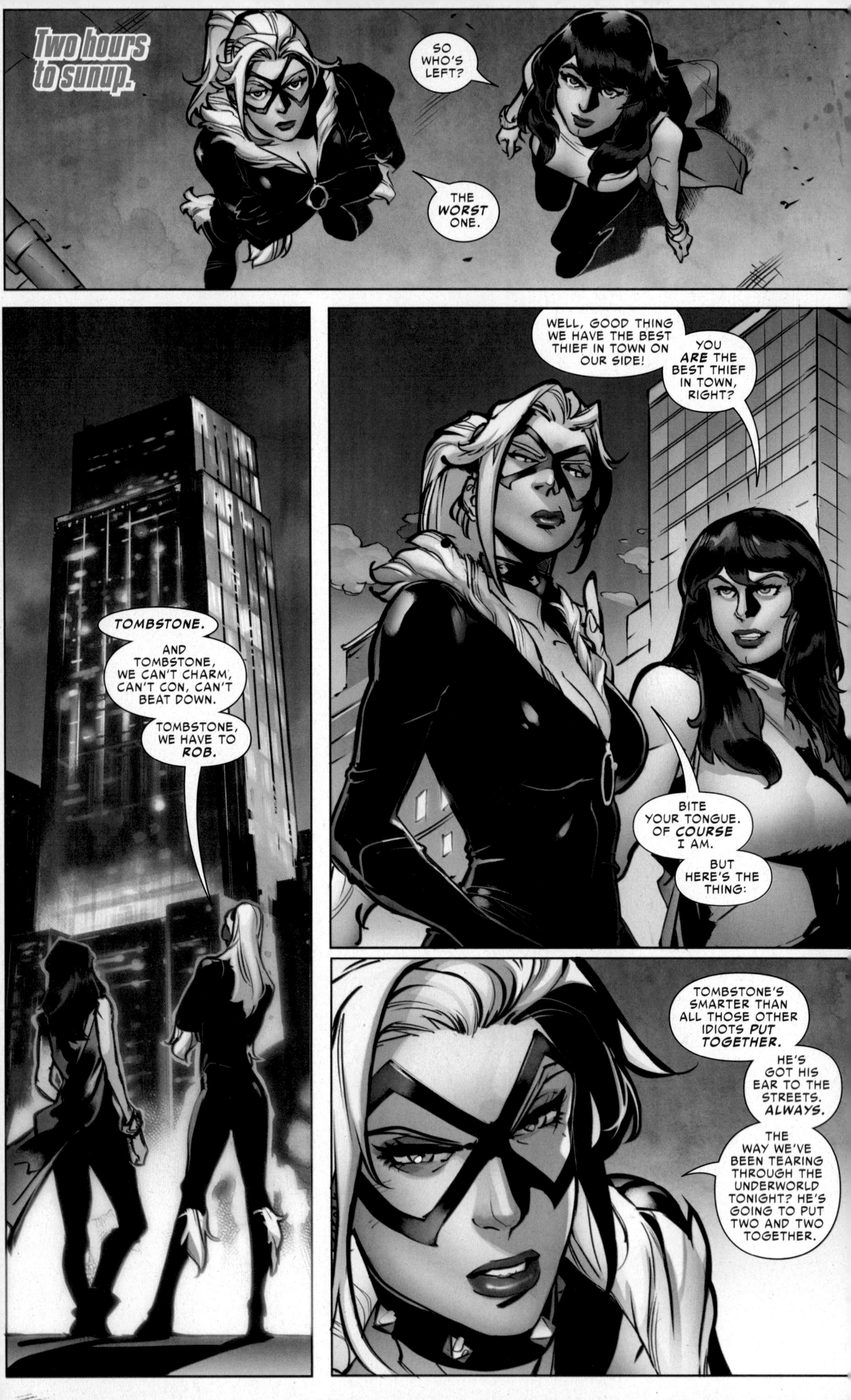
Two hours to sunup.
SO WHO'S LEFT?
THE WORST ONE.
TOMBSTONE.
AND TOMBSTONE, WE CAN'T CHARM, CAN'T CON, CAN'T BEAT DOWN.
TOMBSTONE, WE HAVE TO ROB.
WELL, GOOD THING WE HAVE THE BEST THIEF IN TOWN ON OUR SIDE!
YOU ARE THE BEST THIEF IN TOWN, RIGHT?
BITE YOUR TONGUE. OF COURSE I AM.
BUT HERE'S THE THING:
TOMBSTONE'S SMARTER THAN ALL THOSE OTHER IDIOTS PUT TOGETHER.
HE'S GOT HIS EAR TO THE STREETS. ALWAYS.
THE WAY WE'VE BEEN TEARING THROUGH THE UNDERWORLD TONIGHT? HE'S GOING TO PUT TWO AND TWO TOGETHER.

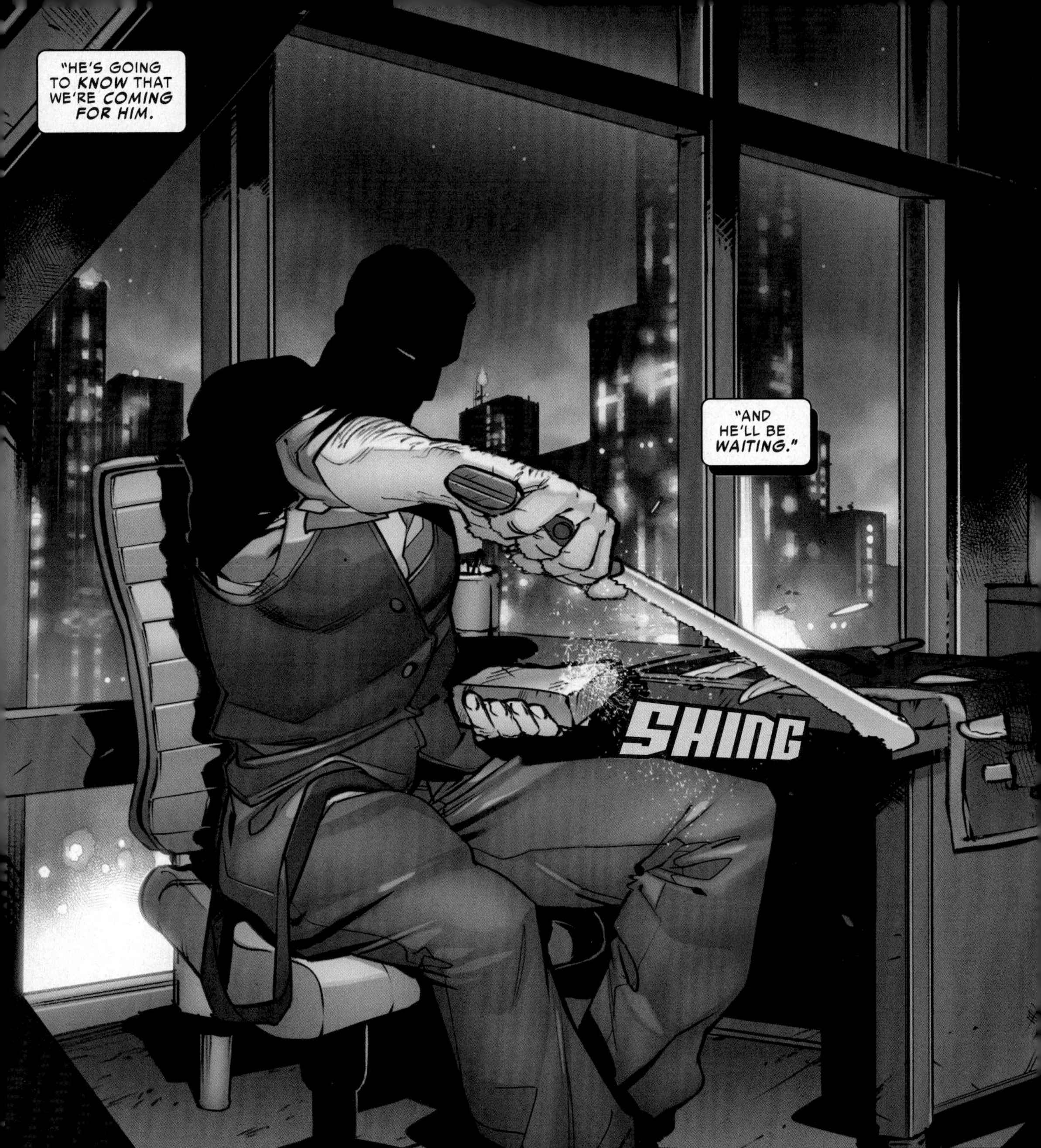
"HE'S GOING TO KNOW THAT WE'RE COMING FOR HIM.
"AND HE'LL BE WAITING."
SHING

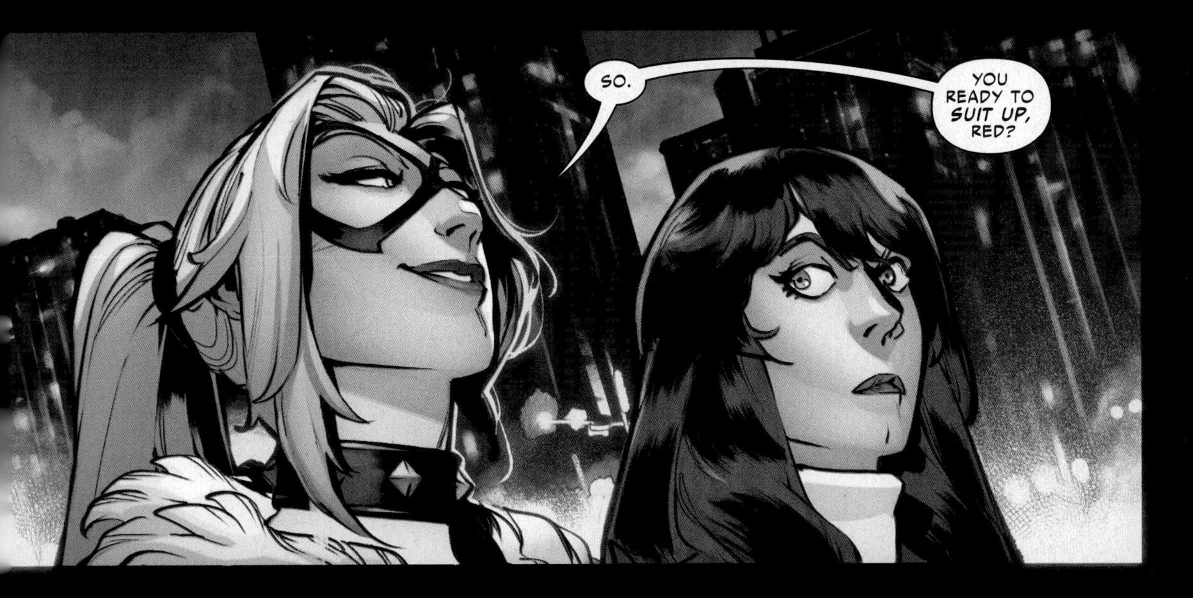
SO.
YOU READY TO SUIT UP, RED?

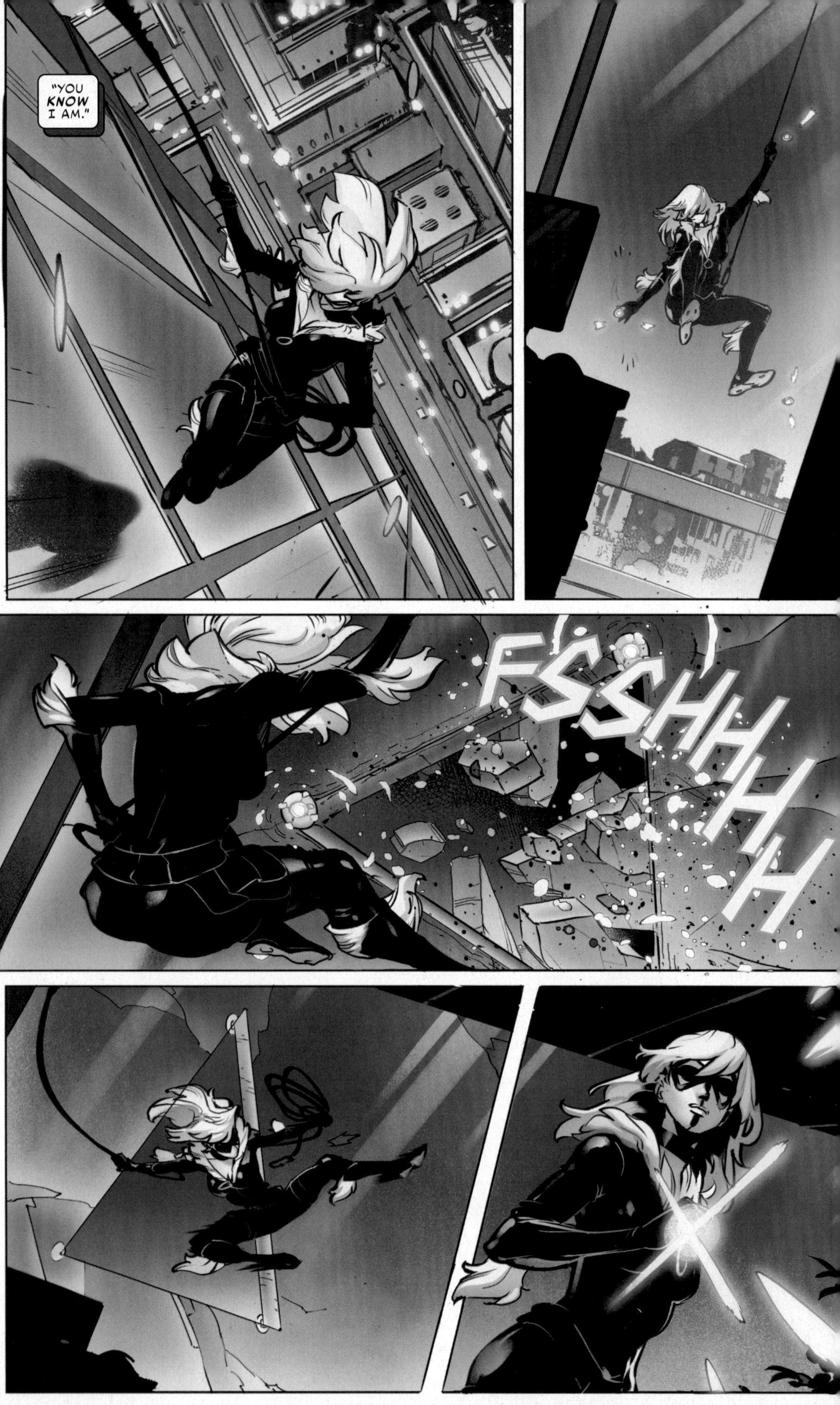
"YOU KNOW I AM."
FSSHHHHH

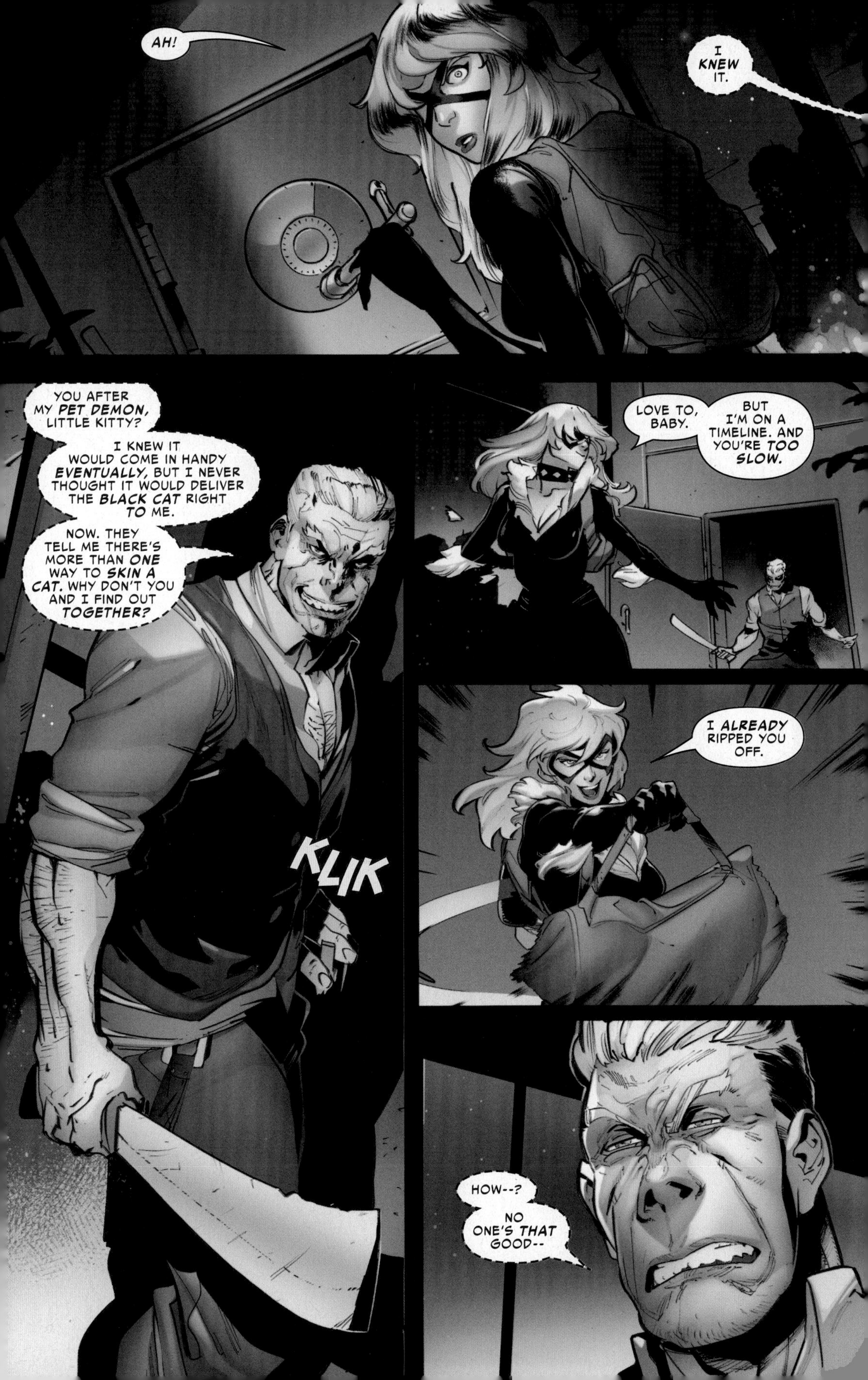
AH!
I KNEW IT.
YOU AFTER MY PET DEMON, LITTLE KITTY?
I KNEW IT WOULD COME IN HANDY EVENTUALLY, BUT I NEVER THOUGHT IT WOULD DELIVER THE BLACK CAT RIGHT TO ME.
NOW. THEY TELL ME THERE'S MORE THAN ONE WAY TO SKIN A CAT. WHY DON'T YOU AND I FIND OUT TOGETHER?
KLIK
LOVE TO, BABY.
BUT I'M ON A TIMELINE. AND YOU'RE TOO SLOW.
I ALREADY RIPPED YOU OFF.
HOW--?
NO ONE'S THAT GOOD--

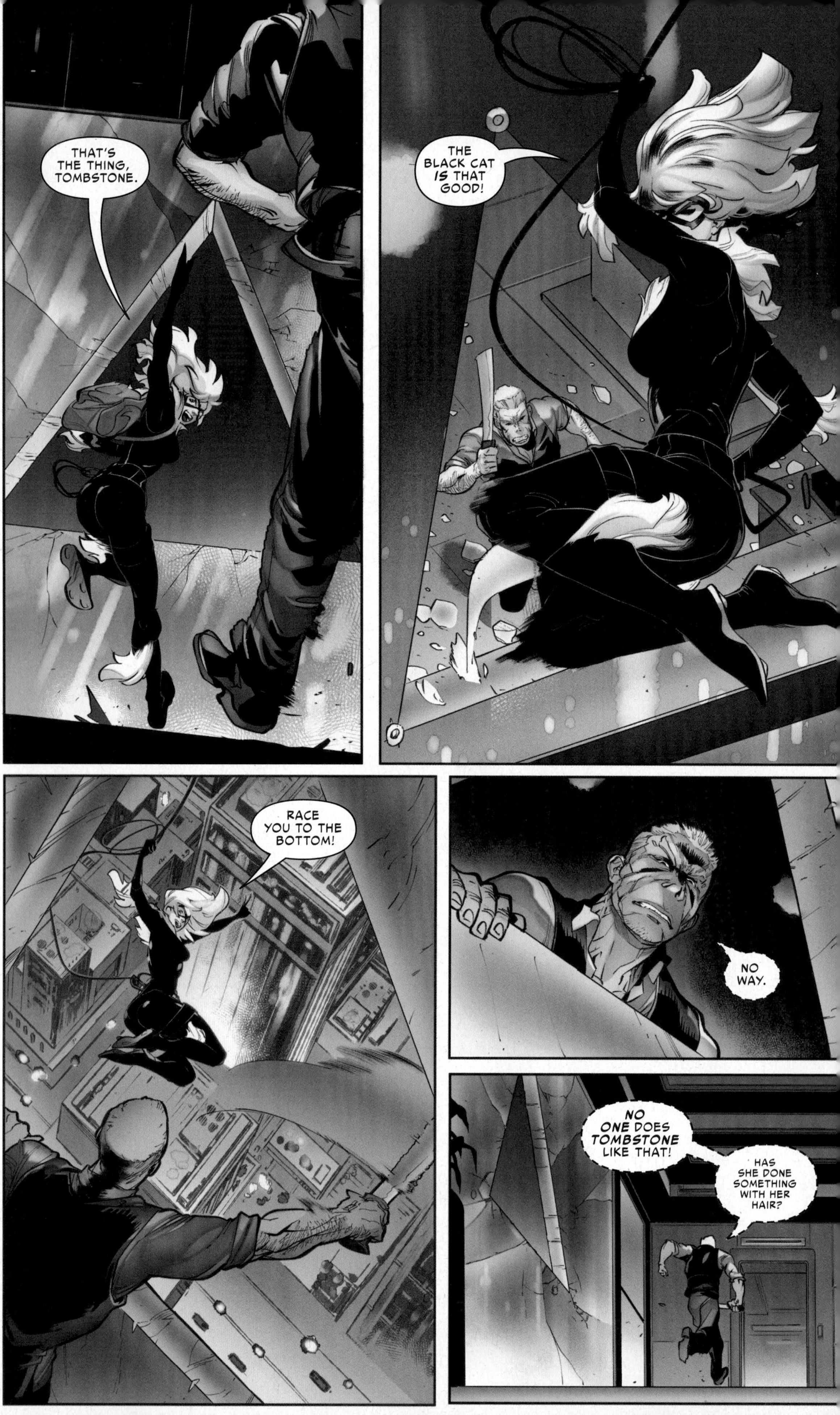
THAT'S THE THING, TOMBSTONE.
THE BLACK CAT IS THAT GOOD!
RACE YOU TO THE BOTTOM!
NO WAY.
NO ONE DOES TOMBSTONE LIKE THAT!
HAS SHE DONE SOMETHING WITH HER HAIR?

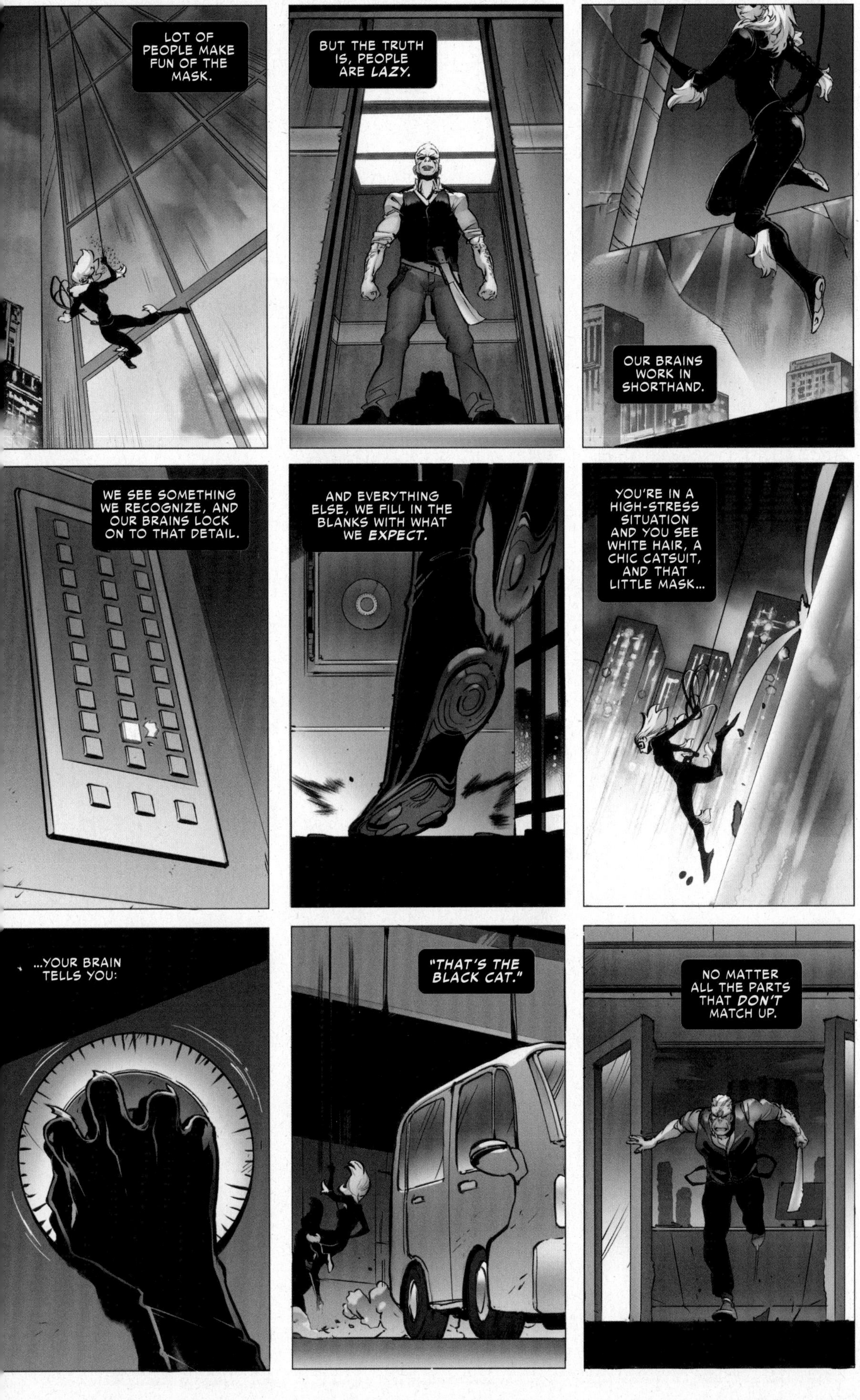
LOT OF PEOPLE MAKE FUN OF THE MASK.
BUT THE TRUTH IS, PEOPLE ARE *LAZY.*
OUR BRAINS WORK IN SHORTHAND.
WE SEE SOMETHING WE RECOGNIZE, AND OUR BRAINS LOCK ON TO THAT DETAIL.
AND EVERYTHING ELSE, WE FILL IN THE BLANKS WITH WHAT WE *EXPECT.*
YOU'RE IN A HIGH-STRESS SITUATION AND YOU SEE WHITE HAIR, A CHIC CATSUIT, AND THAT LITTLE MASK...
...YOUR BRAIN TELLS YOU:
"THAT'S THE BLACK CAT."
NO MATTER ALL THE PARTS THAT *DON'T* MATCH UP.

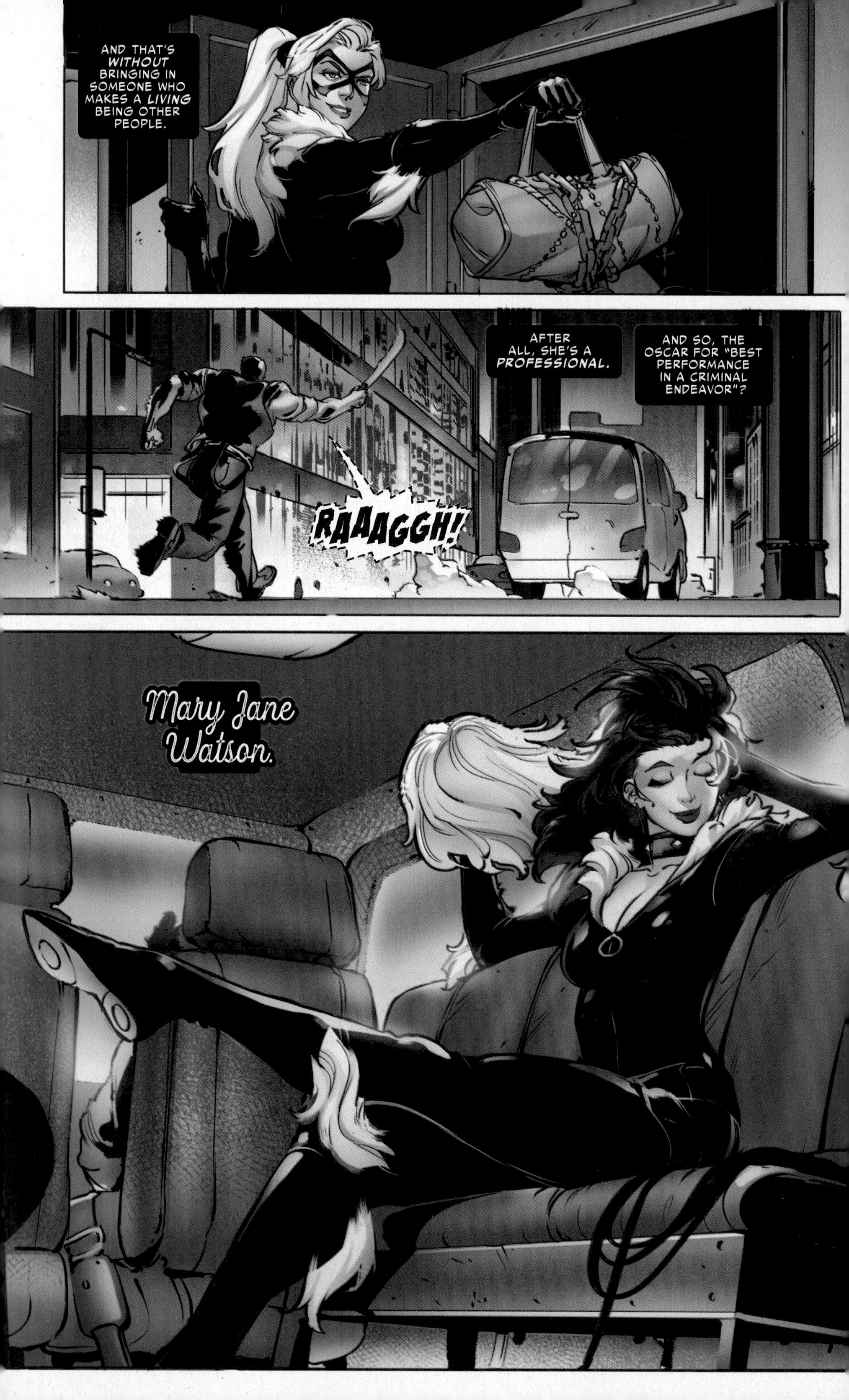
AND THAT'S WITHOUT BRINGING IN SOMEONE WHO MAKES A LIVING BEING OTHER PEOPLE.
AFTER ALL, SHE'S A PROFESSIONAL.
AND SO, THE OSCAR FOR "BEST PERFORMANCE IN A CRIMINAL ENDEAVOR"?
RAAAGGH!
Mary Jane Watson.

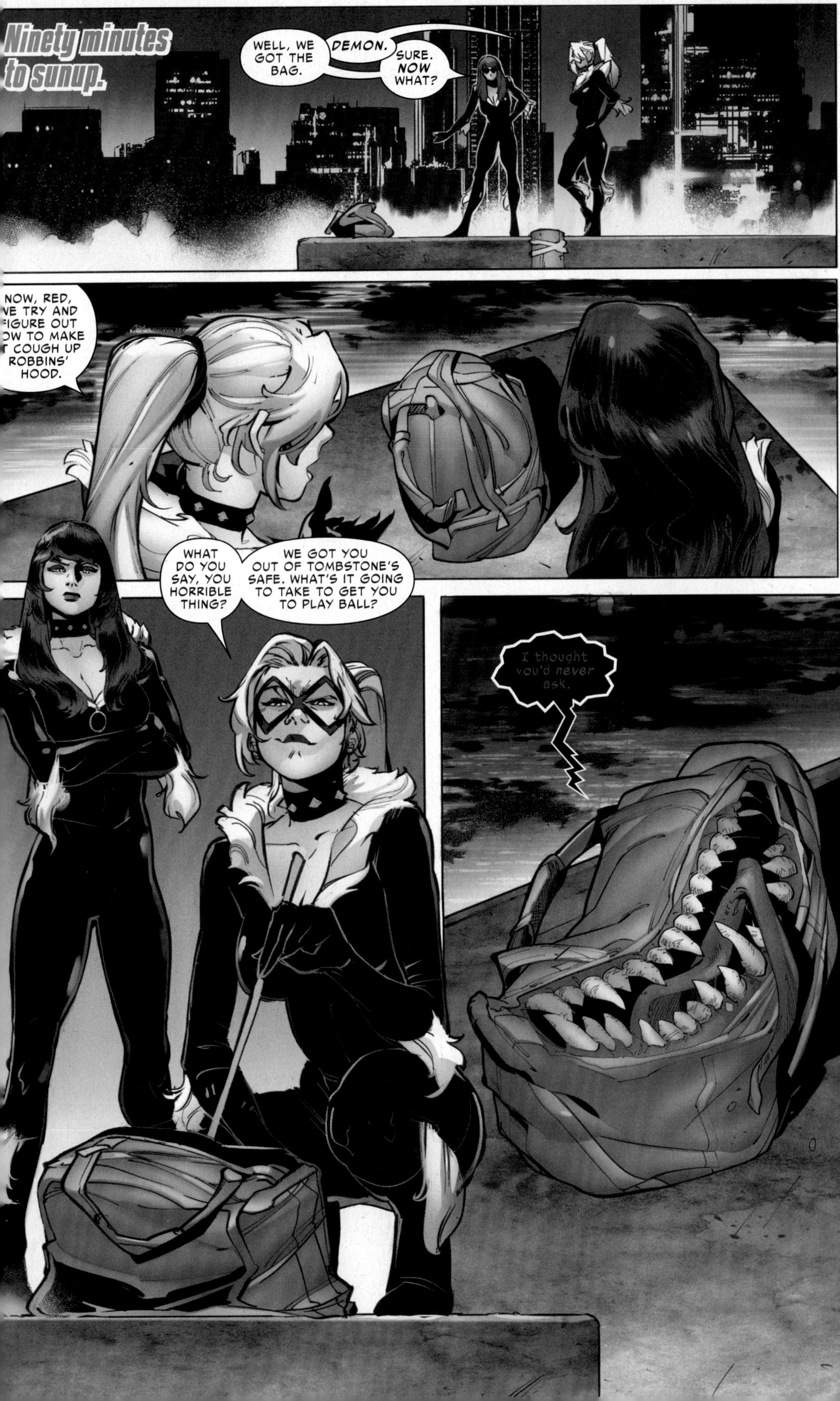
Ninety minutes to sunup.
WELL, WE GOT THE BAG.
DEMON.
SURE. NOW WHAT?
NOW, RED, VE TRY AND FIGURE OUT OW TO MAKE T COUGH UP ROBBINS' HOOD.
WHAT DO YOU SAY, YOU HORRIBLE THING?
WE GOT YOU OUT OF TOMBSTONE'S SAFE. WHAT'S IT GOING TO TAKE TO GET YOU TO PLAY BALL?
I thought you'd never ask.

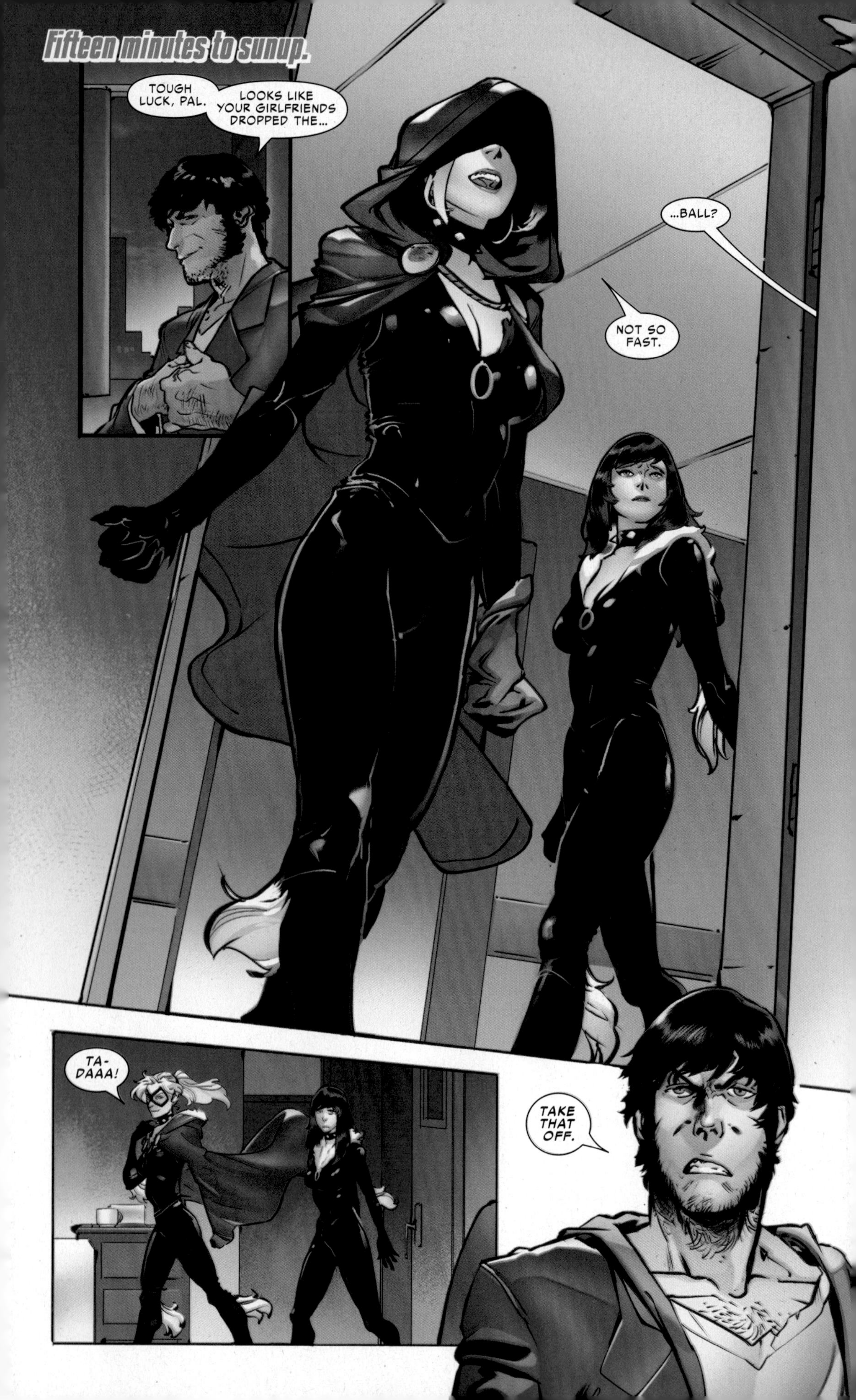

Fifteen minutes to sunup.
TOUGH LUCK, PAL.
LOOKS LIKE YOUR GIRLFRIENDS DROPPED THE...
...BALL?
NOT SO FAST.
TA-DAAA!
TAKE THAT OFF.

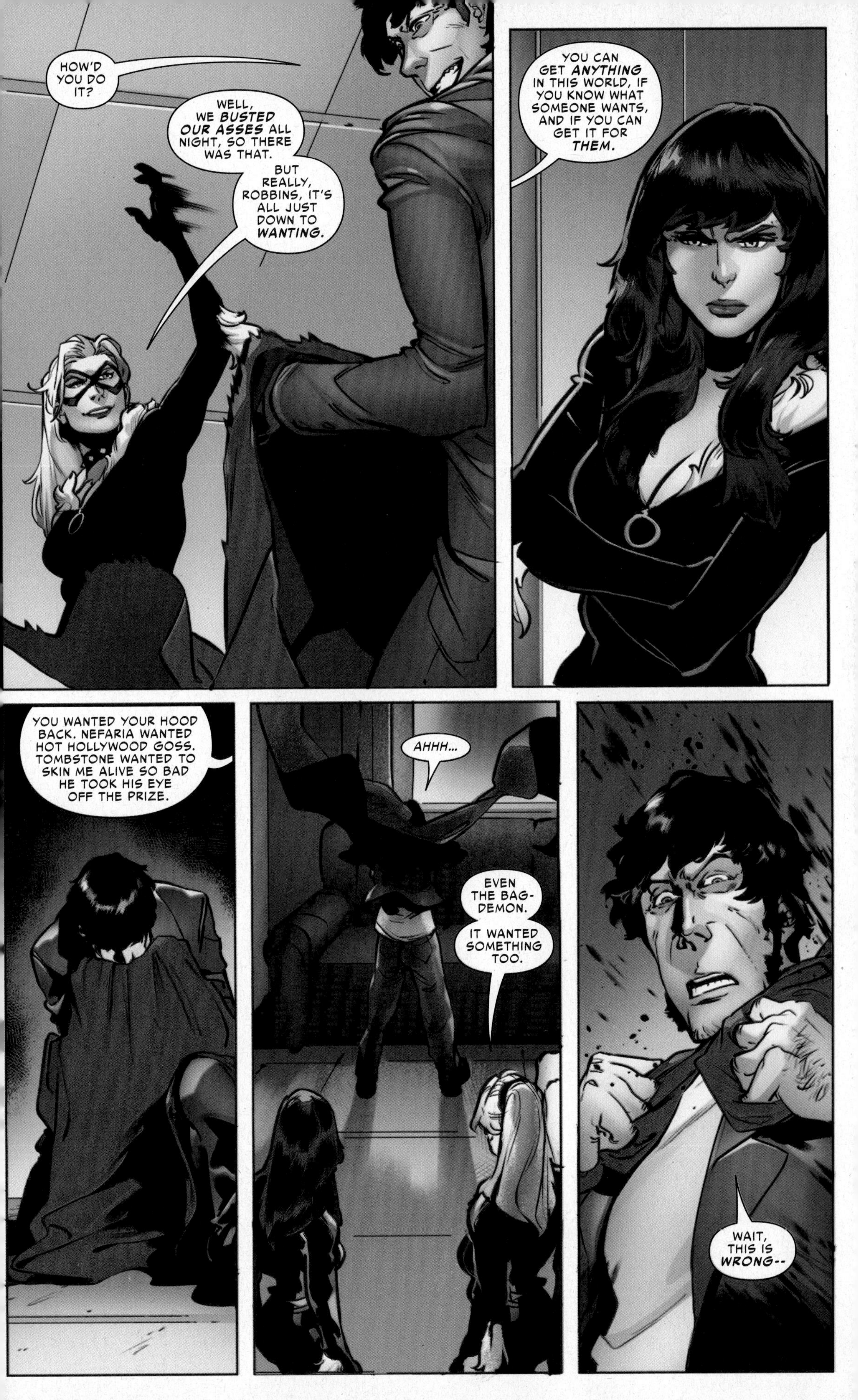
HOW'D YOU DO IT?
WELL, WE BUSTED OUR ASSES ALL NIGHT, SO THERE WAS THAT.
BUT REALLY, ROBBINS, IT'S ALL JUST DOWN TO WANTING.
YOU CAN GET ANYTHING IN THIS WORLD, IF YOU KNOW WHAT SOMEONE WANTS, AND IF YOU CAN GET IT FOR THEM.
YOU WANTED YOUR HOOD BACK. NEFARIA WANTED HOT HOLLYWOOD GOSS. TOMBSTONE WANTED TO SKIN ME ALIVE SO BAD HE TOOK HIS EYE OFF THE PRIZE.
AHHH...
EVEN THE BAG-DEMON.
IT WANTED SOMETHING TOO.
WAIT, THIS IS WRONG--

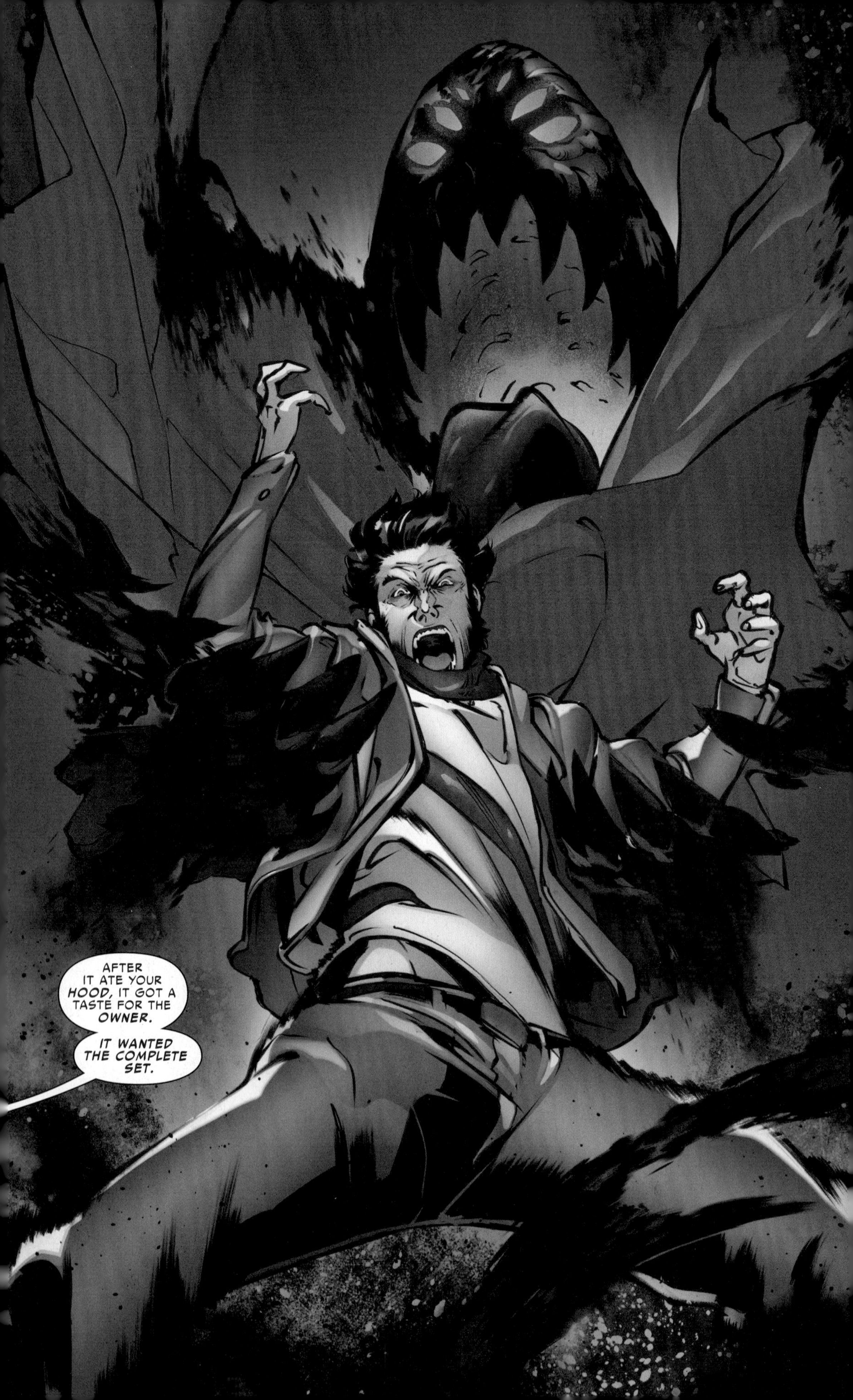
AFTER IT ATE YOUR *HOOD*, IT GOT A TASTE FOR THE *OWNER*.
IT WANTED THE COMPLETE SET.

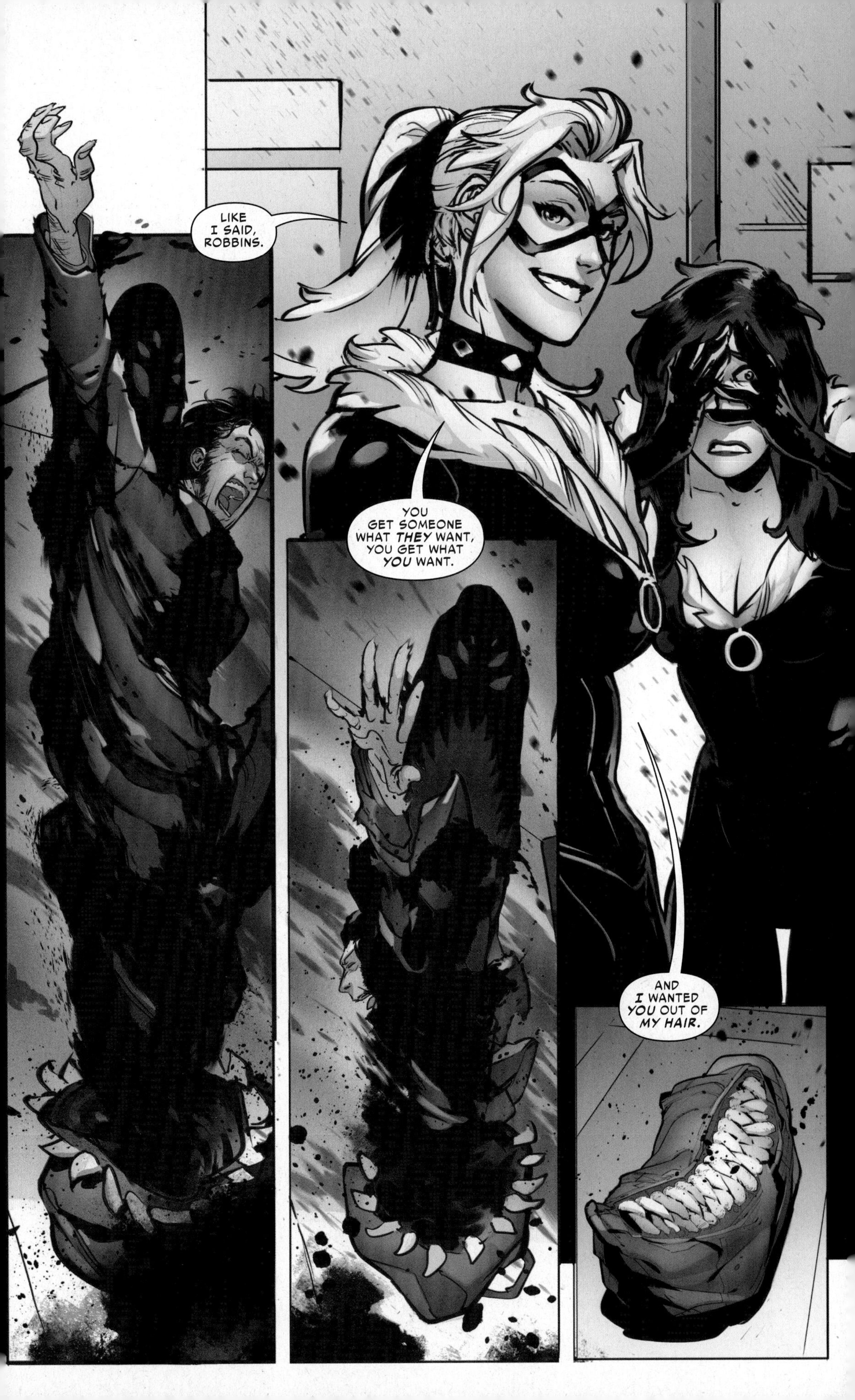
LIKE I SAID, ROBBINS.
YOU GET SOMEONE WHAT *THEY* WANT, YOU GET WHAT *YOU* WANT.
AND I WANTED *YOU* OUT OF MY *HAIR*.

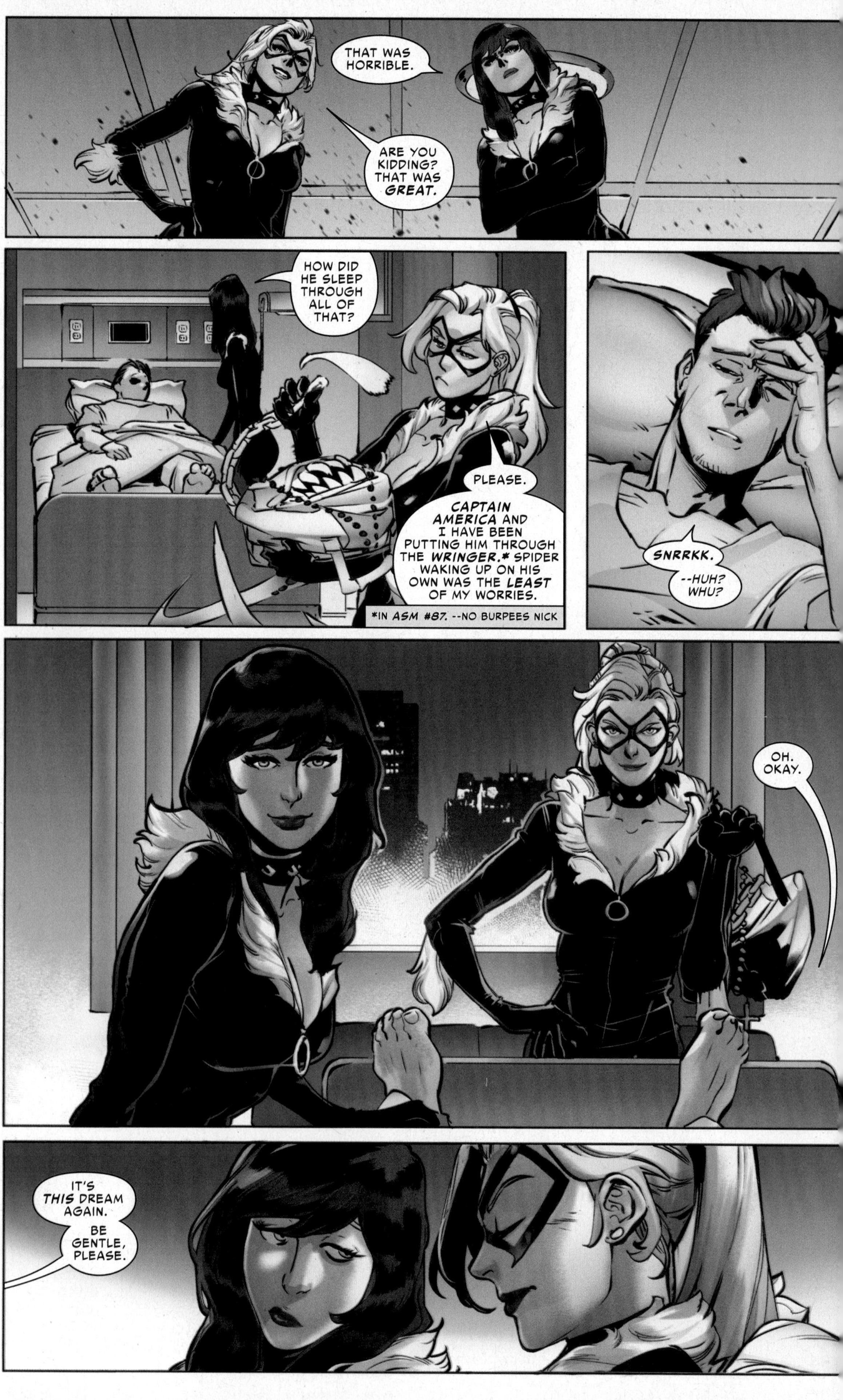
THAT WAS HORRIBLE.
ARE YOU KIDDING? THAT WAS GREAT.
HOW DID HE SLEEP THROUGH ALL OF THAT?
PLEASE.
CAPTAIN AMERICA AND I HAVE BEEN PUTTING HIM THROUGH THE WRINGER.* SPIDER WAKING UP ON HIS OWN WAS THE LEAST OF MY WORRIES.
*IN ASM #87. --NO BURPEES NICK
SNRRKK.
--HUH? WHU?
OH. OKAY.
IT'S THIS DREAM AGAIN.
BE GENTLE, PLEASE.

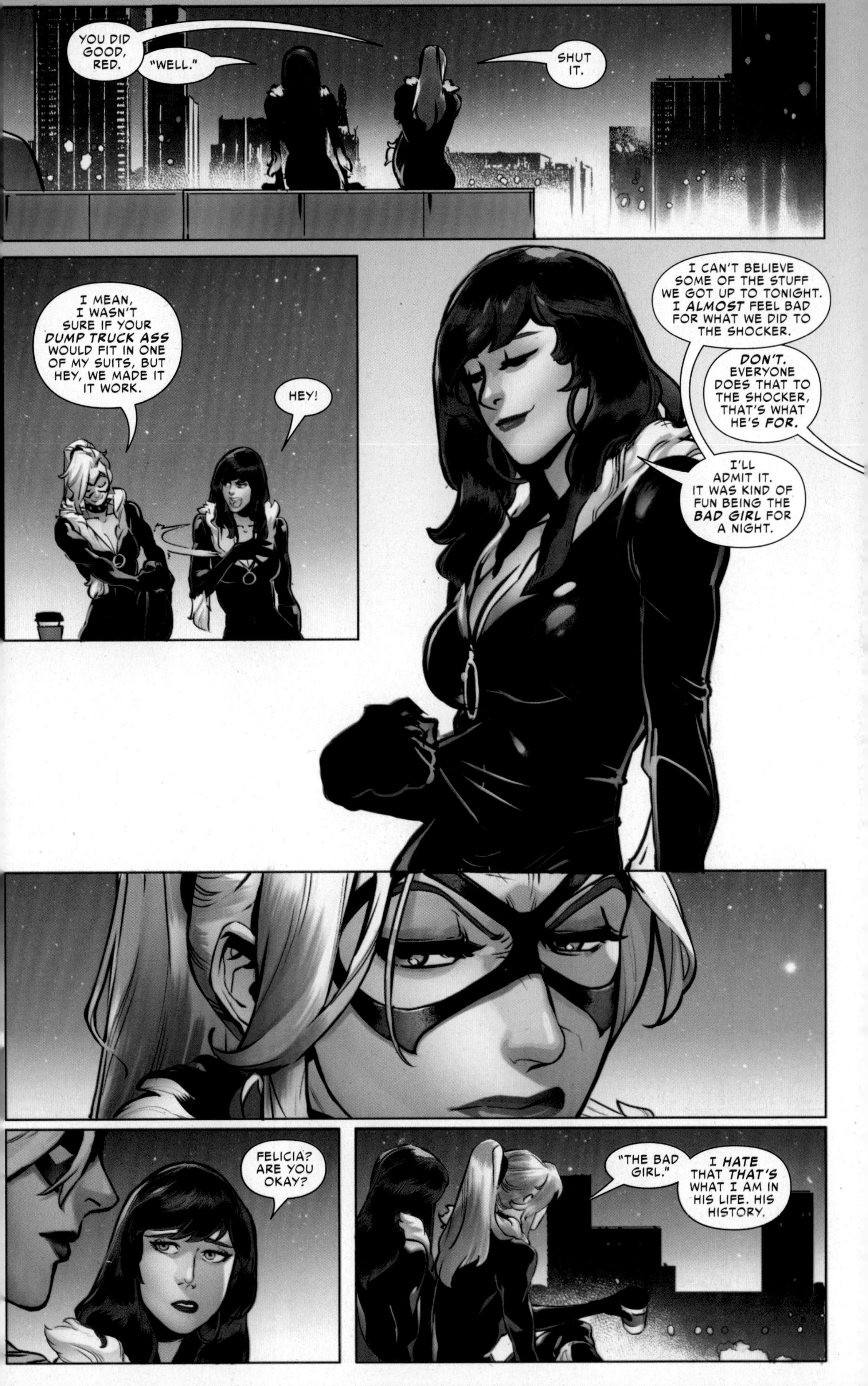
YOU DID GOOD, RED.
"WELL."
SHUT IT.
I MEAN, I WASN'T SURE IF YOUR DUMP TRUCK ASS WOULD FIT IN ONE OF MY SUITS, BUT HEY, WE MADE IT IT WORK.
HEY!
I CAN'T BELIEVE SOME OF THE STUFF WE GOT UP TO TONIGHT. I ALMOST FEEL BAD FOR WHAT WE DID TO THE SHOCKER.
DON'T. EVERYONE DOES THAT TO THE SHOCKER, THAT'S WHAT HE'S FOR.
I'LL ADMIT IT. IT WAS KIND OF FUN BEING THE BAD GIRL FOR A NIGHT.
FELICIA? ARE YOU OKAY?
"THE BAD GIRL."
I HATE THAT THAT'S WHAT I AM IN HIS LIFE. HIS HISTORY.

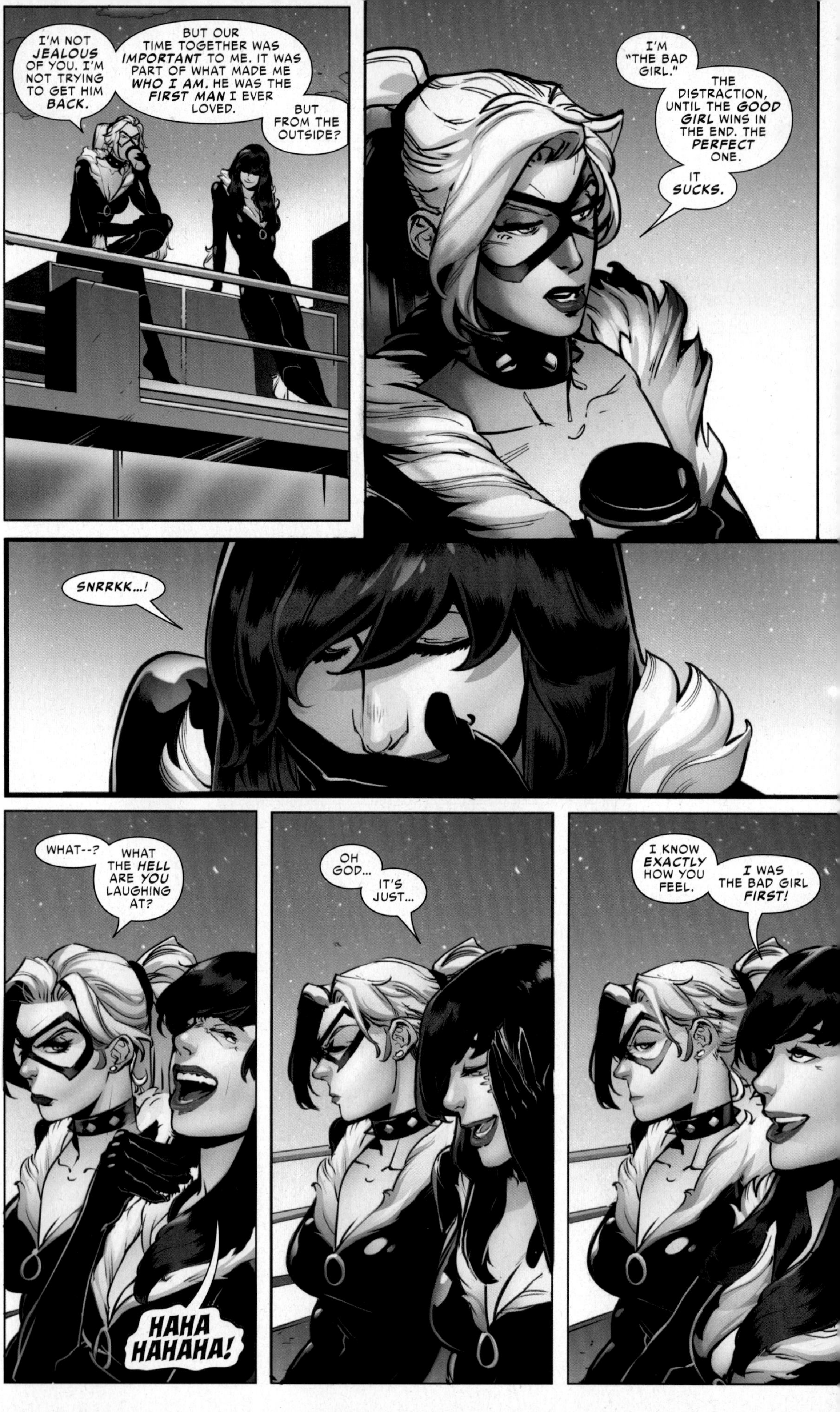

I'M NOT JEALOUS OF YOU. I'M NOT TRYING TO GET HIM BACK.
BUT OUR TIME TOGETHER WAS IMPORTANT TO ME. IT WAS PART OF WHAT MADE ME WHO I AM. HE WAS THE FIRST MAN I EVER LOVED.
BUT FROM THE OUTSIDE?
I'M "THE BAD GIRL."
THE DISTRACTION, UNTIL THE GOOD GIRL WINS IN THE END. THE PERFECT ONE.
IT SUCKS.
SNRRKK...!
WHAT--?
WHAT THE HELL ARE YOU LAUGHING AT?
HAHA HAHAHA!
OH GOD...
IT'S JUST...
I KNOW EXACTLY HOW YOU FEEL.
I WAS THE BAD GIRL FIRST!

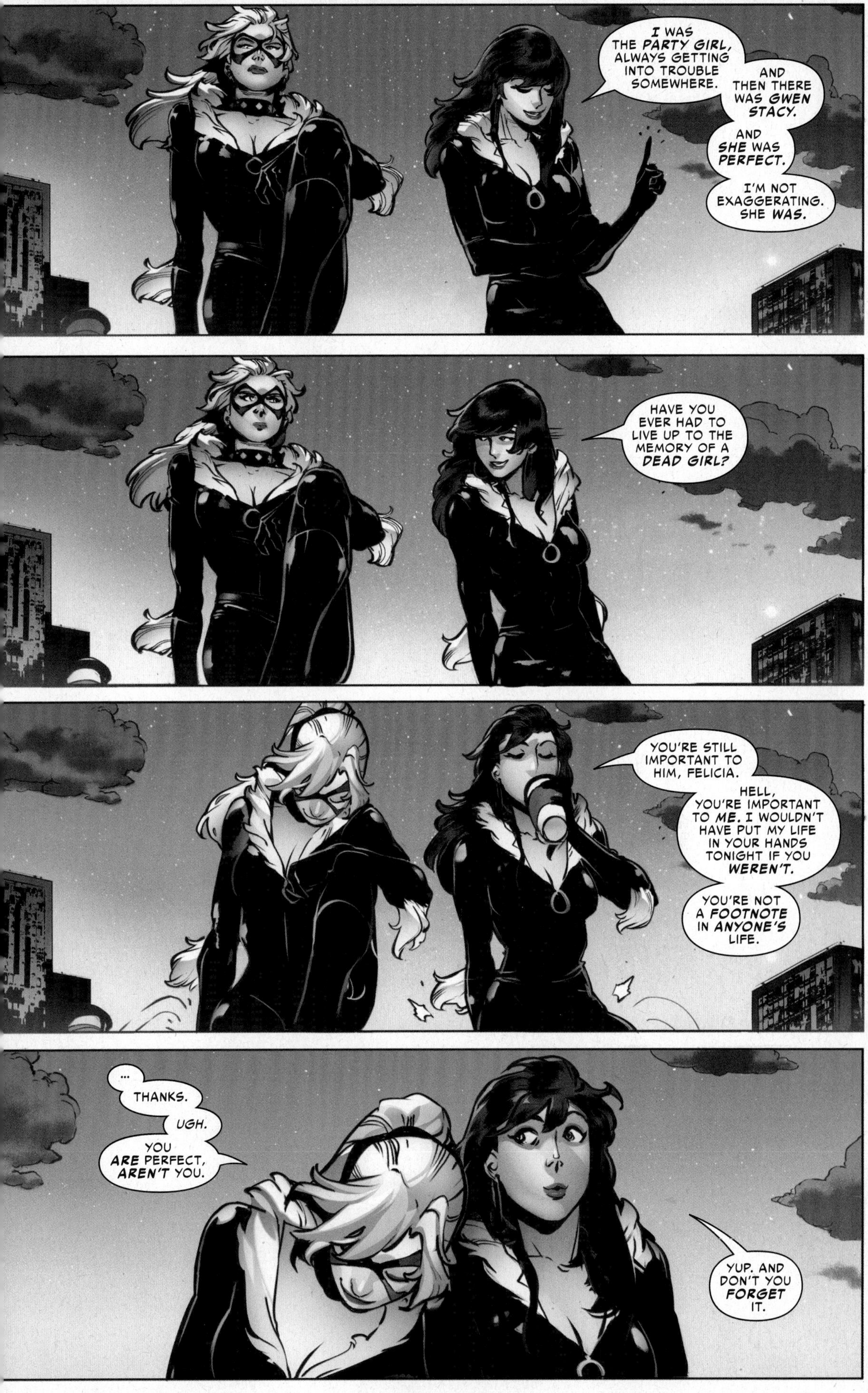
I WAS THE PARTY GIRL, ALWAYS GETTING INTO TROUBLE SOMEWHERE.
AND THEN THERE WAS GWEN STACY.
AND SHE WAS PERFECT.
I'M NOT EXAGGERATING. SHE WAS.
HAVE YOU EVER HAD TO LIVE UP TO THE MEMORY OF A DEAD GIRL?
YOU'RE STILL IMPORTANT TO HIM, FELICIA.
HELL, YOU'RE IMPORTANT TO ME. I WOULDN'T HAVE PUT MY LIFE IN YOUR HANDS TONIGHT IF YOU WEREN'T.
YOU'RE NOT A FOOTNOTE IN ANYONE'S LIFE.
...
THANKS.
UGH.
YOU ARE PERFECT, AREN'T YOU.
YUP. AND DON'T YOU FORGET IT.

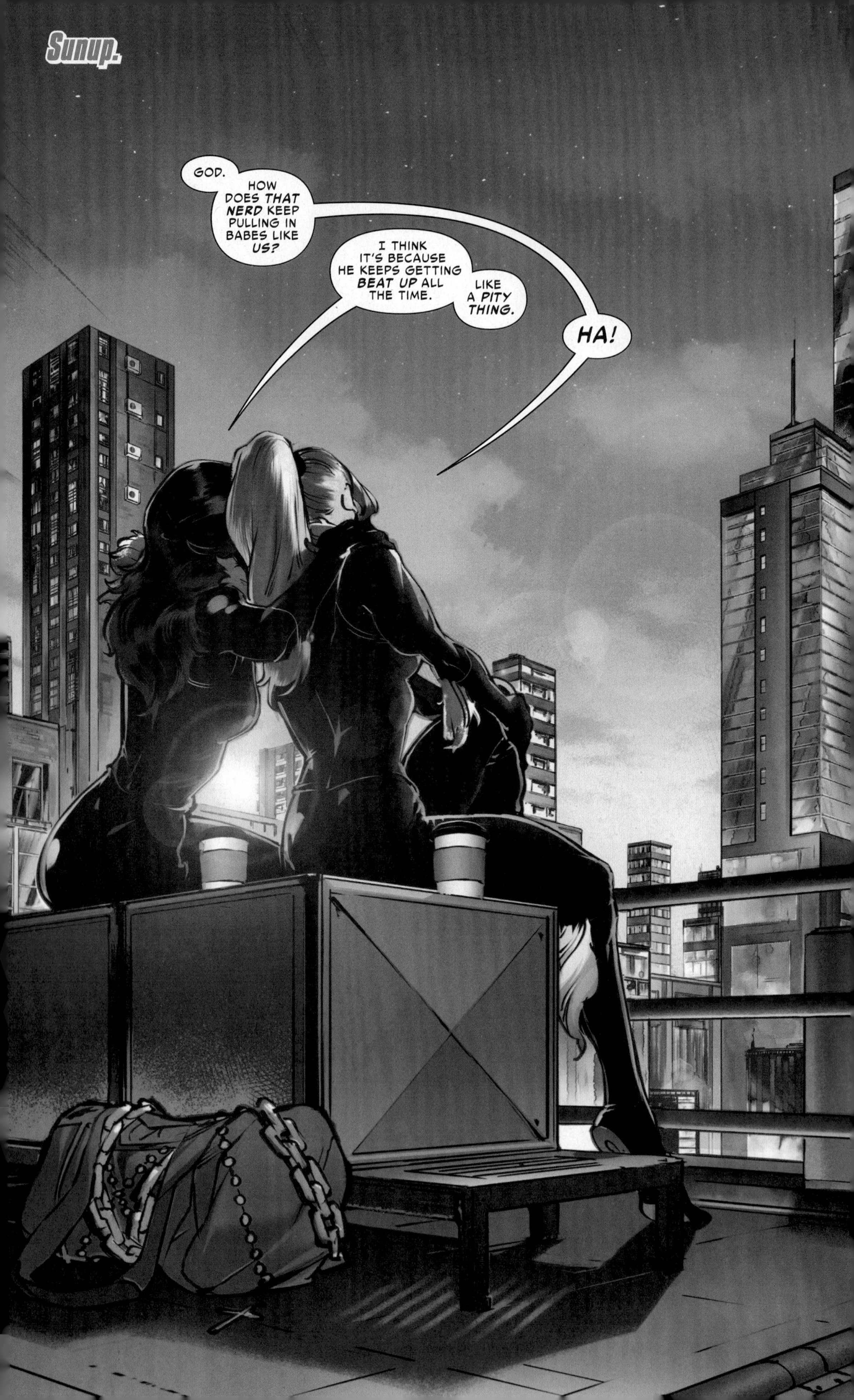
Sunup.
GOD.
HOW DOES THAT NERD KEEP PULLING IN BABES LIKE US?
I THINK IT'S BECAUSE HE KEEPS GETTING BEAT UP ALL THE TIME.
LIKE A PITY THING.
HA!

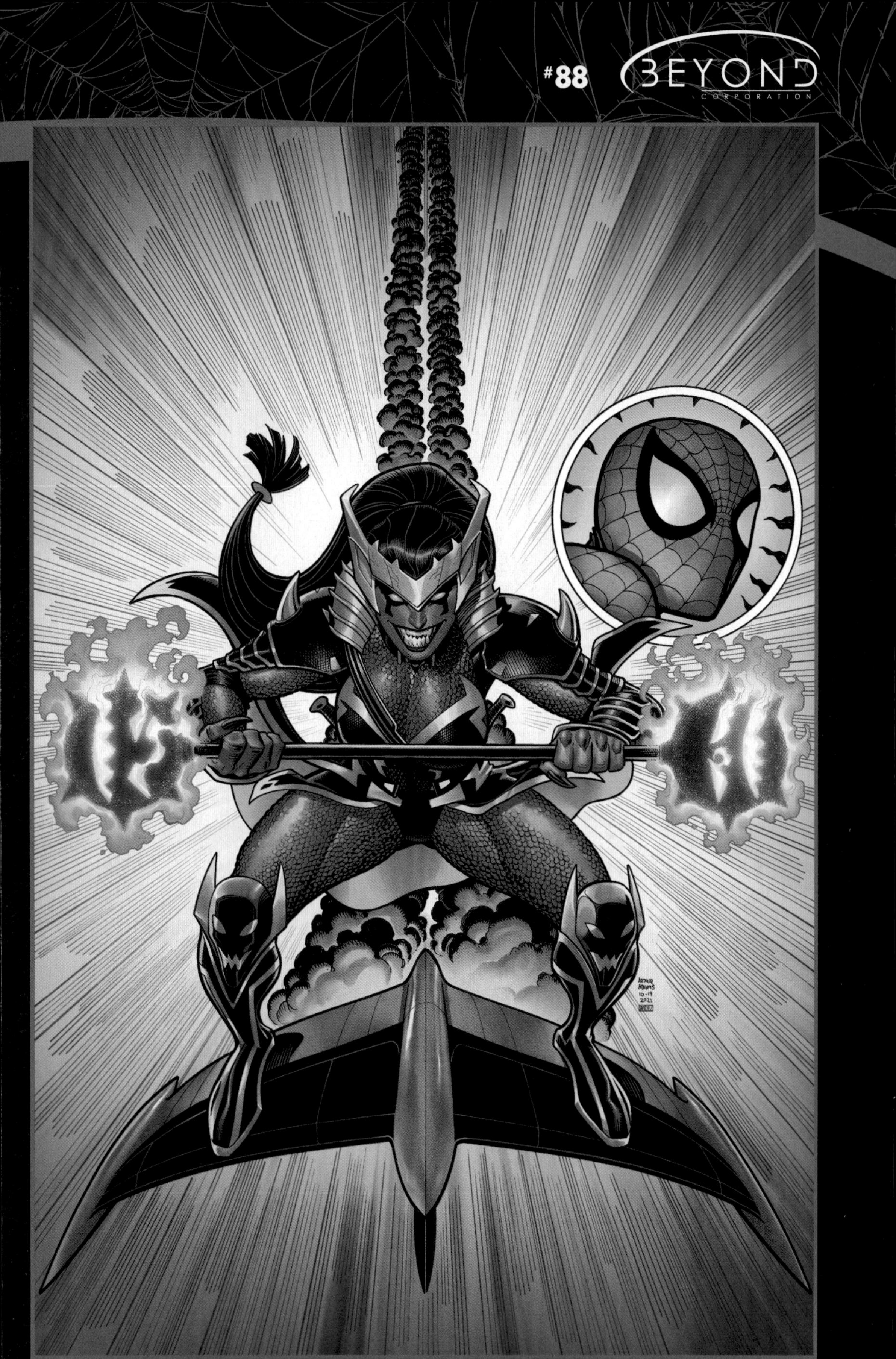
#88
BEYOND
CORPORATION

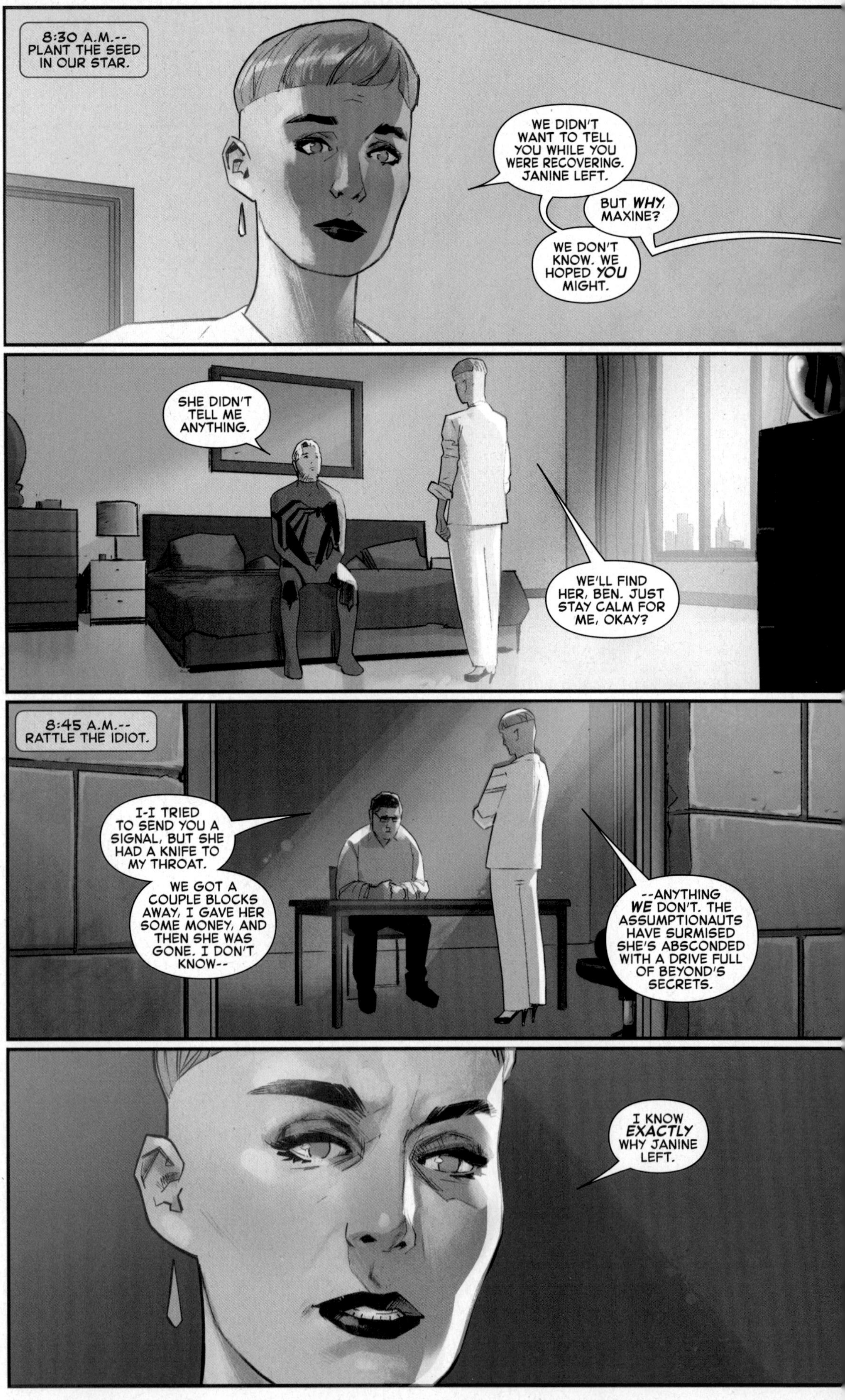
8:30 A.M.-- PLANT THE SEED IN OUR STAR.
WE DIDN'T WANT TO TELL YOU WHILE YOU WERE RECOVERING. JANINE LEFT.
BUT WHY, MAXINE?
WE DON'T KNOW. WE HOPED YOU MIGHT.
SHE DIDN'T TELL ME ANYTHING.
WE'LL FIND HER, BEN. JUST STAY CALM FOR ME, OKAY?
8:45 A.M.-- RATTLE THE IDIOT.
I-I TRIED TO SEND YOU A SIGNAL, BUT SHE HAD A KNIFE TO MY THROAT.
WE GOT A COUPLE BLOCKS AWAY, I GAVE HER SOME MONEY, AND THEN SHE WAS GONE. I DON'T KNOW--
--ANYTHING WE DON'T. THE ASSUMPTIONAUTS HAVE SURMISED SHE'S ABSCONDED WITH A DRIVE FULL OF BEYOND'S SECRETS.
I KNOW EXACTLY WHY JANINE LEFT.

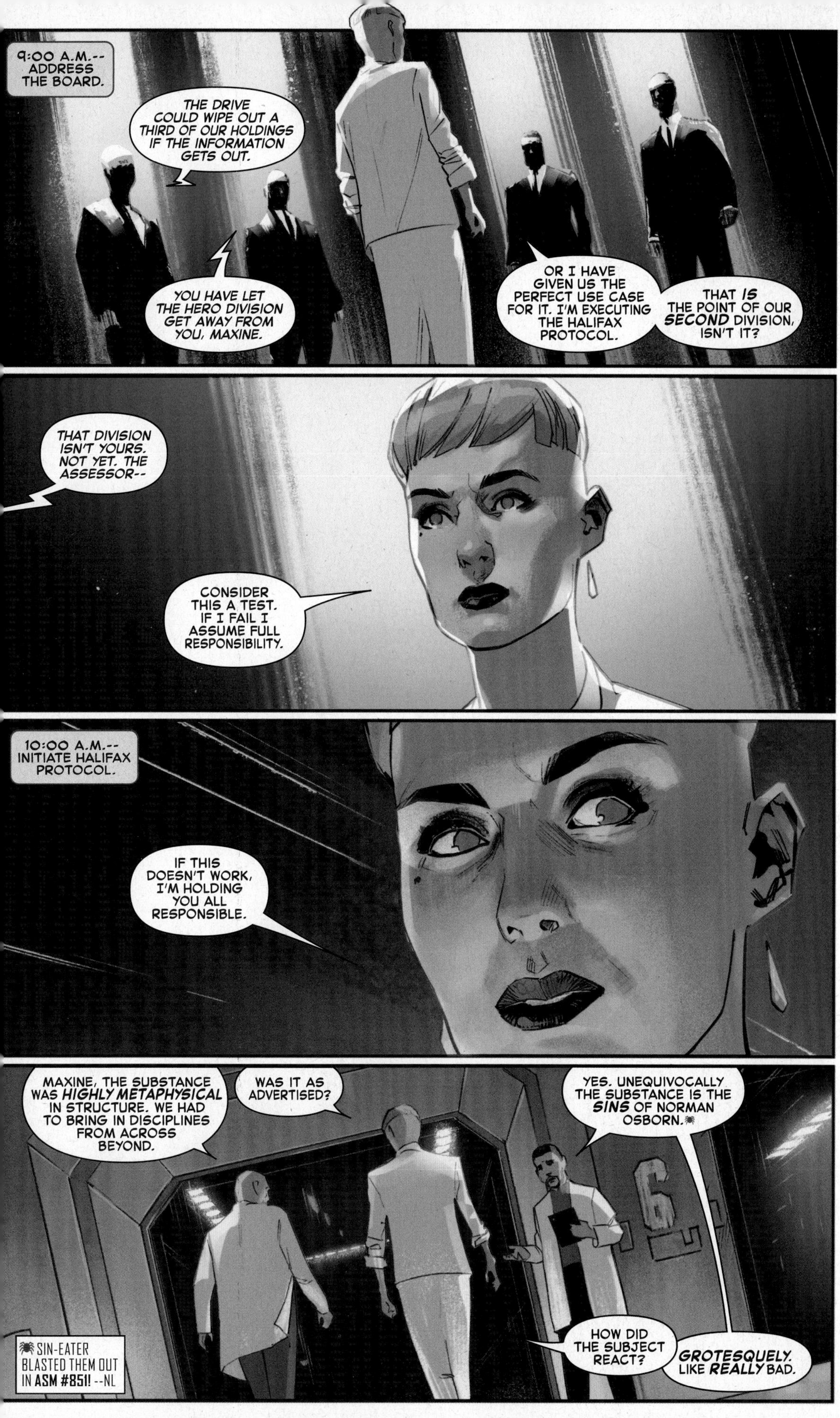
9:00 A.M.-- ADDRESS THE BOARD.
THE DRIVE COULD WIPE OUT A THIRD OF OUR HOLDINGS IF THE INFORMATION GETS OUT.
YOU HAVE LET THE HERO DIVISION GET AWAY FROM YOU, MAXINE.
OR I HAVE GIVEN US THE PERFECT USE CASE FOR IT. I'M EXECUTING THE HALIFAX PROTOCOL.
THAT IS THE POINT OF OUR SECOND DIVISION, ISN'T IT?
THAT DIVISION ISN'T YOURS. NOT YET. THE ASSESSOR--
CONSIDER THIS A TEST. IF I FAIL I ASSUME FULL RESPONSIBILITY.
10:00 A.M.-- INITIATE HALIFAX PROTOCOL.
IF THIS DOESN'T WORK, I'M HOLDING YOU ALL RESPONSIBLE.
MAXINE, THE SUBSTANCE WAS HIGHLY METAPHYSICAL IN STRUCTURE. WE HAD TO BRING IN DISCIPLINES FROM ACROSS BEYOND.
WAS IT AS ADVERTISED?
YES. UNEQUIVOCALLY THE SUBSTANCE IS THE SINS OF NORMAN OSBORN.
HOW DID THE SUBJECT REACT?
GROTESQUELY. LIKE REALLY BAD.
SIN-EATER BLASTED THEM OUT IN ASM #851! --NL

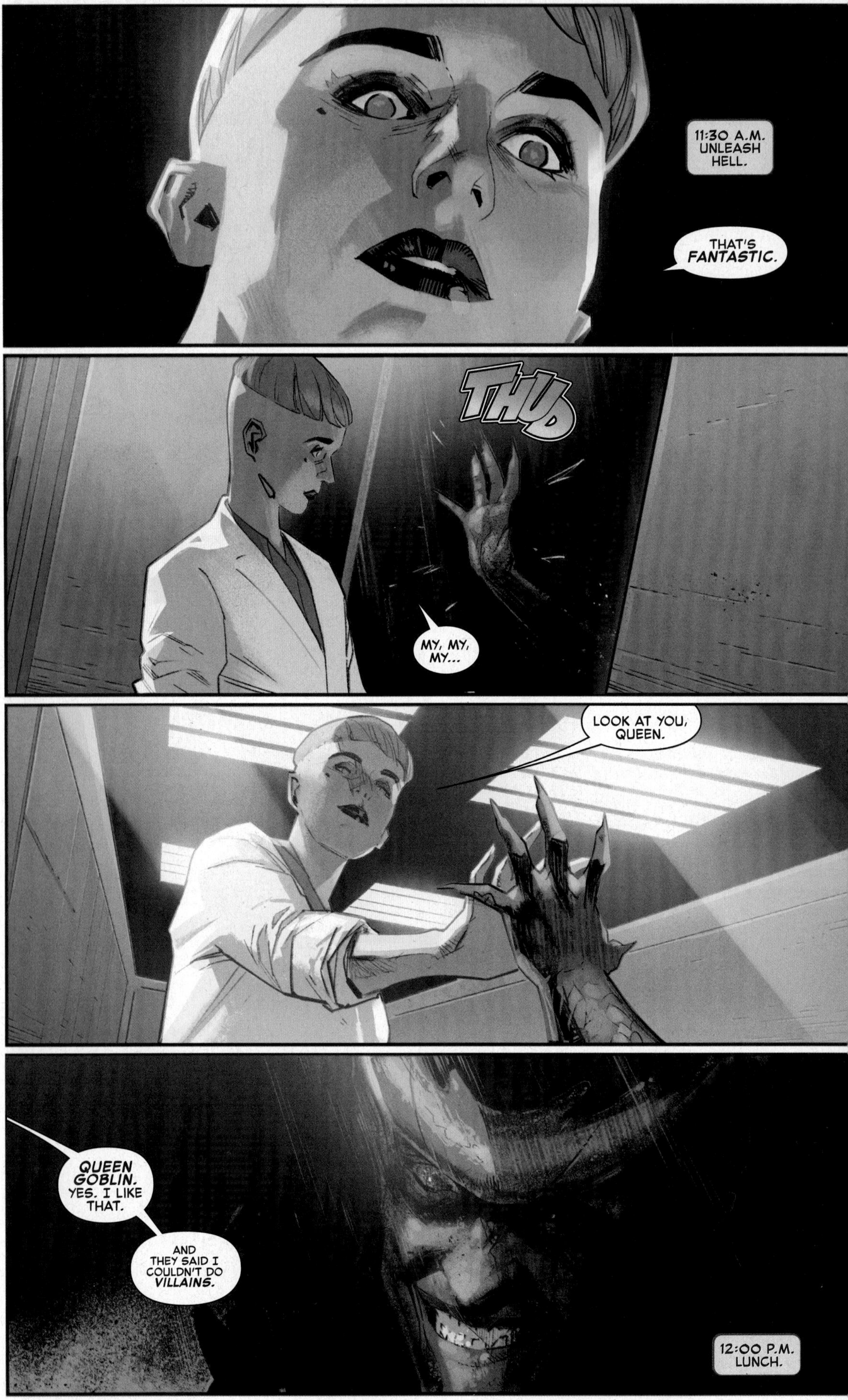
11:30 A.M. UNLEASH HELL.
THAT'S FANTASTIC.
THUD
MY, MY, MY...
LOOK AT YOU, QUEEN.
QUEEN GOBLIN. YES. I LIKE THAT.
AND THEY SAID I COULDN'T DO VILLAINS.
12:00 P.M. LUNCH.

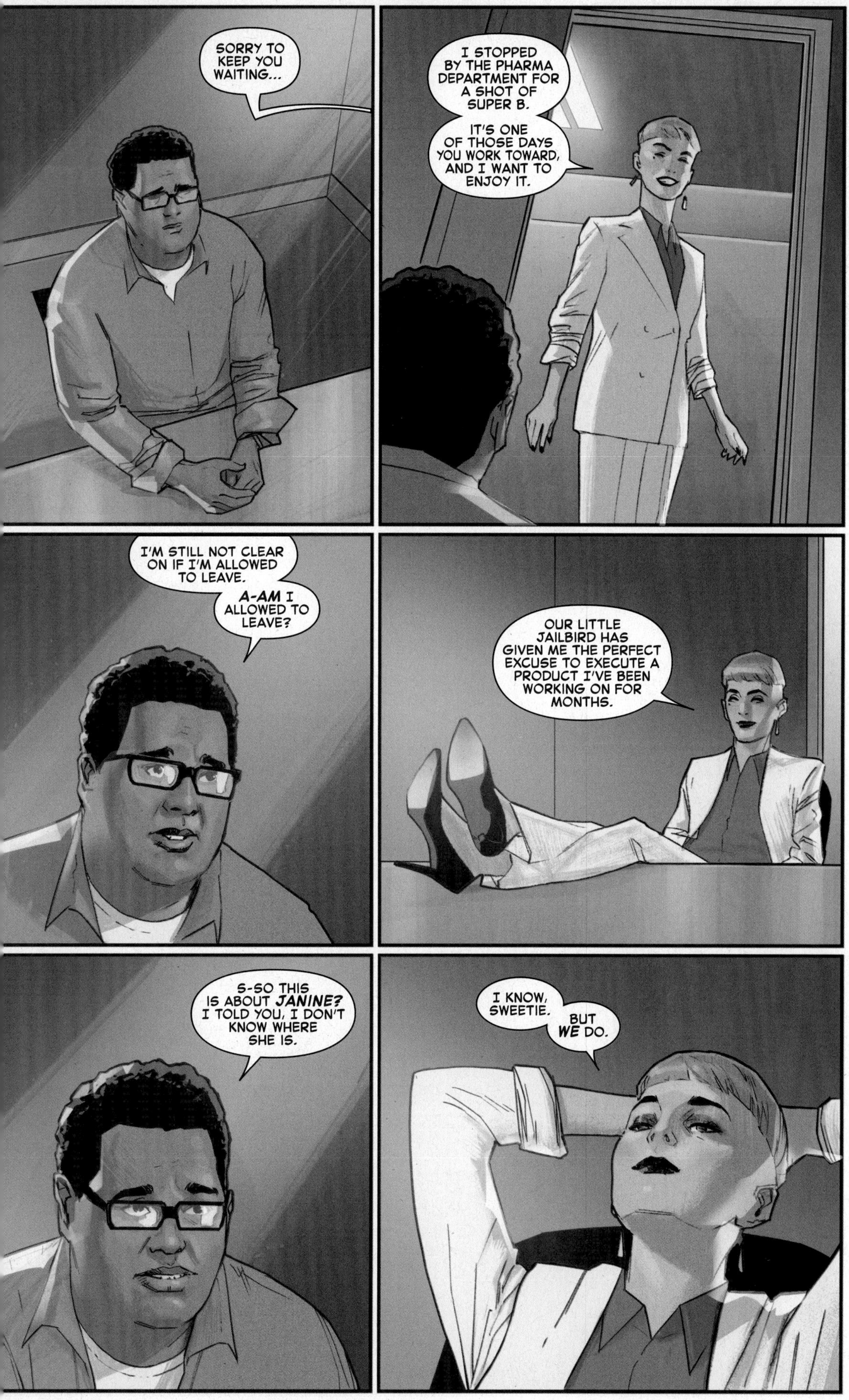
SORRY TO KEEP YOU WAITING...
I STOPPED BY THE PHARMA DEPARTMENT FOR A SHOT OF SUPER B.
IT'S ONE OF THOSE DAYS YOU WORK TOWARD, AND I WANT TO ENJOY IT.
I'M STILL NOT CLEAR ON IF I'M ALLOWED TO LEAVE.
A-AM I ALLOWED TO LEAVE?
OUR LITTLE JAILBIRD HAS GIVEN ME THE PERFECT EXCUSE TO EXECUTE A PRODUCT I'VE BEEN WORKING ON FOR MONTHS.
S-SO THIS IS ABOUT JANINE? I TOLD YOU, I DON'T KNOW WHERE SHE IS.
I KNOW, SWEETIE.
BUT WE DO.

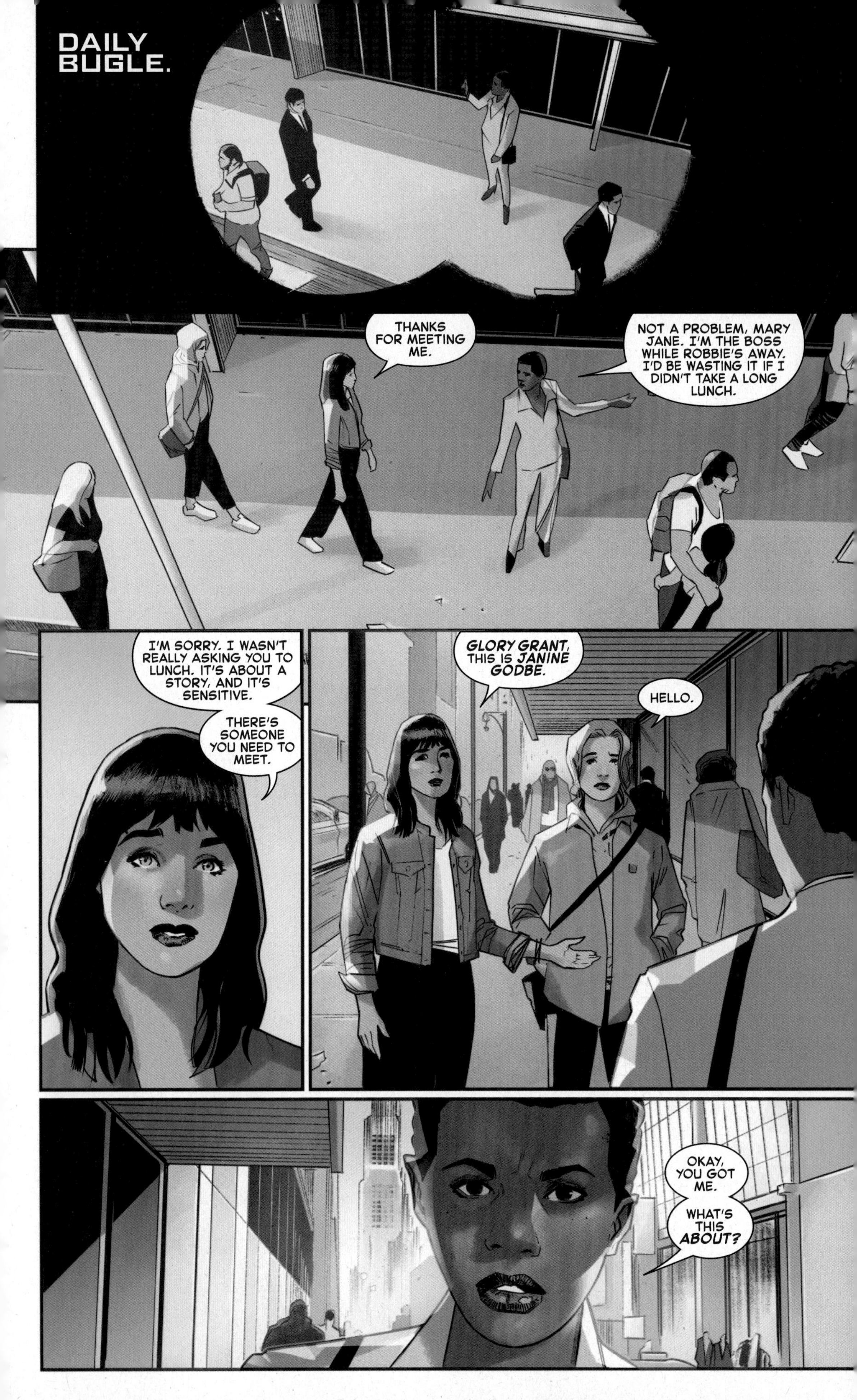
DAILY BUGLE.
THANKS FOR MEETING ME.
NOT A PROBLEM, MARY JANE. I'M THE BOSS WHILE ROBBIE'S AWAY. I'D BE WASTING IT IF I DIDN'T TAKE A LONG LUNCH.
I'M SORRY. I WASN'T REALLY ASKING YOU TO LUNCH. IT'S ABOUT A STORY, AND IT'S SENSITIVE.
THERE'S SOMEONE YOU NEED TO MEET.
GLORY GRANT, THIS IS JANINE GODBE.
HELLO.
OKAY, YOU GOT ME.
WHAT'S THIS ABOUT?

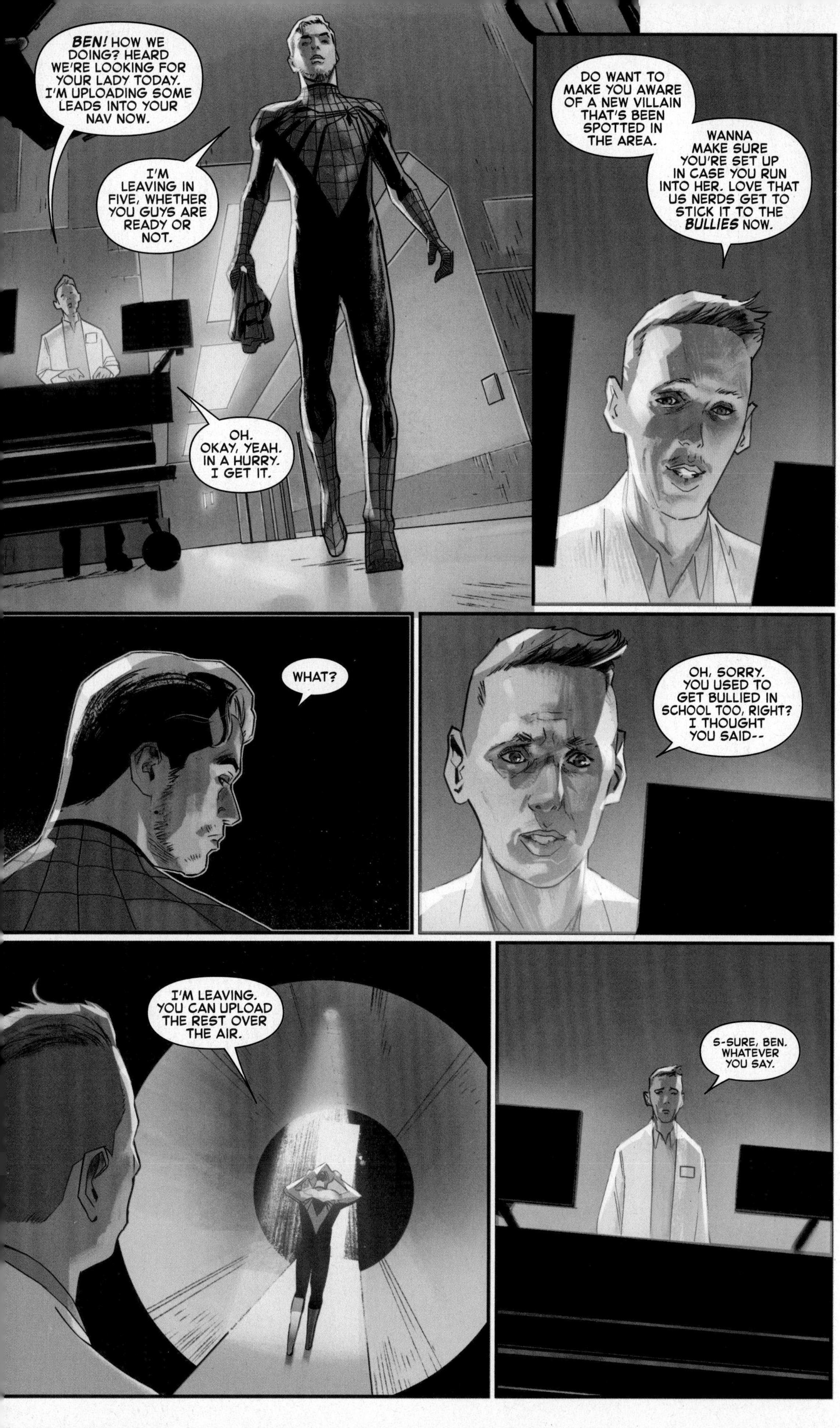
BEN! HOW WE DOING? HEARD WE'RE LOOKING FOR YOUR LADY TODAY. I'M UPLOADING SOME LEADS INTO YOUR NAV NOW.
I'M LEAVING IN FIVE, WHETHER YOU GUYS ARE READY OR NOT.
OH. OKAY, YEAH. IN A HURRY. I GET IT.
DO WANT TO MAKE YOU AWARE OF A NEW VILLAIN THAT'S BEEN SPOTTED IN THE AREA.
WANNA MAKE SURE YOU'RE SET UP IN CASE YOU RUN INTO HER. LOVE THAT US NERDS GET TO STICK IT TO THE BULLIES NOW.
WHAT?
OH, SORRY. YOU USED TO GET BULLIED IN SCHOOL TOO, RIGHT? I THOUGHT YOU SAID--
I'M LEAVING. YOU CAN UPLOAD THE REST OVER THE AIR.
S-SURE, BEN. WHATEVER YOU SAY.

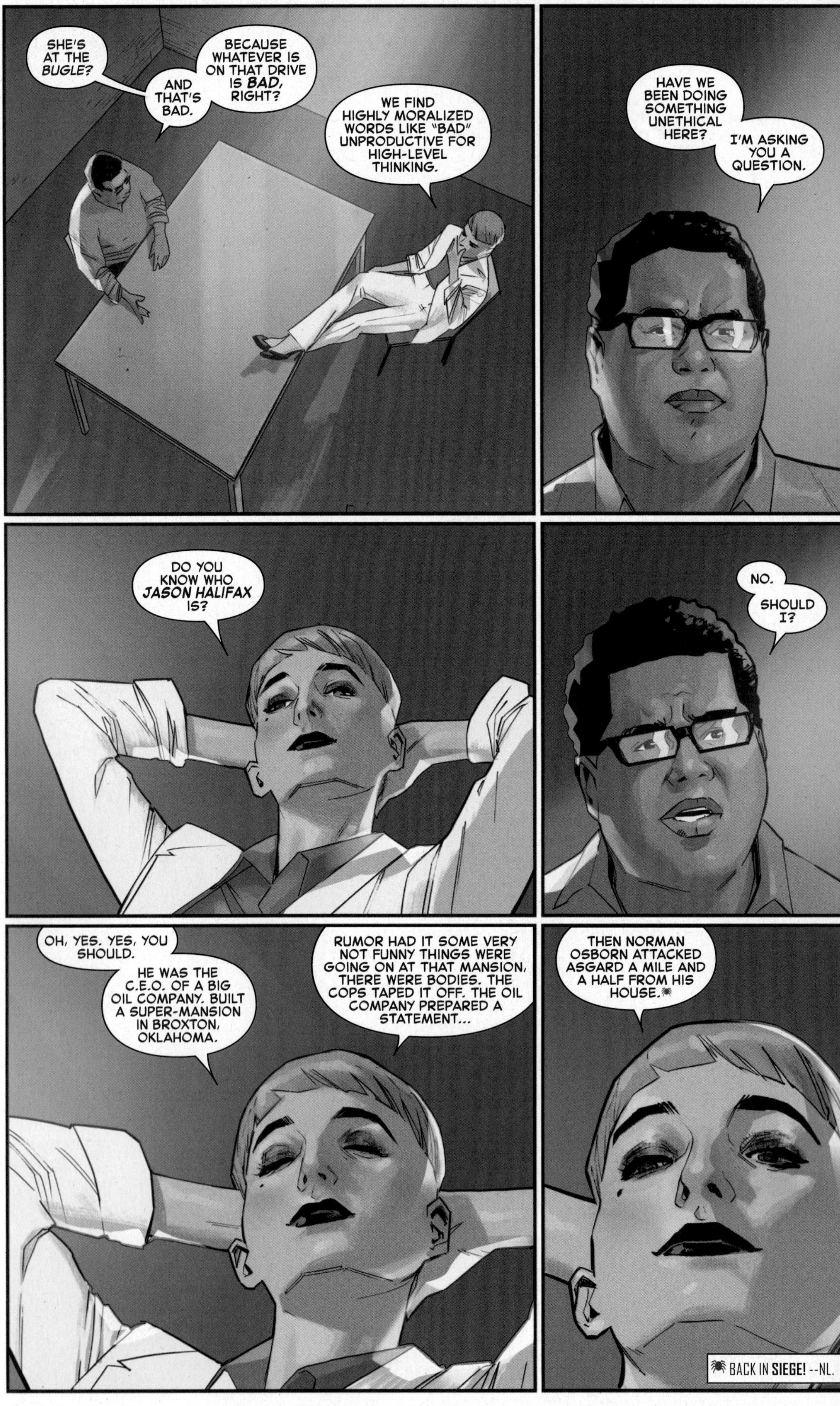
SHE'S AT THE *BUGLE*?
AND THAT'S BAD.
BECAUSE WHATEVER IS ON THAT DRIVE IS **BAD**, RIGHT?
WE FIND HIGHLY MORALIZED WORDS LIKE "BAD" UNPRODUCTIVE FOR HIGH-LEVEL THINKING.
HAVE WE BEEN DOING SOMETHING UNETHICAL HERE?
I'M ASKING YOU A QUESTION.
DO YOU KNOW WHO **JASON HALIFAX** IS?
NO.
SHOULD I?
OH, YES. YES, YOU SHOULD.
HE WAS THE C.E.O. OF A BIG OIL COMPANY. BUILT A SUPER-MANSION IN BROXTON, OKLAHOMA.
RUMOR HAD IT SOME VERY NOT FUNNY THINGS WERE GOING ON AT THAT MANSION, THERE WERE BODIES. THE COPS TAPED IT OFF. THE OIL COMPANY PREPARED A STATEMENT...
THEN NORMAN OSBORN ATTACKED ASGARD A MILE AND A HALF FROM HIS HOUSE.
BACK IN **SIEGE!** --NL.

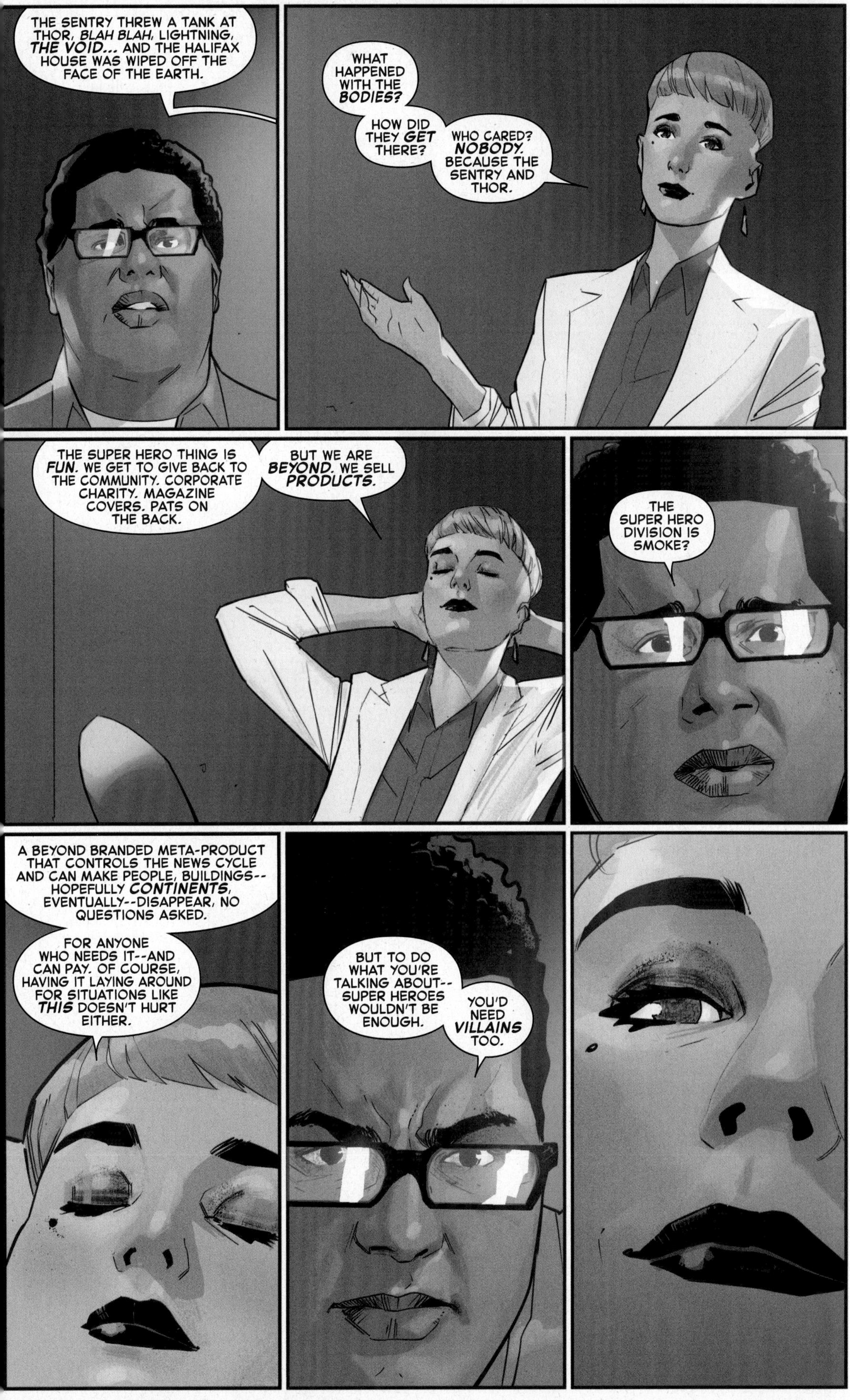
THE SENTRY THREW A TANK AT THOR, *BLAH BLAH*, LIGHTNING, ***THE VOID...*** AND THE HALIFAX HOUSE WAS WIPED OFF THE FACE OF THE EARTH.
WHAT HAPPENED WITH THE ***BODIES?***
HOW DID THEY ***GET*** THERE?
WHO CARED? ***NOBODY.*** BECAUSE THE SENTRY AND THOR.
THE SUPER HERO THING IS ***FUN.*** WE GET TO GIVE BACK TO THE COMMUNITY. CORPORATE CHARITY. MAGAZINE COVERS. PATS ON THE BACK.
BUT WE ARE ***BEYOND.*** WE SELL ***PRODUCTS.***
THE SUPER HERO DIVISION IS SMOKE?
A BEYOND BRANDED META-PRODUCT THAT CONTROLS THE NEWS CYCLE AND CAN MAKE PEOPLE, BUILDINGS--HOPEFULLY ***CONTINENTS,*** EVENTUALLY--DISAPPEAR, NO QUESTIONS ASKED.
FOR ANYONE WHO NEEDS IT--AND CAN PAY. OF COURSE, HAVING IT LAYING AROUND FOR SITUATIONS LIKE ***THIS*** DOESN'T HURT EITHER.
BUT TO DO WHAT YOU'RE TALKING ABOUT--SUPER HEROES WOULDN'T BE ENOUGH.
YOU'D NEED ***VILLAINS*** TOO.

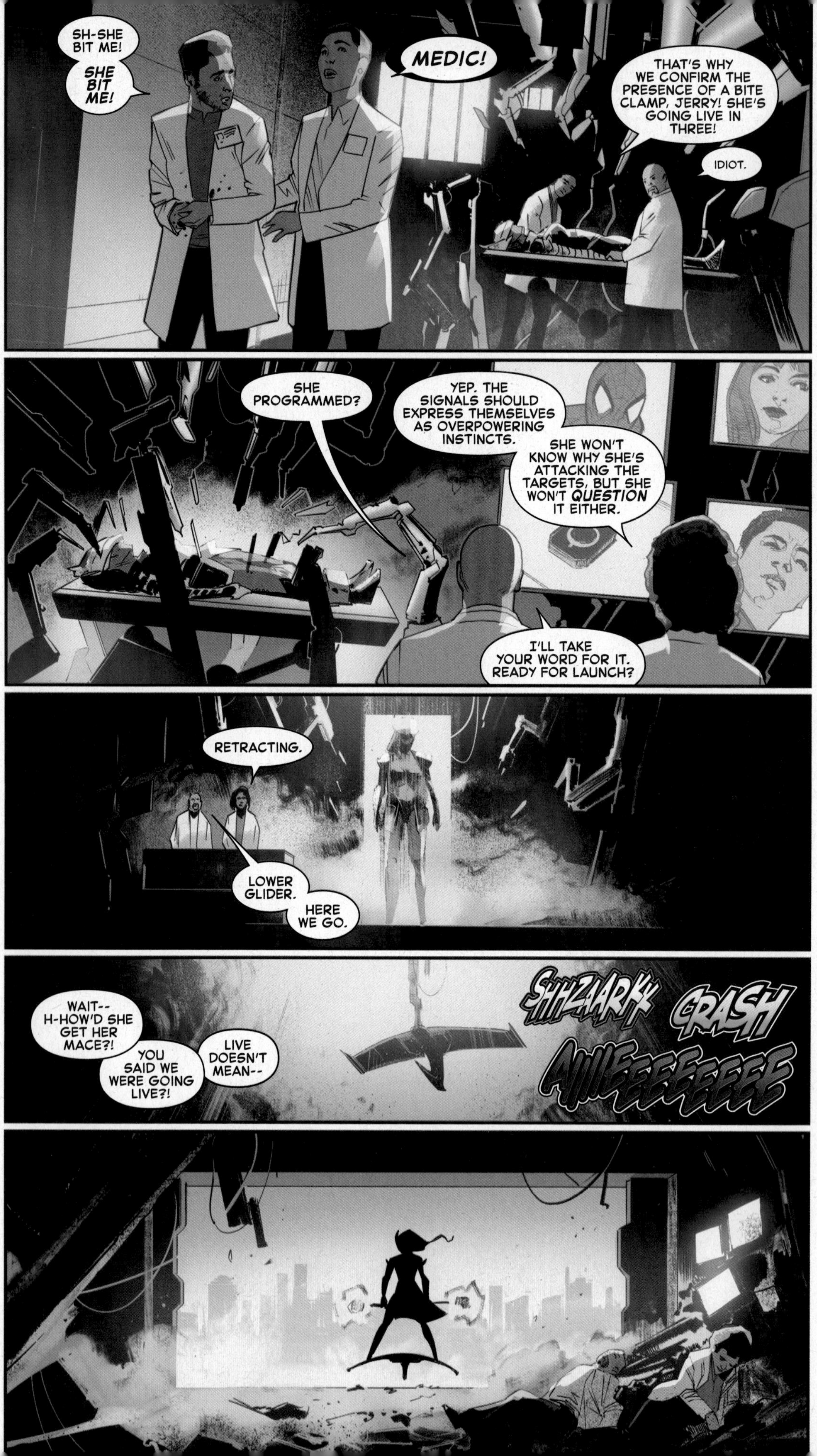
SH-SHE BIT ME!
SHE BIT ME!
MEDIC!
THAT'S WHY WE CONFIRM THE PRESENCE OF A BITE CLAMP, JERRY! SHE'S GOING LIVE IN THREE!
IDIOT.
SHE PROGRAMMED?
YEP. THE SIGNALS SHOULD EXPRESS THEMSELVES AS OVERPOWERING INSTINCTS.
SHE WON'T KNOW WHY SHE'S ATTACKING THE TARGETS, BUT SHE WON'T QUESTION IT EITHER.
I'LL TAKE YOUR WORD FOR IT. READY FOR LAUNCH?
RETRACTING.
LOWER GLIDER.
HERE WE GO.
WAIT-- H-HOW'D SHE GET HER MACE?!
YOU SAID WE WERE GOING LIVE?!
LIVE DOESN'T MEAN--
SHHZAARKK
CRASH
AIIIEEEEEEEE

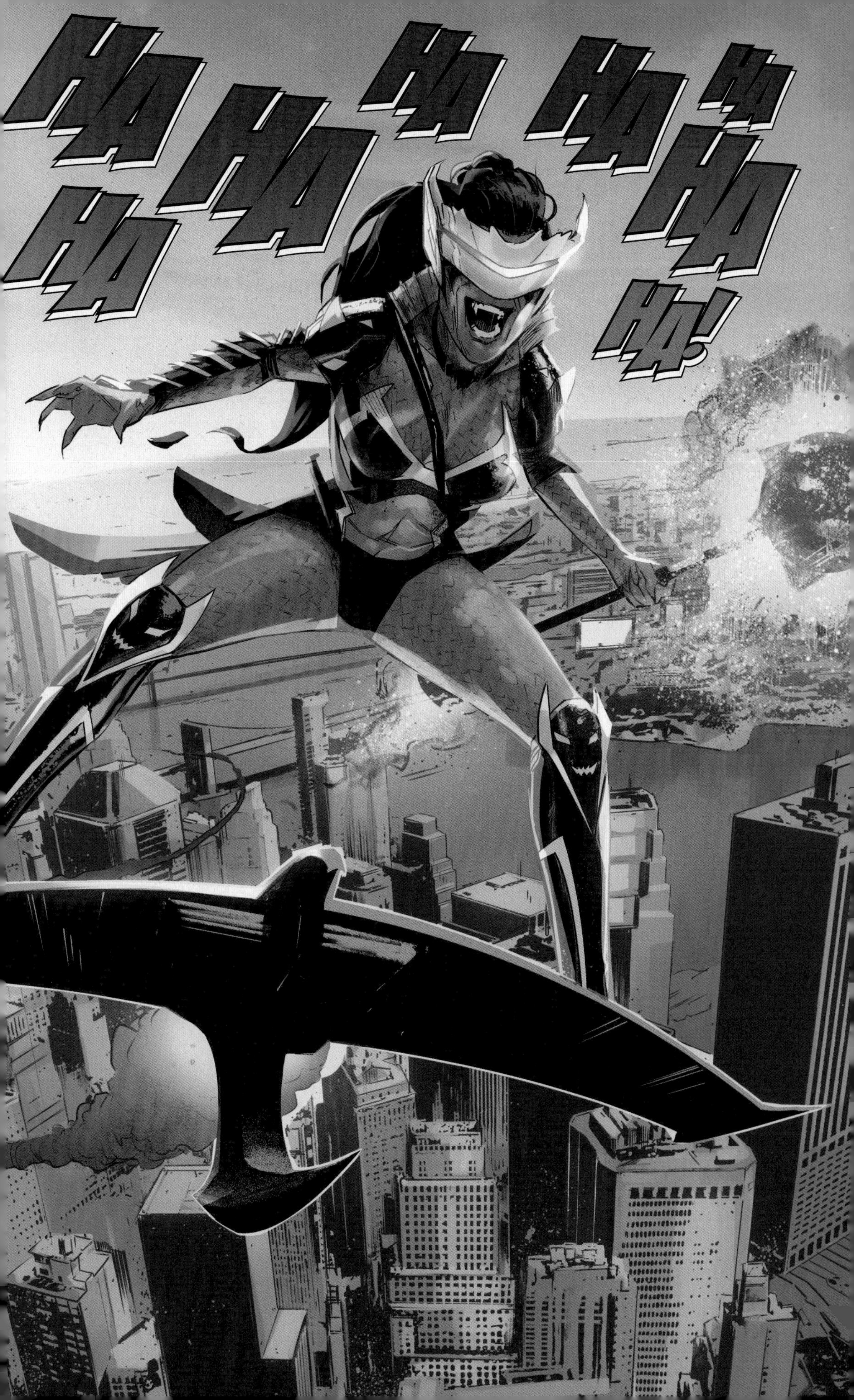
HA HA HA HA HA HA HA HA!

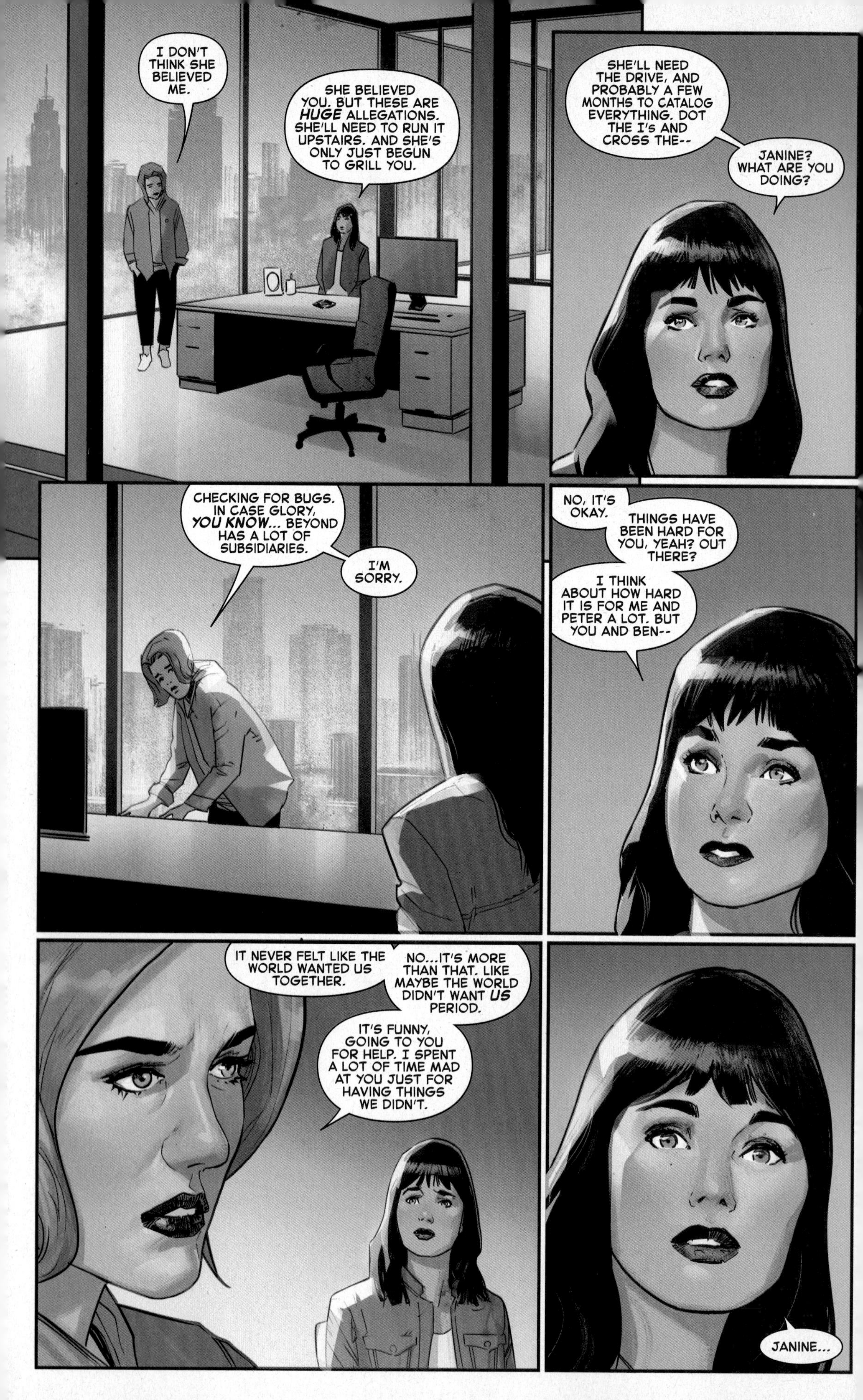
I DON'T THINK SHE BELIEVED ME.
SHE BELIEVED YOU. BUT THESE ARE *HUGE* ALLEGATIONS. SHE'LL NEED TO RUN IT UPSTAIRS. AND SHE'S ONLY JUST BEGUN TO GRILL YOU.
SHE'LL NEED THE DRIVE, AND PROBABLY A FEW MONTHS TO CATALOG EVERYTHING. DOT THE I'S AND CROSS THE--
JANINE? WHAT ARE YOU DOING?
CHECKING FOR BUGS. IN CASE GLORY, *YOU KNOW...* BEYOND HAS A LOT OF SUBSIDIARIES.
I'M SORRY.
NO, IT'S OKAY.
THINGS HAVE BEEN HARD FOR YOU, YEAH? OUT THERE?
I THINK ABOUT HOW HARD IT IS FOR ME AND PETER A LOT. BUT YOU AND BEN--
IT NEVER FELT LIKE THE WORLD WANTED US TOGETHER.
NO...IT'S MORE THAN THAT. LIKE MAYBE THE WORLD DIDN'T WANT *US* PERIOD.
IT'S FUNNY, GOING TO YOU FOR HELP. I SPENT A LOT OF TIME MAD AT YOU JUST FOR HAVING THINGS WE DIDN'T.
JANINE...

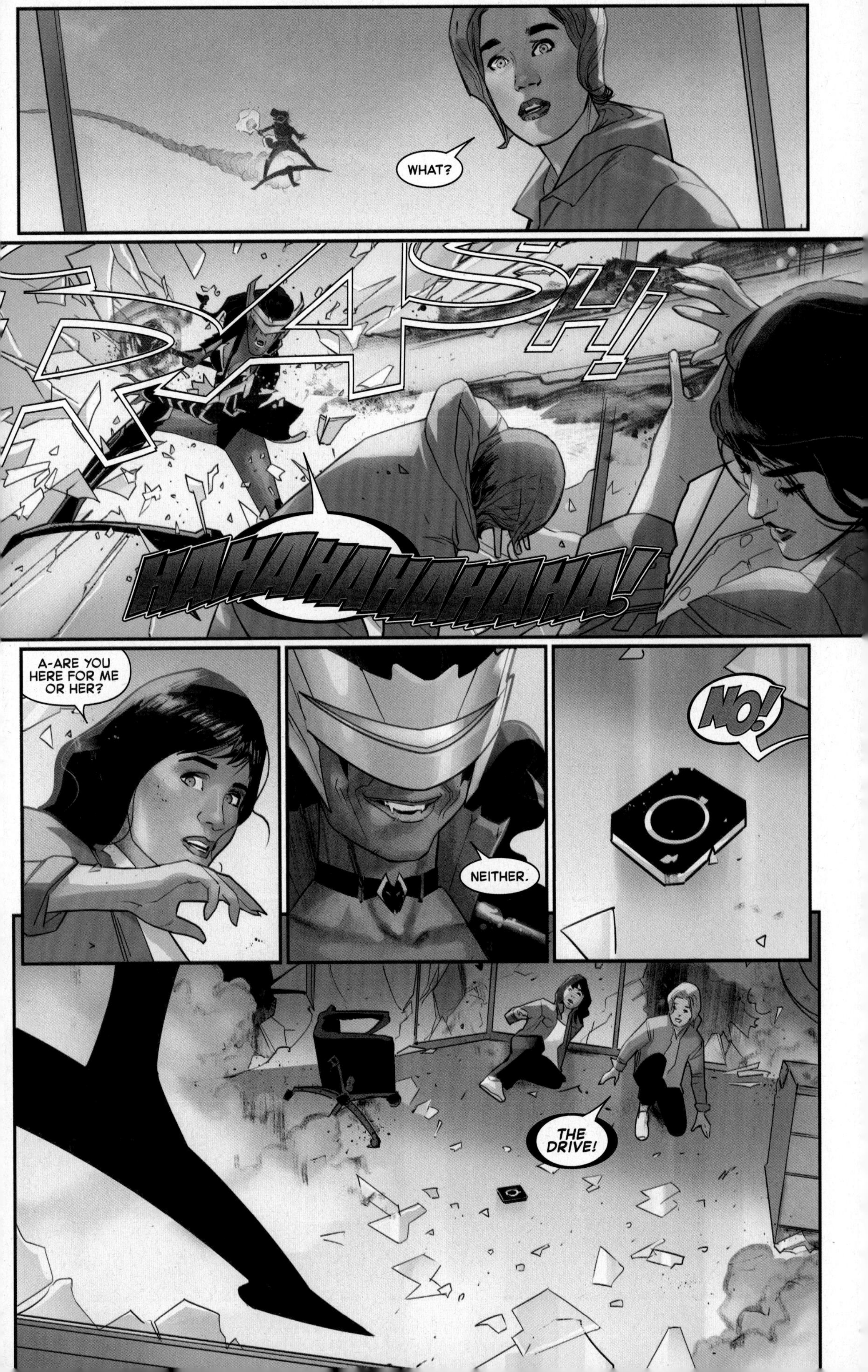
WHAT?
CRASH!
HAHAHAHAHAHAHAHA!
A-ARE YOU HERE FOR ME OR HER?
NEITHER.
NO!
THE DRIVE!

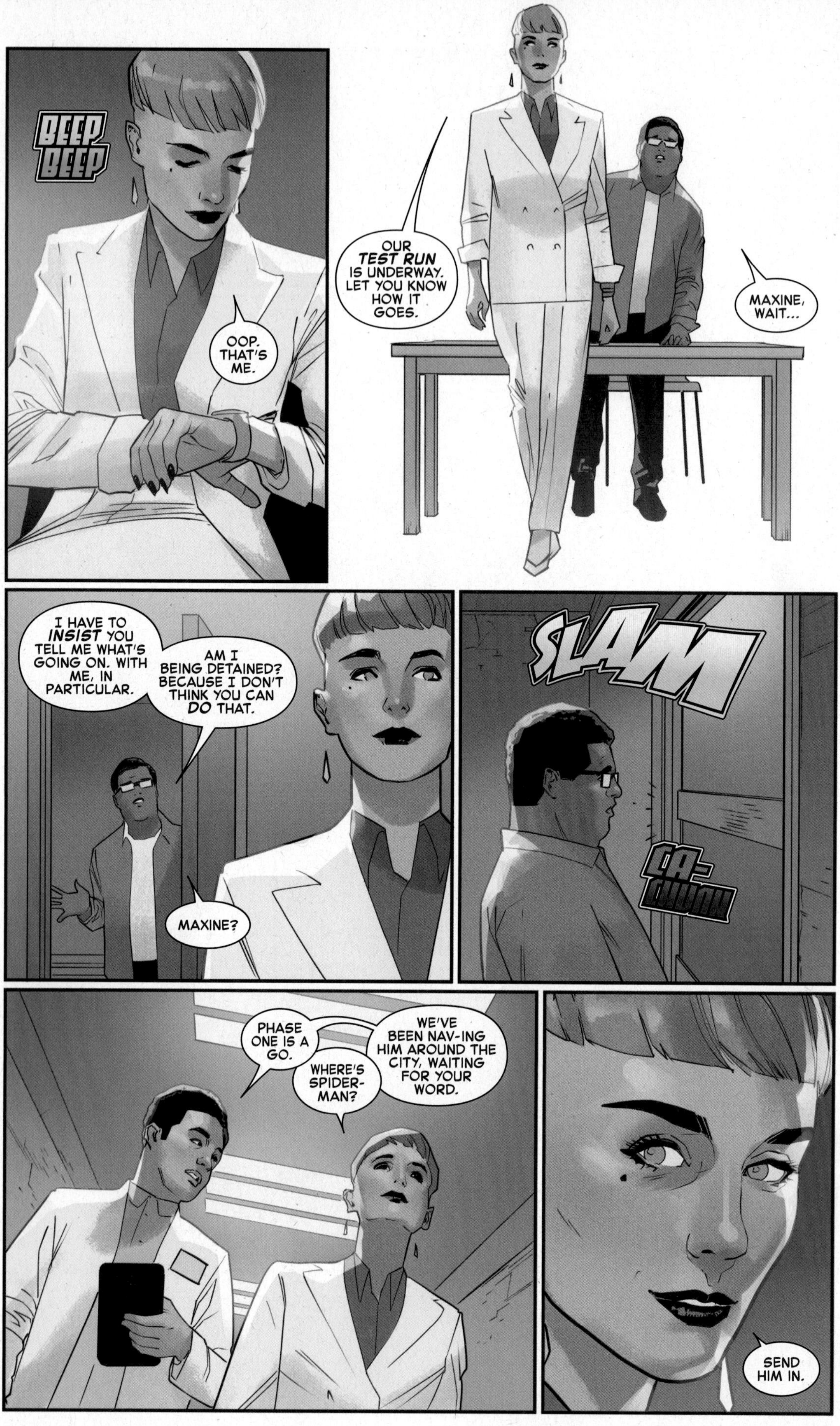
BEEP BEEP
OOP. THAT'S ME.
OUR TEST RUN IS UNDERWAY. LET YOU KNOW HOW IT GOES.
MAXINE, WAIT...
I HAVE TO INSIST YOU TELL ME WHAT'S GOING ON. WITH ME, IN PARTICULAR.
AM I BEING DETAINED? BECAUSE I DON'T THINK YOU CAN DO THAT.
MAXINE?
SLAM
CA-CHUNK
PHASE ONE IS A GO.
WHERE'S SPIDER-MAN?
WE'VE BEEN NAV-ING HIM AROUND THE CITY, WAITING FOR YOUR WORD.
SEND HIM IN.

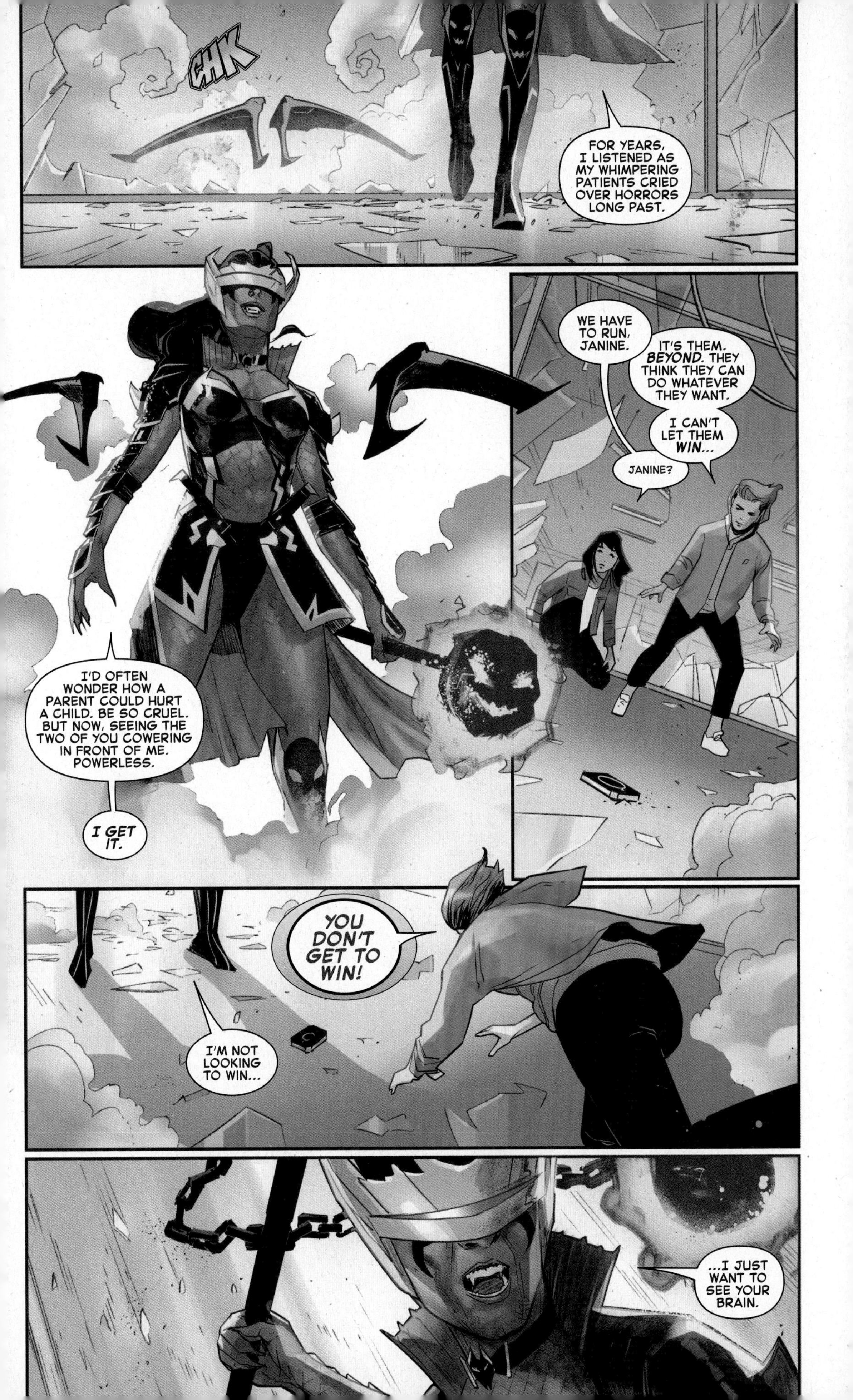
CHK
FOR YEARS, I LISTENED AS MY WHIMPERING PATIENTS CRIED OVER HORRORS LONG PAST.
I'D OFTEN WONDER HOW A PARENT COULD HURT A CHILD. BE SO CRUEL. BUT NOW, SEEING THE TWO OF YOU COWERING IN FRONT OF ME. POWERLESS.
I GET IT.
WE HAVE TO RUN, JANINE.
IT'S THEM. BEYOND. THEY THINK THEY CAN DO WHATEVER THEY WANT.
I CAN'T LET THEM WIN...
JANINE?
YOU DON'T GET TO WIN!
I'M NOT LOOKING TO WIN...
...I JUST WANT TO SEE YOUR BRAIN.

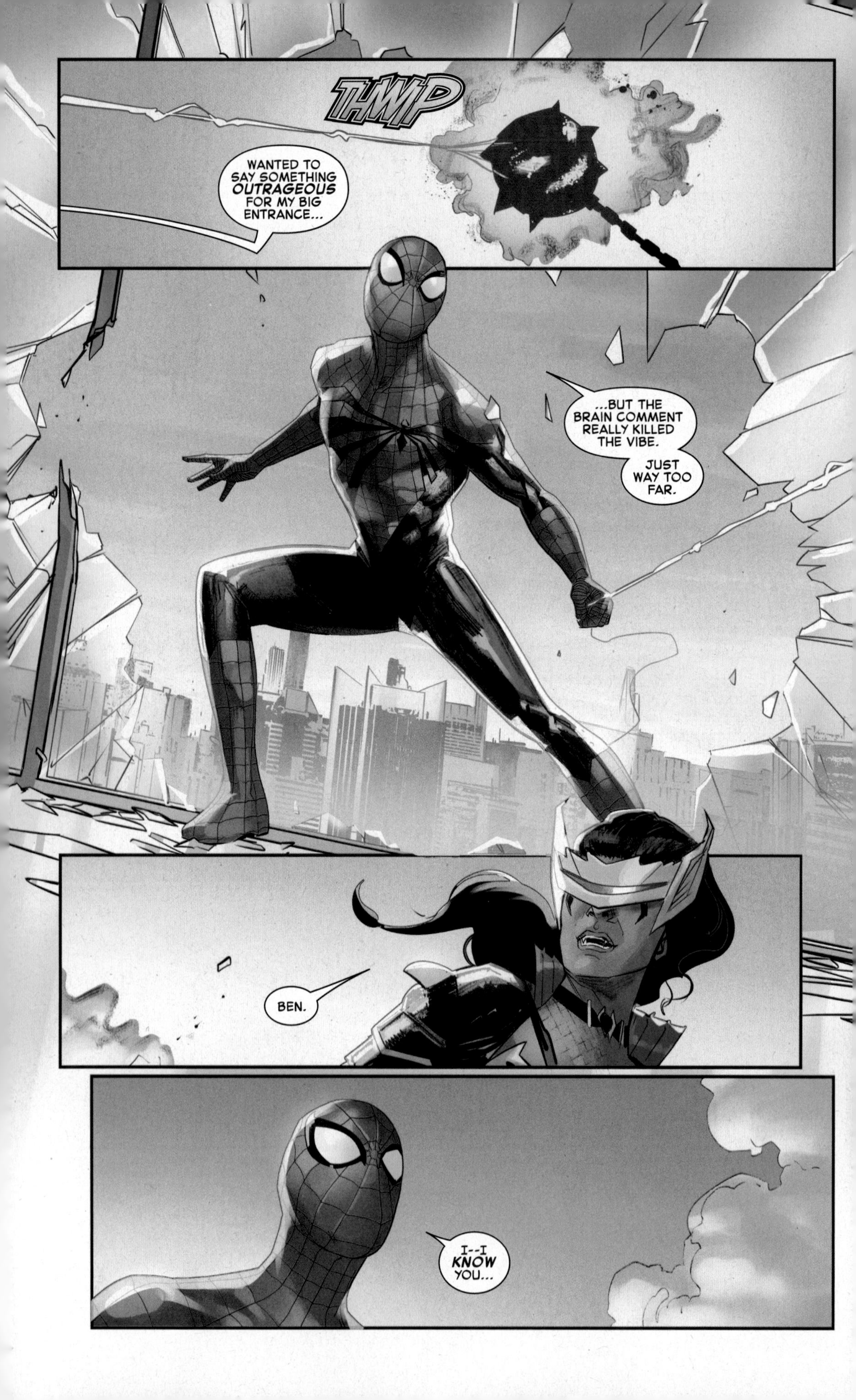
THWIP
WANTED TO SAY SOMETHING OUTRAGEOUS FOR MY BIG ENTRANCE...
...BUT THE BRAIN COMMENT REALLY KILLED THE VIBE.
JUST WAY TOO FAR.
BEN.
I--I KNOW YOU...

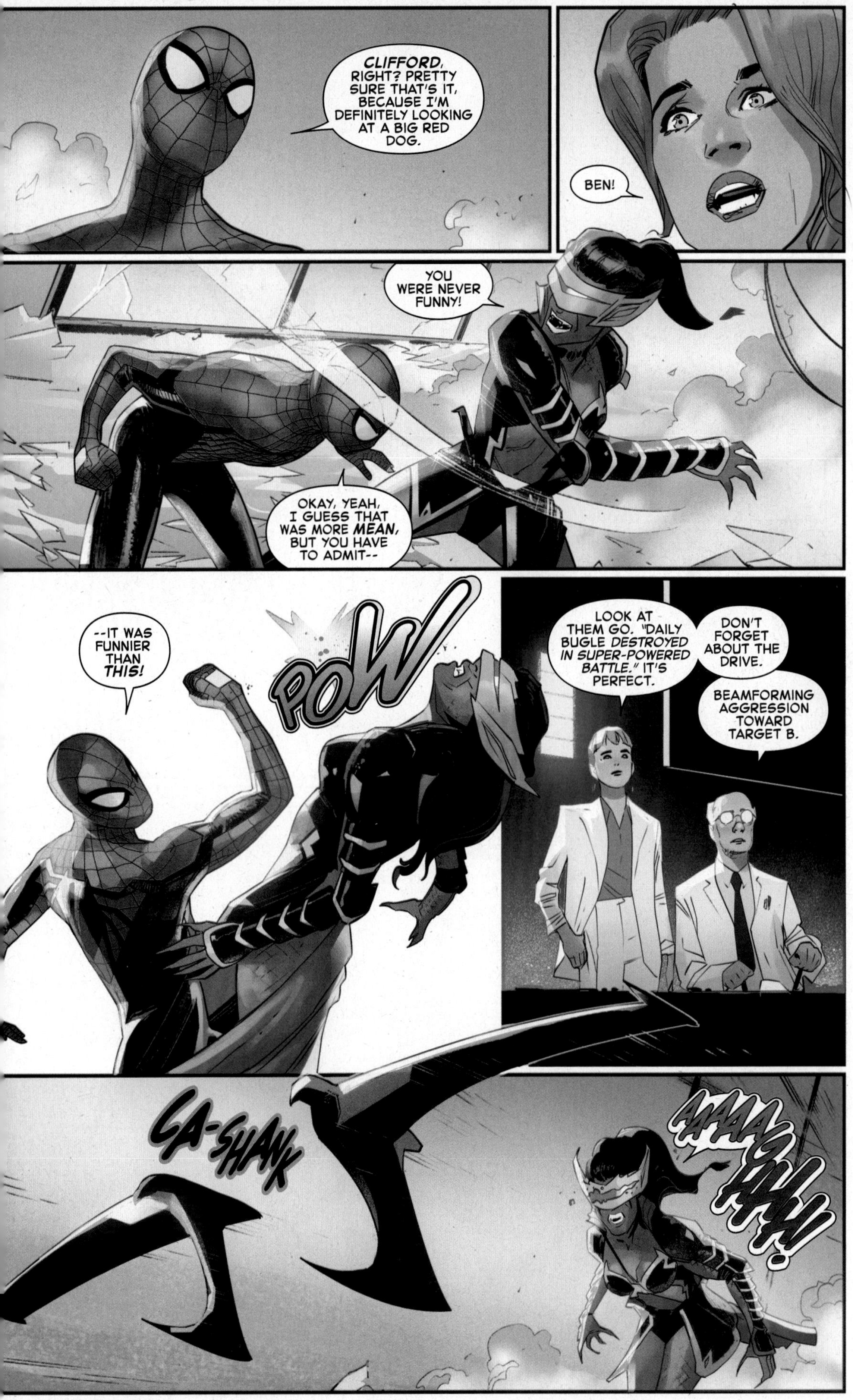
CLIFFORD, RIGHT? PRETTY SURE THAT'S IT, BECAUSE I'M DEFINITELY LOOKING AT A BIG RED DOG.
BEN!
YOU WERE NEVER FUNNY!
OKAY, YEAH, I GUESS THAT WAS MORE MEAN, BUT YOU HAVE TO ADMIT--
--IT WAS FUNNIER THAN THIS!
POW
LOOK AT THEM GO. "DAILY BUGLE DESTROYED IN SUPER-POWERED BATTLE." IT'S PERFECT.
DON'T FORGET ABOUT THE DRIVE.
BEAMFORMING AGGRESSION TOWARD TARGET B.
CA-SHANK
AAAAAGHHH!

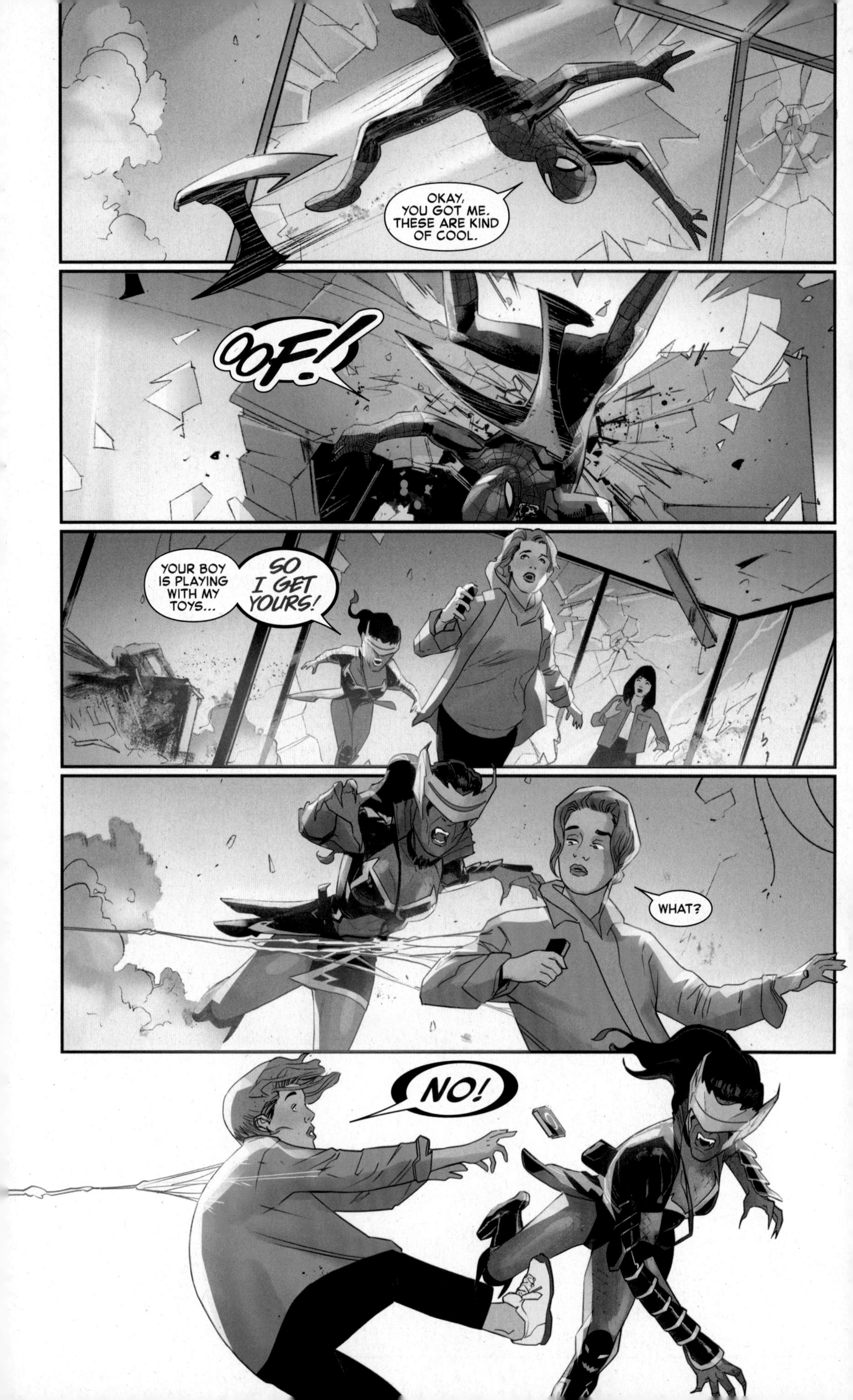
OKAY, YOU GOT ME. THESE ARE KIND OF COOL.
OOF!
YOUR BOY IS PLAYING WITH MY TOYS...
SO I GET YOURS!
WHAT?
NO!

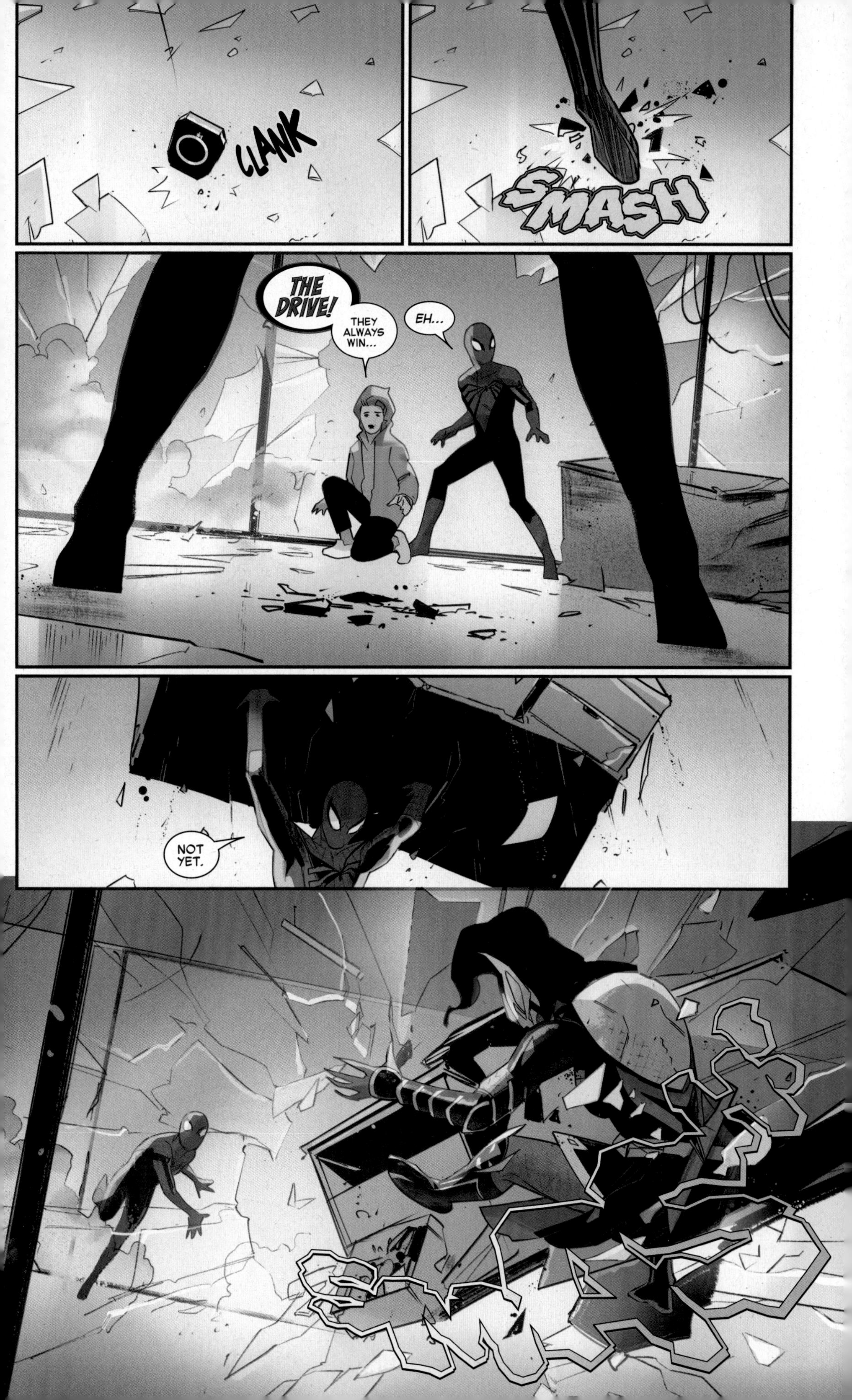
CLANK
SMASH
THE DRIVE!
THEY ALWAYS WIN...
EH...
NOT YET.

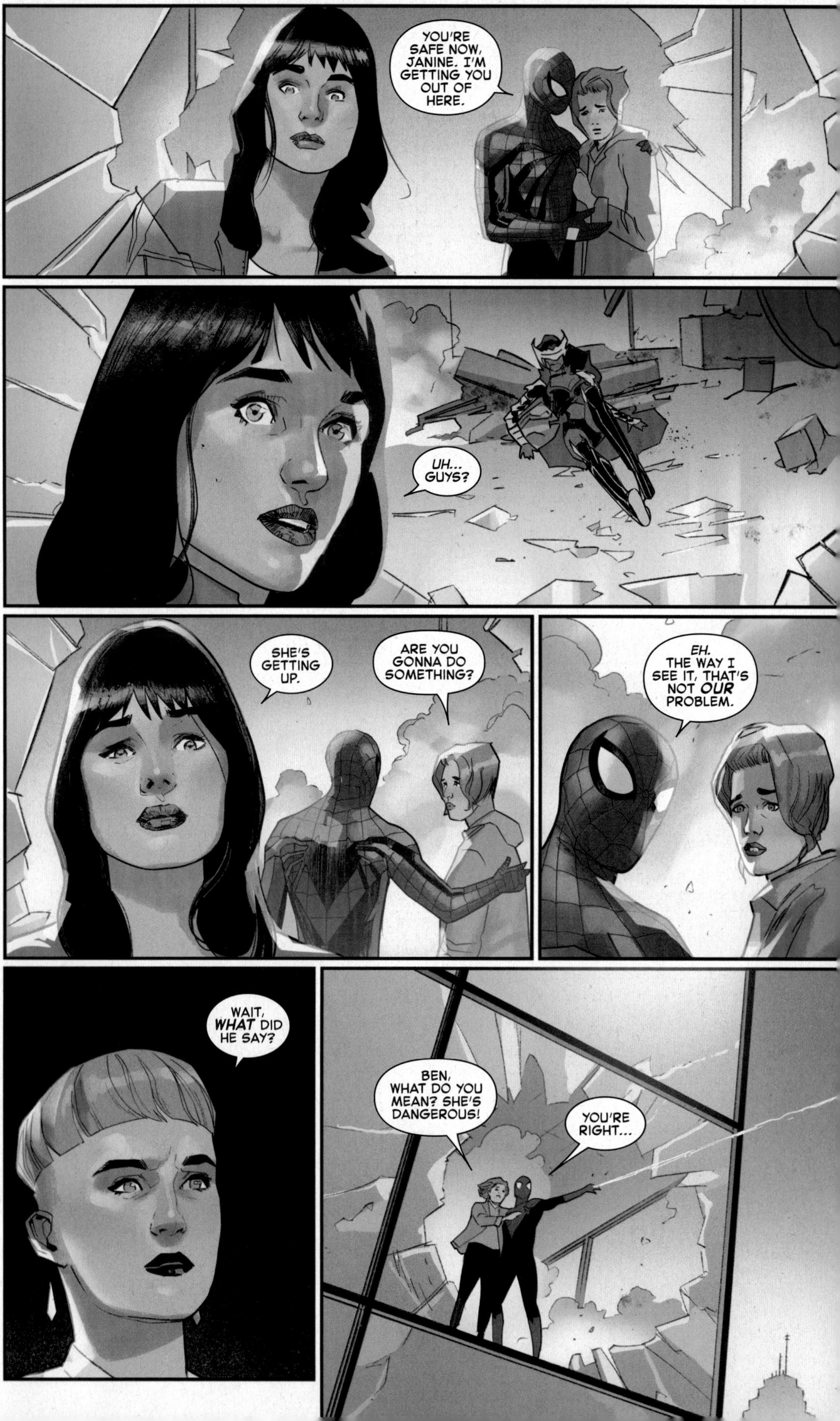
YOU'RE SAFE NOW, JANINE. I'M GETTING YOU OUT OF HERE.
UH... GUYS?
SHE'S GETTING UP.
ARE YOU GONNA DO SOMETHING?
EH. THE WAY I SEE IT, THAT'S NOT *OUR* PROBLEM.
WAIT, *WHAT* DID HE SAY?
BEN, WHAT DO YOU MEAN? SHE'S DANGEROUS!
YOU'RE RIGHT...

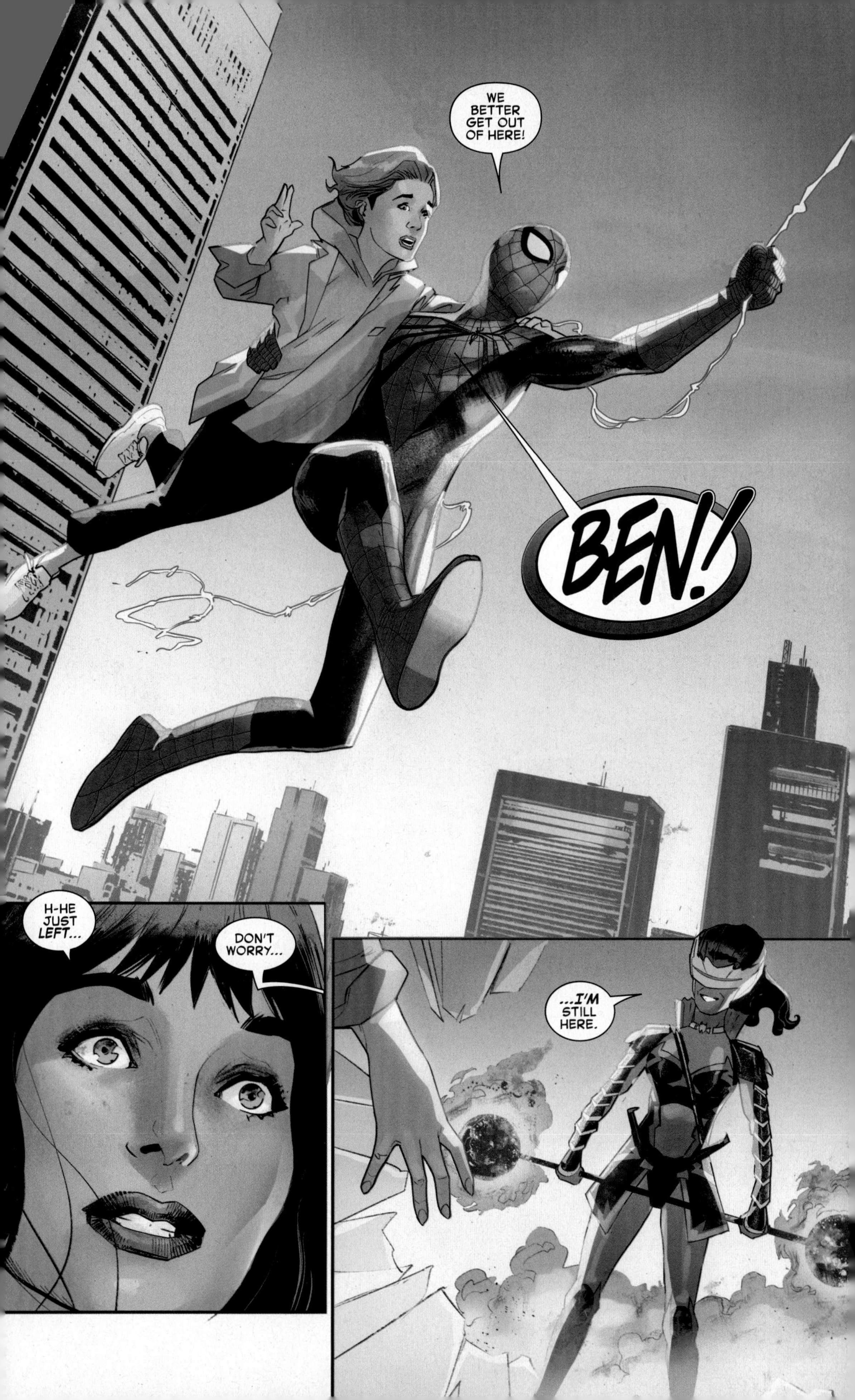
WE BETTER GET OUT OF HERE!
BEN!
H-HE JUST LEFT...
DON'T WORRY...
...I'M STILL HERE.

BEYOND CORPORATION #88.BEY

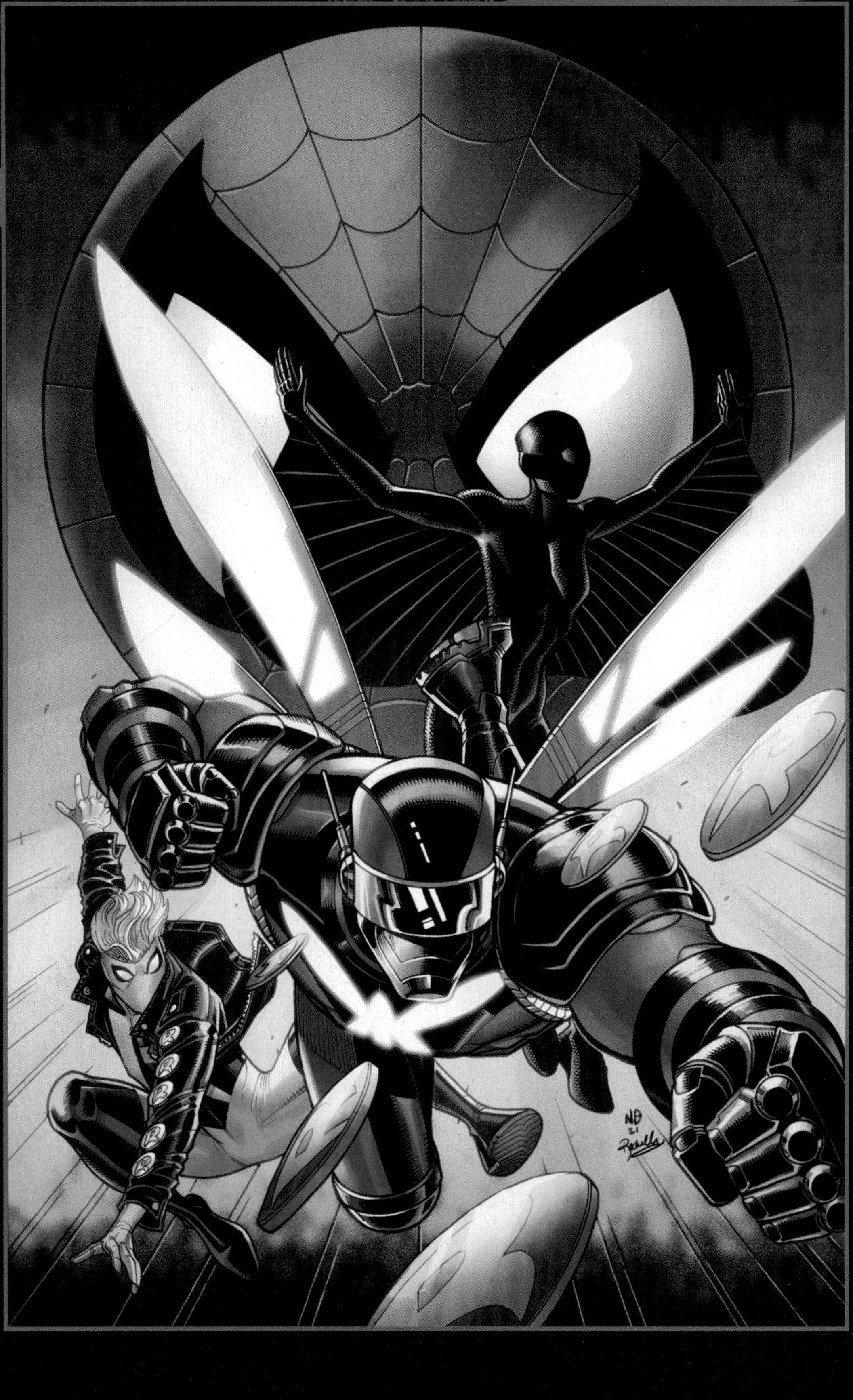

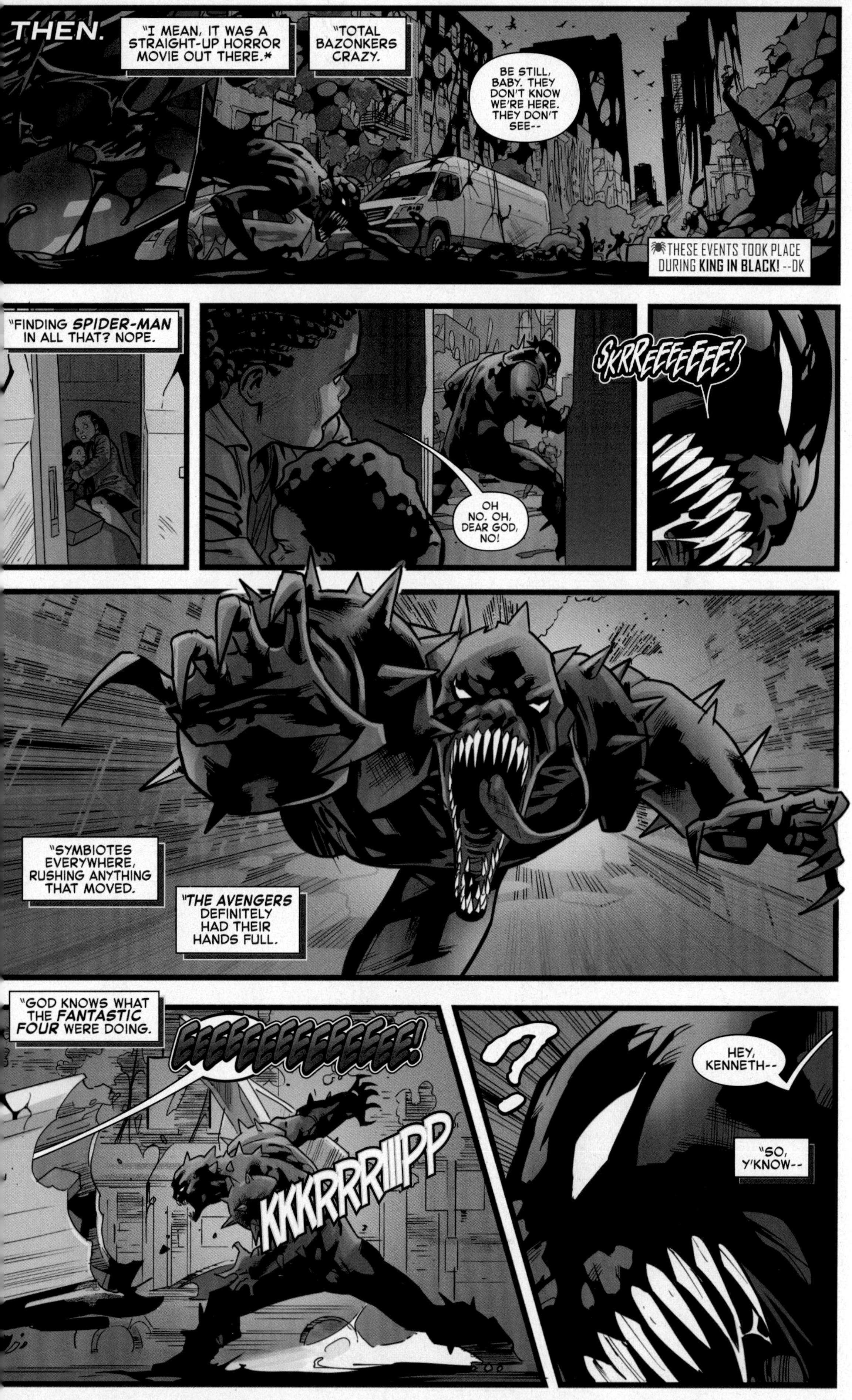
THEN.
"I MEAN, IT WAS A STRAIGHT-UP HORROR MOVIE OUT THERE.*
"TOTAL BAZONKERS CRAZY.
BE STILL, BABY. THEY DON'T KNOW WE'RE HERE. THEY DON'T SEE--
*THESE EVENTS TOOK PLACE DURING KING IN BLACK! --DK
"FINDING SPIDER-MAN IN ALL THAT? NOPE.
OH NO. OH, DEAR GOD, NO!
SKRREEEEEEE!
"SYMBIOTES EVERYWHERE, RUSHING ANYTHING THAT MOVED.
"THE AVENGERS DEFINITELY HAD THEIR HANDS FULL.
"GOD KNOWS WHAT THE FANTASTIC FOUR WERE DOING.
EEEEEEEEEEEEEEE!
KKKRRRIIIPP
?!
HEY, KENNETH--
"SO, Y'KNOW--

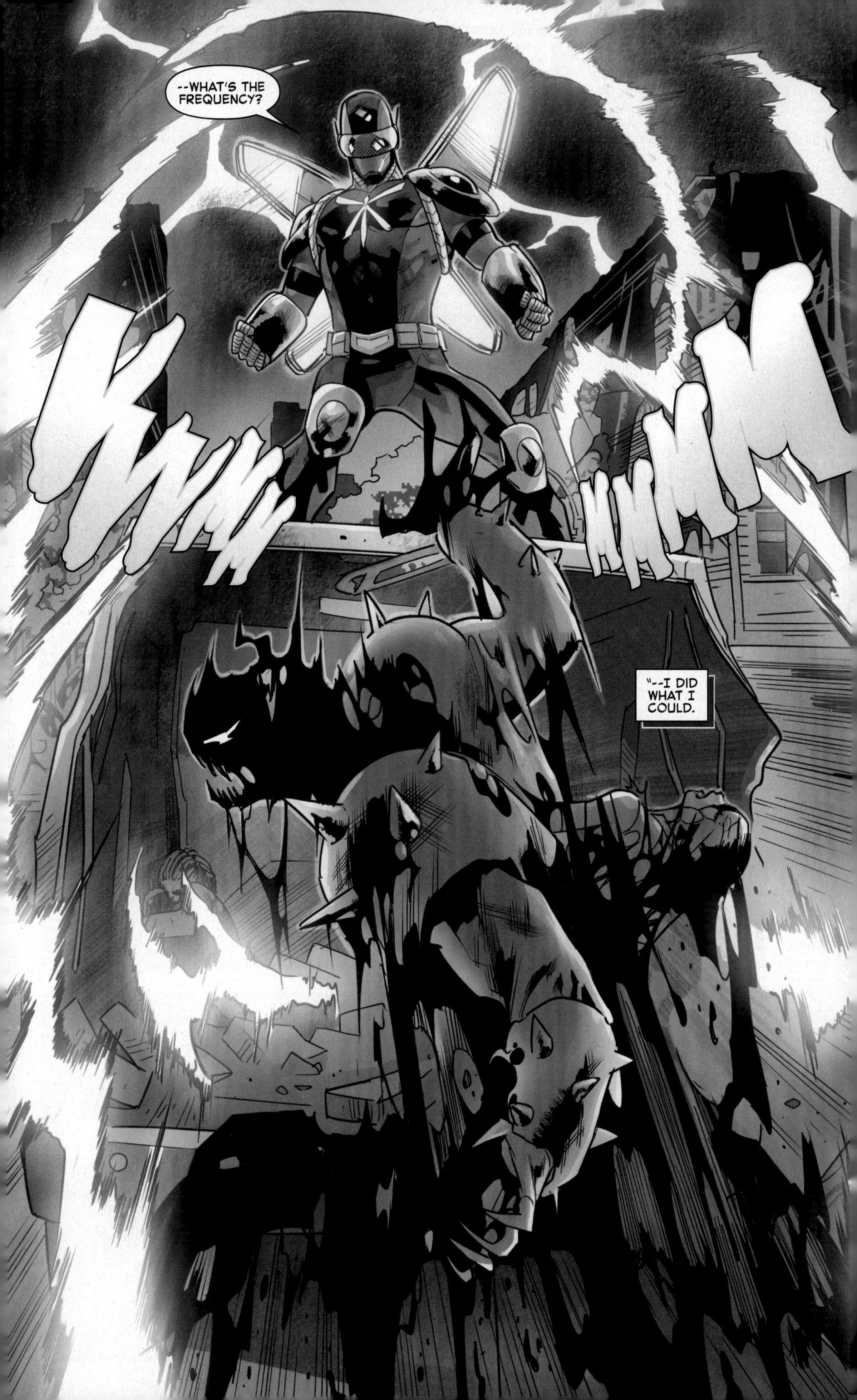
--WHAT'S THE FREQUENCY?
KRWWMMMMMMM
"--I DID WHAT I COULD.

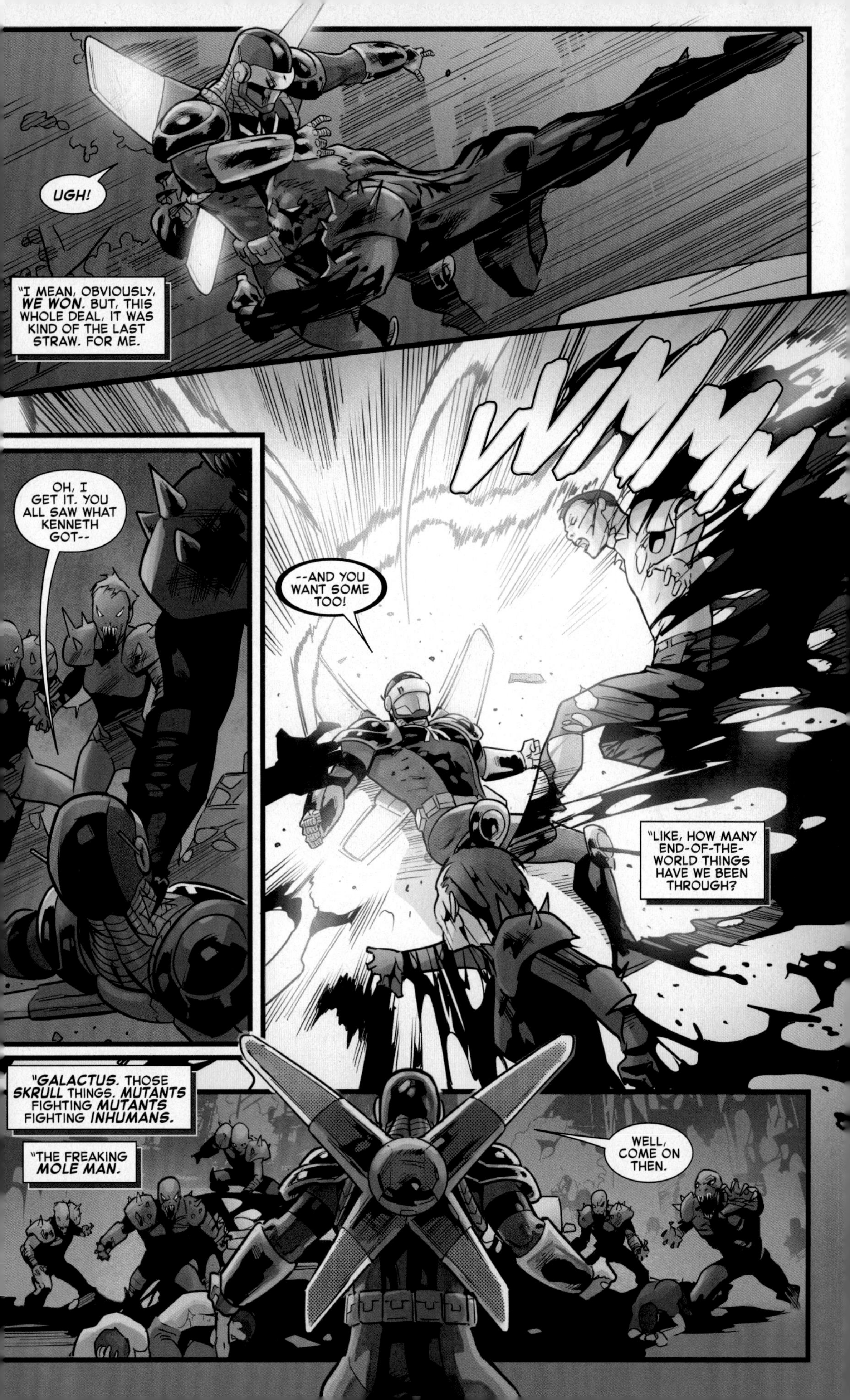

UGH!
"I MEAN, OBVIOUSLY, WE WON. BUT, THIS WHOLE DEAL, IT WAS KIND OF THE LAST STRAW. FOR ME.
VVMMM
OH, I GET IT. YOU ALL SAW WHAT KENNETH GOT--
--AND YOU WANT SOME TOO!
"LIKE, HOW MANY END-OF-THE-WORLD THINGS HAVE WE BEEN THROUGH?
"GALACTUS. THOSE SKRULL THINGS. MUTANTS FIGHTING MUTANTS FIGHTING INHUMANS.
"THE FREAKING MOLE MAN.
WELL, COME ON THEN.

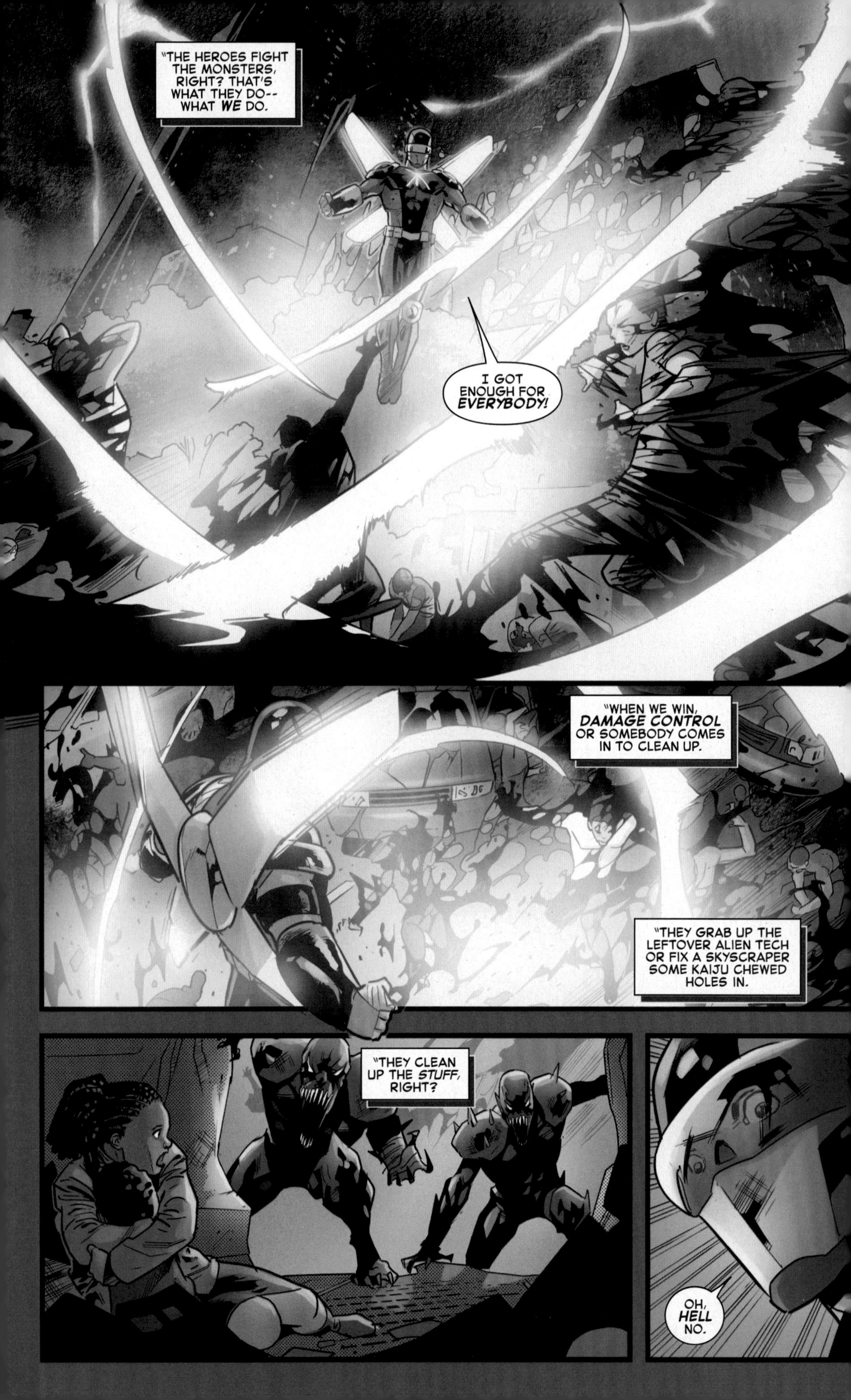
"THE HEROES FIGHT THE MONSTERS, RIGHT? THAT'S WHAT THEY DO-- WHAT *WE* DO.
I GOT ENOUGH FOR *EVERYBODY!*
"WHEN WE WIN, *DAMAGE CONTROL* OR SOMEBODY COMES IN TO CLEAN UP.
"THEY GRAB UP THE LEFTOVER ALIEN TECH OR FIX A SKYSCRAPER SOME KAIJU CHEWED HOLES IN.
"THEY CLEAN UP THE *STUFF*, RIGHT?
OH, *HELL* NO.

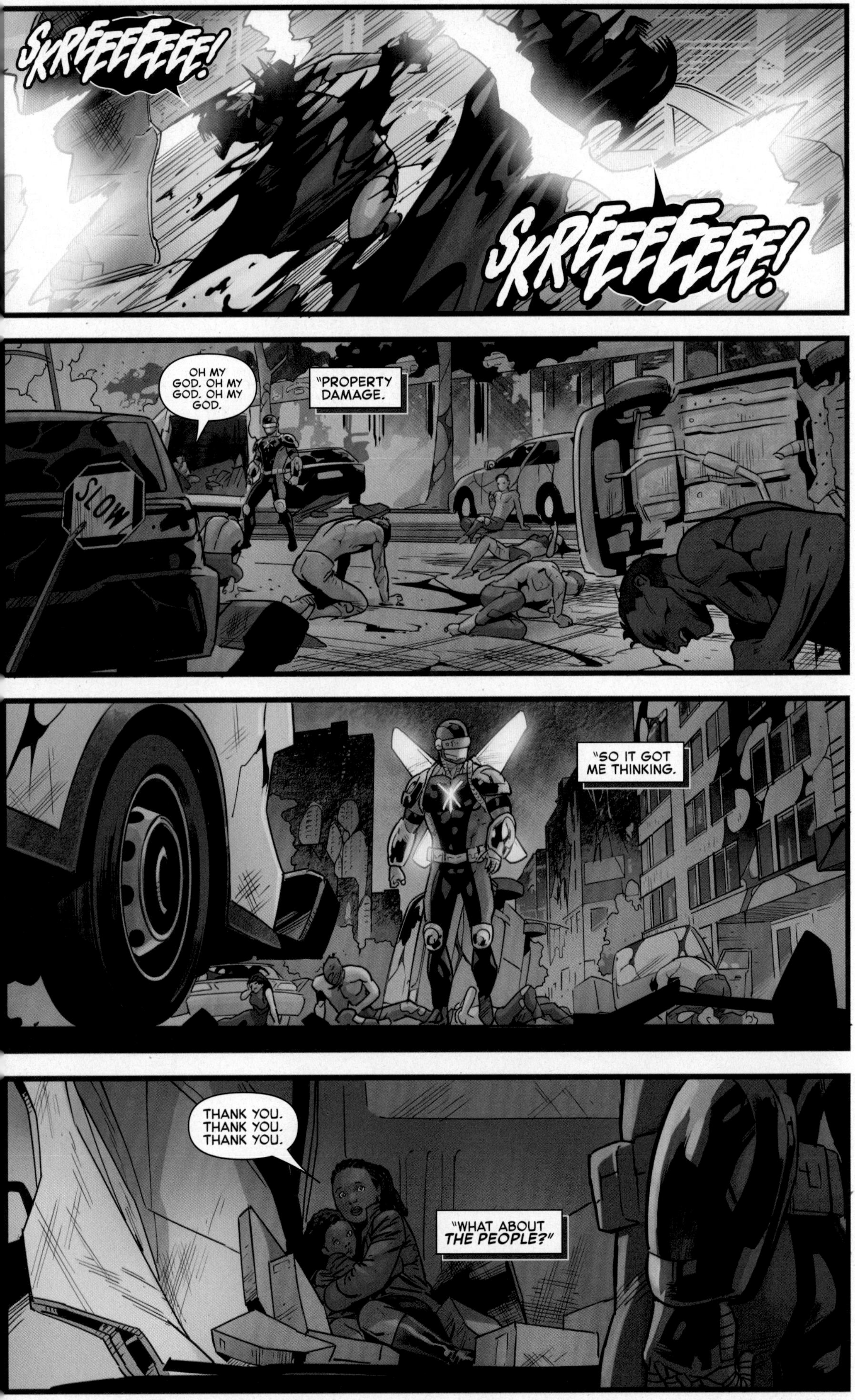
SKREEEEEEE!
SKREEEEEEEE!
OH MY GOD. OH MY GOD. OH MY GOD.
"PROPERTY DAMAGE.
"SO IT GOT ME THINKING.
THANK YOU. THANK YOU. THANK YOU.
"WHAT ABOUT THE PEOPLE?"

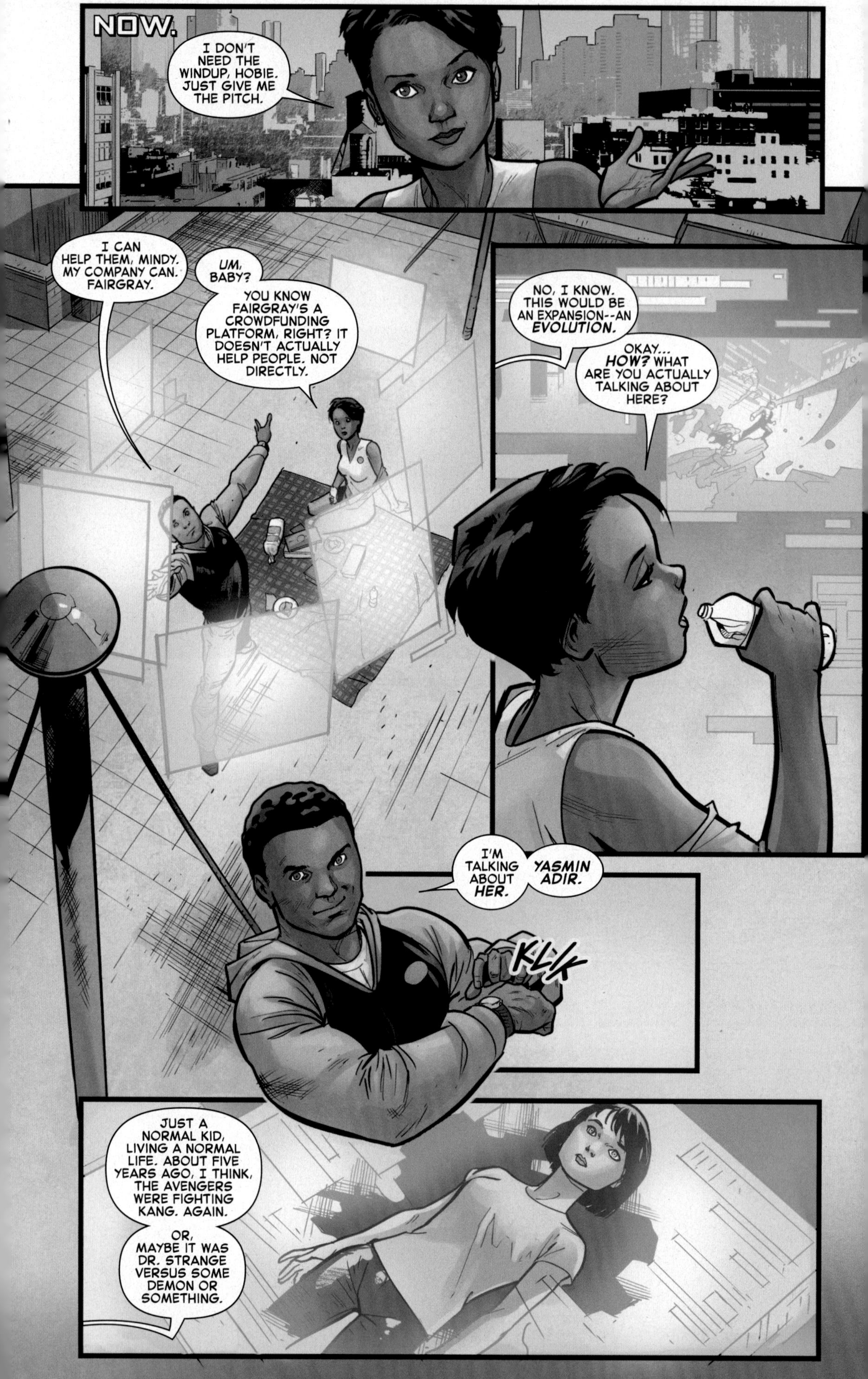
NOW.
I DON'T NEED THE WINDUP, HOBIE. JUST GIVE ME THE PITCH.
I CAN HELP THEM, MINDY. MY COMPANY CAN. FAIRGRAY.
UM, BABY?
YOU KNOW FAIRGRAY'S A CROWDFUNDING PLATFORM, RIGHT? IT DOESN'T ACTUALLY HELP PEOPLE. NOT DIRECTLY.
NO, I KNOW. THIS WOULD BE AN EXPANSION--AN EVOLUTION.
OKAY... HOW? WHAT ARE YOU ACTUALLY TALKING ABOUT HERE?
I'M TALKING ABOUT HER.
YASMIN ADIR.
KLIK
JUST A NORMAL KID, LIVING A NORMAL LIFE. ABOUT FIVE YEARS AGO, I THINK, THE AVENGERS WERE FIGHTING KANG. AGAIN.
OR, MAYBE IT WAS DR. STRANGE VERSUS SOME DEMON OR SOMETHING.

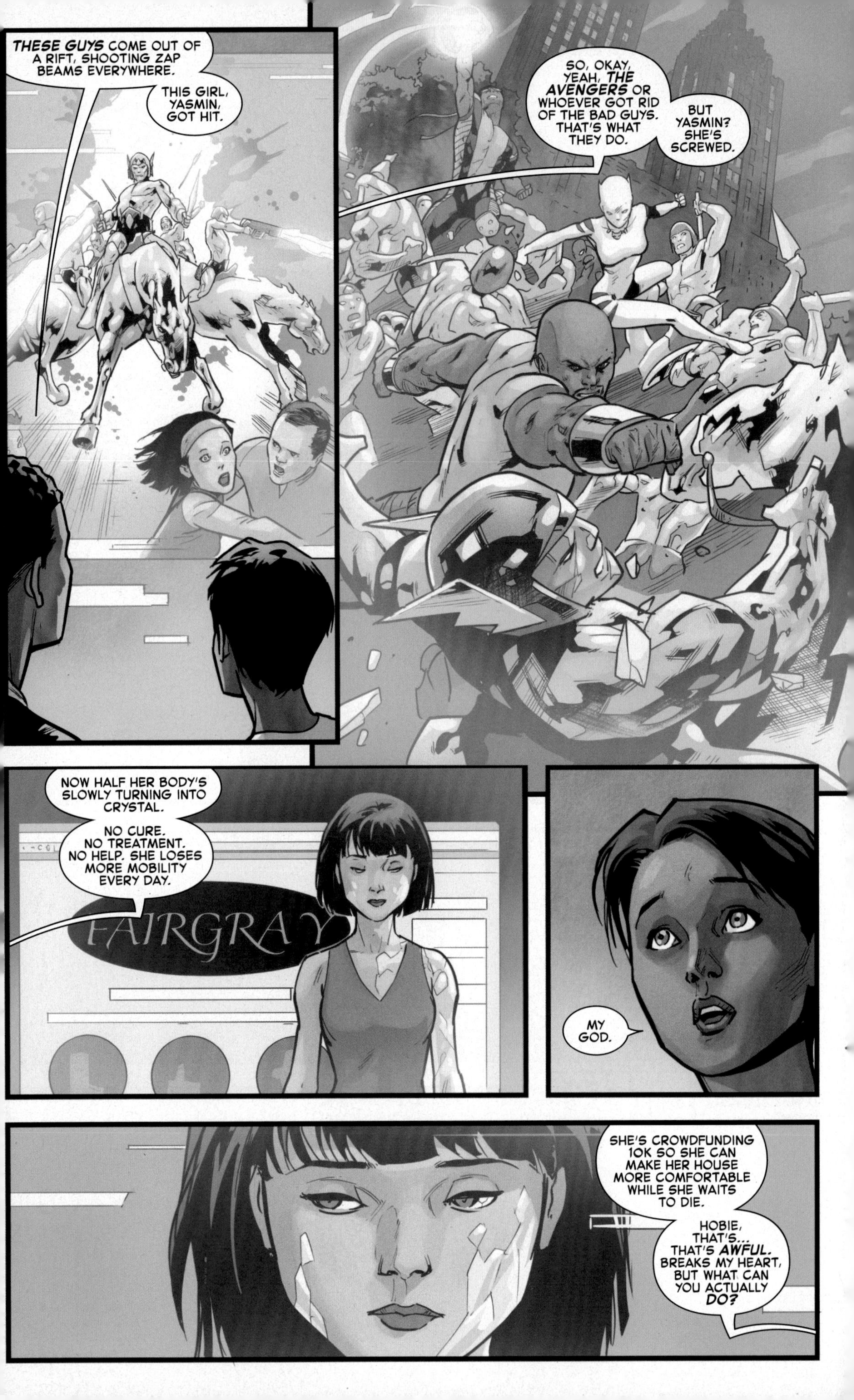
THESE GUYS COME OUT OF A RIFT, SHOOTING ZAP BEAMS EVERYWHERE.
THIS GIRL, YASMIN, GOT HIT.
SO, OKAY, YEAH, THE AVENGERS OR WHOEVER GOT RID OF THE BAD GUYS. THAT'S WHAT THEY DO.
BUT YASMIN? SHE'S SCREWED.
NOW HALF HER BODY'S SLOWLY TURNING INTO CRYSTAL.
NO CURE. NO TREATMENT. NO HELP. SHE LOSES MORE MOBILITY EVERY DAY.
FAIRGRAY
MY GOD.
SHE'S CROWDFUNDING 10K SO SHE CAN MAKE HER HOUSE MORE COMFORTABLE WHILE SHE WAITS TO DIE.
HOBIE, THAT'S... THAT'S AWFUL. BREAKS MY HEART, BUT WHAT CAN YOU ACTUALLY DO?

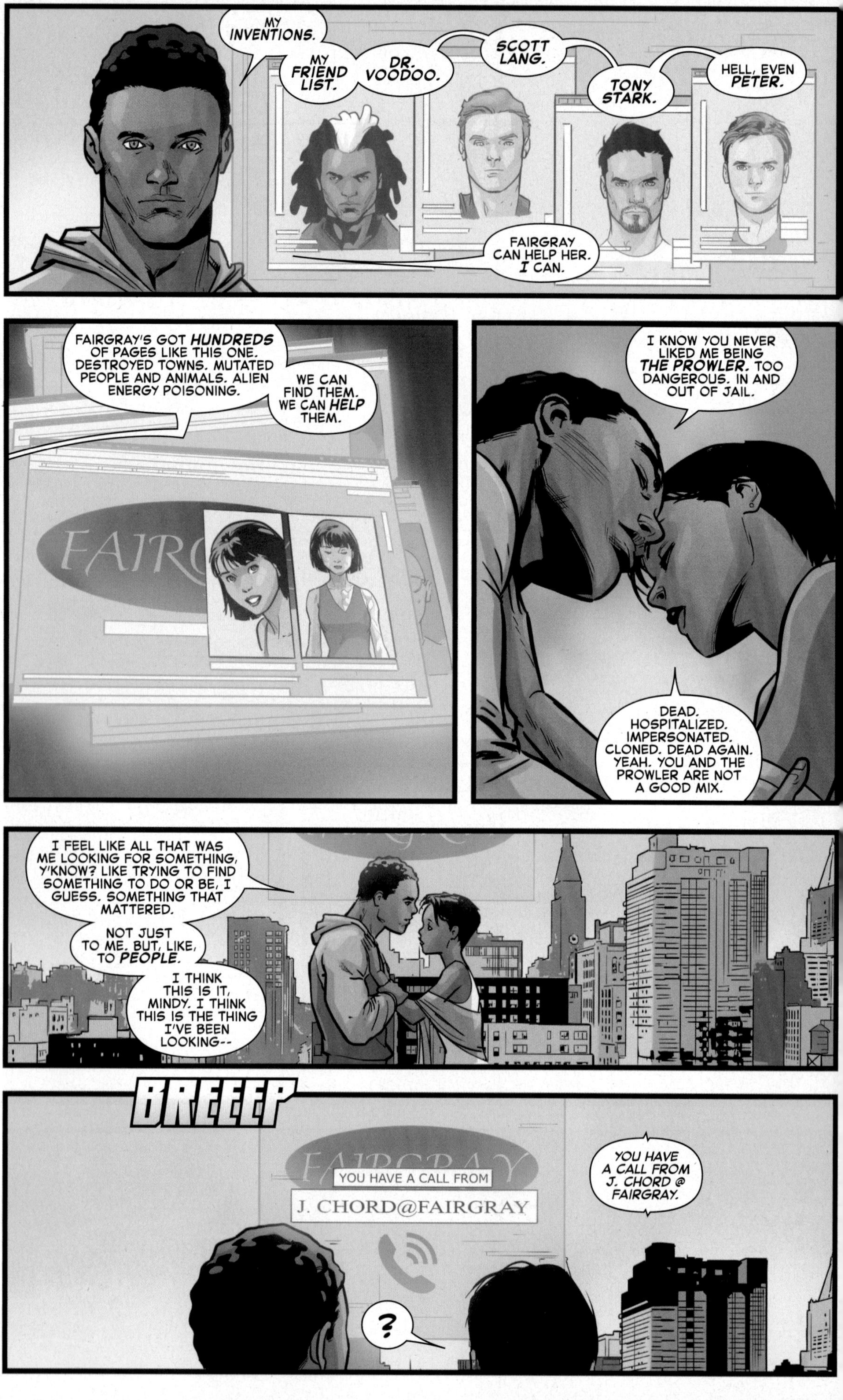
MY INVENTIONS.
MY FRIEND LIST.
DR. VOODOO.
SCOTT LANG.
TONY STARK.
HELL, EVEN PETER.
FAIRGRAY CAN HELP HER. I CAN.
FAIRGRAY'S GOT HUNDREDS OF PAGES LIKE THIS ONE. DESTROYED TOWNS. MUTATED PEOPLE AND ANIMALS. ALIEN ENERGY POISONING.
WE CAN FIND THEM. WE CAN HELP THEM.
FAIRG
I KNOW YOU NEVER LIKED ME BEING THE PROWLER. TOO DANGEROUS. IN AND OUT OF JAIL.
DEAD. HOSPITALIZED. IMPERSONATED. CLONED. DEAD AGAIN. YEAH. YOU AND THE PROWLER ARE NOT A GOOD MIX.
I FEEL LIKE ALL THAT WAS ME LOOKING FOR SOMETHING, Y'KNOW? LIKE TRYING TO FIND SOMETHING TO DO OR BE, I GUESS. SOMETHING THAT MATTERED.
NOT JUST TO ME. BUT, LIKE, TO PEOPLE.
I THINK THIS IS IT, MINDY. I THINK THIS IS THE THING I'VE BEEN LOOKING--
BREEEP
FAIRGRAY
YOU HAVE A CALL FROM
J. CHORD@FAIRGRAY
YOU HAVE A CALL FROM J. CHORD @ FAIRGRAY.
?

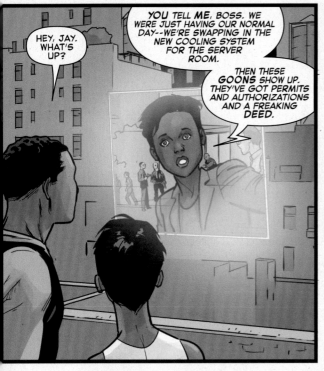

HEY, JAY. WHAT'S UP?

YOU TELL *ME*, BOSS. WE WERE JUST HAVING OUR NORMAL DAY--WE'RE SWAPPING IN THE NEW COOLING SYSTEM FOR THE SERVER ROOM.

THEN THESE *GOONS* SHOW UP. THEY'VE GOT PERMITS AND AUTHORIZATIONS AND A FREAKING *DEED.*

THEY KICKED US ALL OUT. NOW THEY'RE TAKING ALL THE WORK STATIONS AND SERVERS.

THEY SAY THEY OWN THE PLACE. WE'RE ALL *TERMINATED.*

WAIT... *WHAT?*

WHAT THE HELL ARE YOU TALKING ABOUT, JANELLE? WHO'S *THEY?* THEY *WHO?*

THEM, BOSS. WHO DO YOU THINK?

DIVISION OF BEYOND CORPORATION AUTHORIZED PERSONNEL ONLY

RODDY CONFIRMED THEIR PAPERWORK'S LEGIT.

DIVISION OF BEYOND CORPORATION
AUTHORIZED PERSONNEL ONLY

DID YOU REALLY SELL FAIRGRAY WITHOUT TELLING US, BOSS?

BECAUSE THAT WOULD BE REALLY #$%& UP.

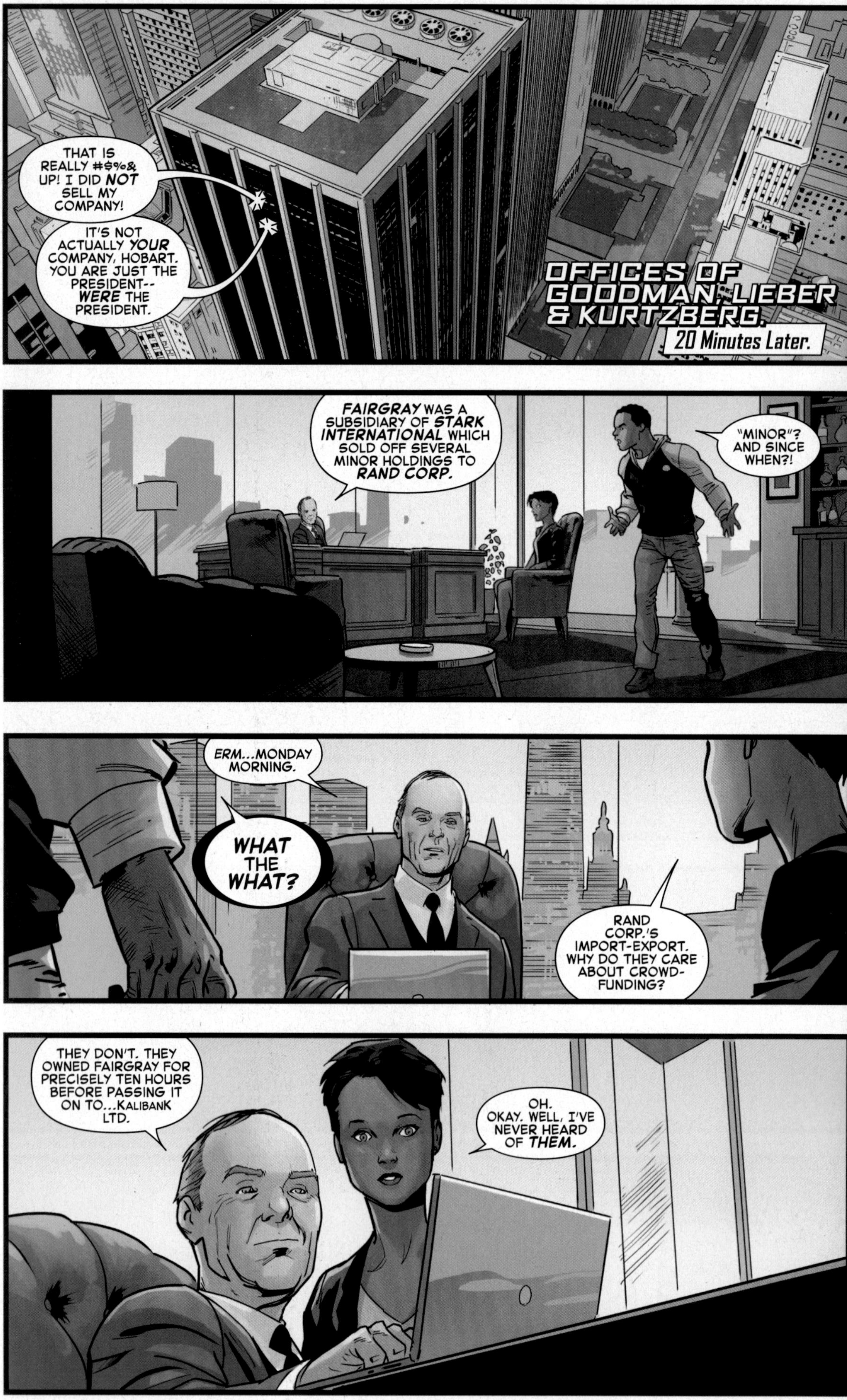
THAT IS REALLY #$%& UP! I DID NOT SELL MY COMPANY!
IT'S NOT ACTUALLY YOUR COMPANY, HOBART. YOU ARE JUST THE PRESIDENT-- WERE THE PRESIDENT.
OFFICES OF GOODMAN, LIEBER & KURTZBERG.
20 Minutes Later.
FAIRGRAY WAS A SUBSIDIARY OF STARK INTERNATIONAL WHICH SOLD OFF SEVERAL MINOR HOLDINGS TO RAND CORP.
"MINOR"? AND SINCE WHEN?!
ERM...MONDAY MORNING.
WHAT THE WHAT?
RAND CORP.'S IMPORT-EXPORT. WHY DO THEY CARE ABOUT CROWD-FUNDING?
THEY DON'T. THEY OWNED FAIRGRAY FOR PRECISELY TEN HOURS BEFORE PASSING IT ON TO...KALIBANK LTD.
OH. OKAY. WELL, I'VE NEVER HEARD OF THEM.

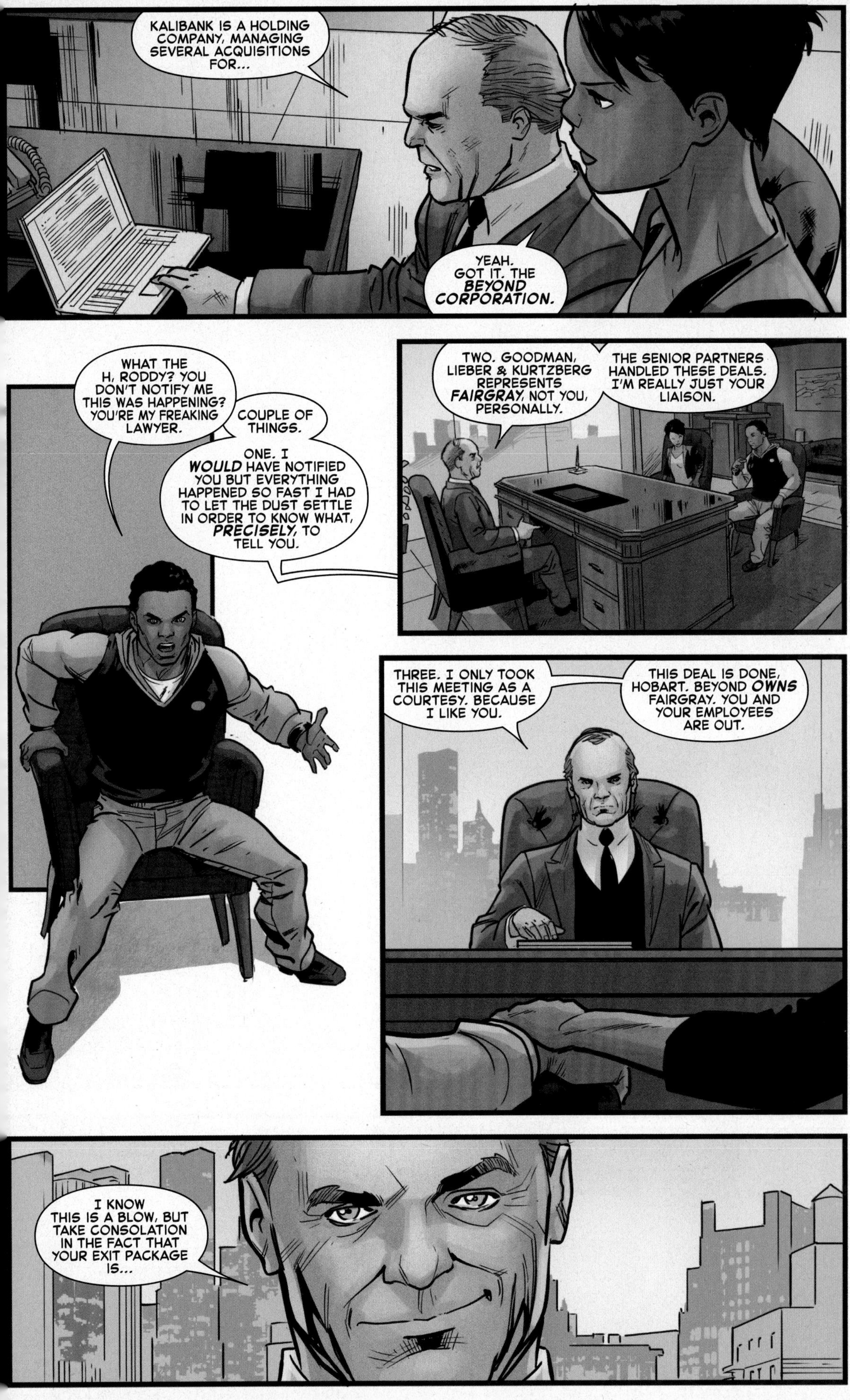
KALIBANK IS A HOLDING COMPANY, MANAGING SEVERAL ACQUISITIONS FOR...
YEAH. GOT IT. THE BEYOND CORPORATION.
WHAT THE H, RODDY? YOU DON'T NOTIFY ME THIS WAS HAPPENING? YOU'RE MY FREAKING LAWYER.
COUPLE OF THINGS.
ONE. I WOULD HAVE NOTIFIED YOU BUT EVERYTHING HAPPENED SO FAST I HAD TO LET THE DUST SETTLE IN ORDER TO KNOW WHAT, PRECISELY, TO TELL YOU.
TWO. GOODMAN, LIEBER & KURTZBERG REPRESENTS FAIRGRAY, NOT YOU, PERSONALLY.
THE SENIOR PARTNERS HANDLED THESE DEALS. I'M REALLY JUST YOUR LIAISON.
THREE. I ONLY TOOK THIS MEETING AS A COURTESY. BECAUSE I LIKE YOU.
THIS DEAL IS DONE, HOBART. BEYOND OWNS FAIRGRAY. YOU AND YOUR EMPLOYEES ARE OUT.
I KNOW THIS IS A BLOW, BUT TAKE CONSOLATION IN THE FACT THAT YOUR EXIT PACKAGE IS...

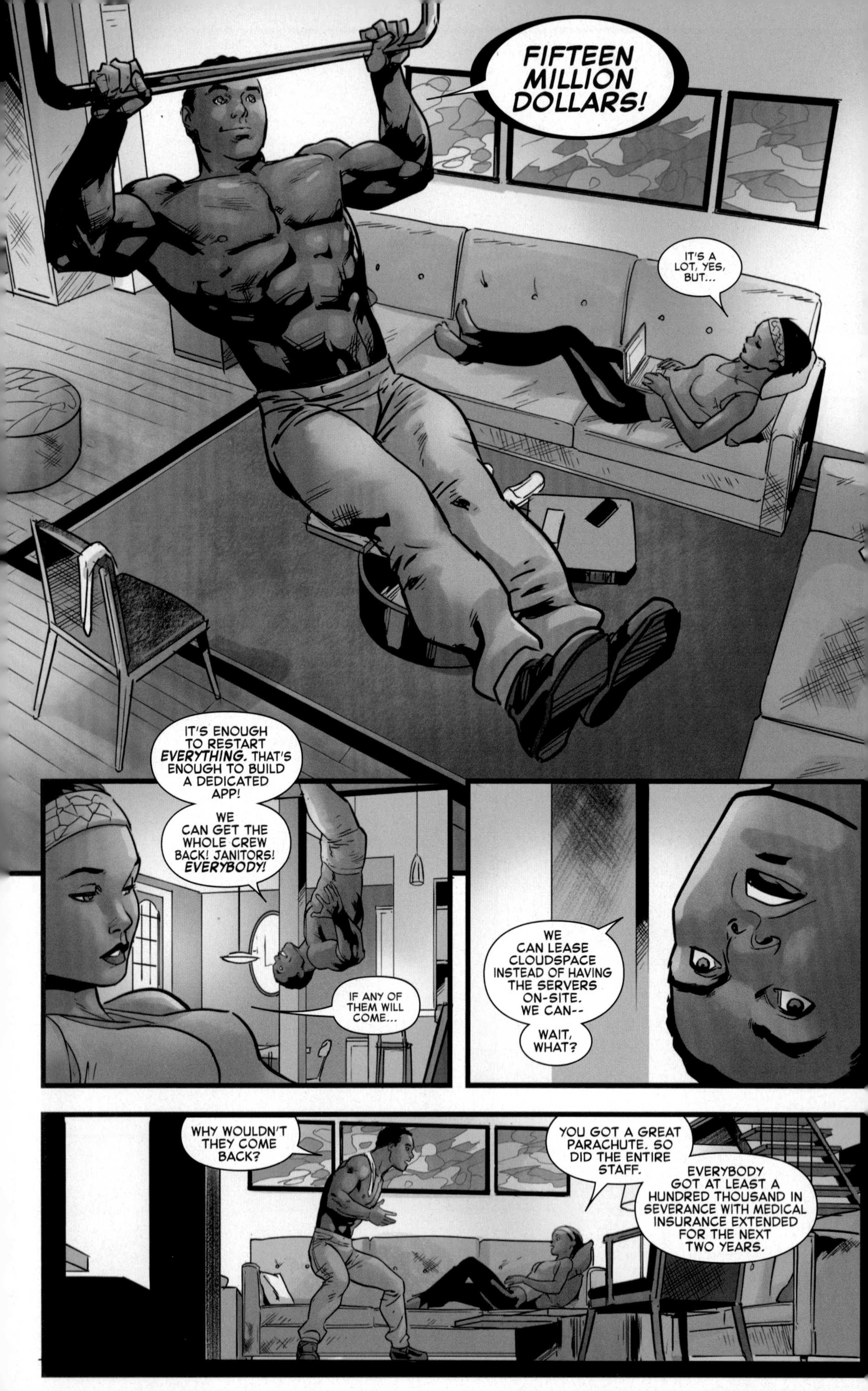
FIFTEEN MILLION DOLLARS!
IT'S A LOT, YES, BUT...
IT'S ENOUGH TO RESTART EVERYTHING. THAT'S ENOUGH TO BUILD A DEDICATED APP!
WE CAN GET THE WHOLE CREW BACK! JANITORS! EVERYBODY!
IF ANY OF THEM WILL COME...
WE CAN LEASE CLOUDSPACE INSTEAD OF HAVING THE SERVERS ON-SITE. WE CAN--
WAIT, WHAT?
WHY WOULDN'T THEY COME BACK?
YOU GOT A GREAT PARACHUTE. SO DID THE ENTIRE STAFF.
EVERYBODY GOT AT LEAST A HUNDRED THOUSAND IN SEVERANCE WITH MEDICAL INSURANCE EXTENDED FOR THE NEXT TWO YEARS.

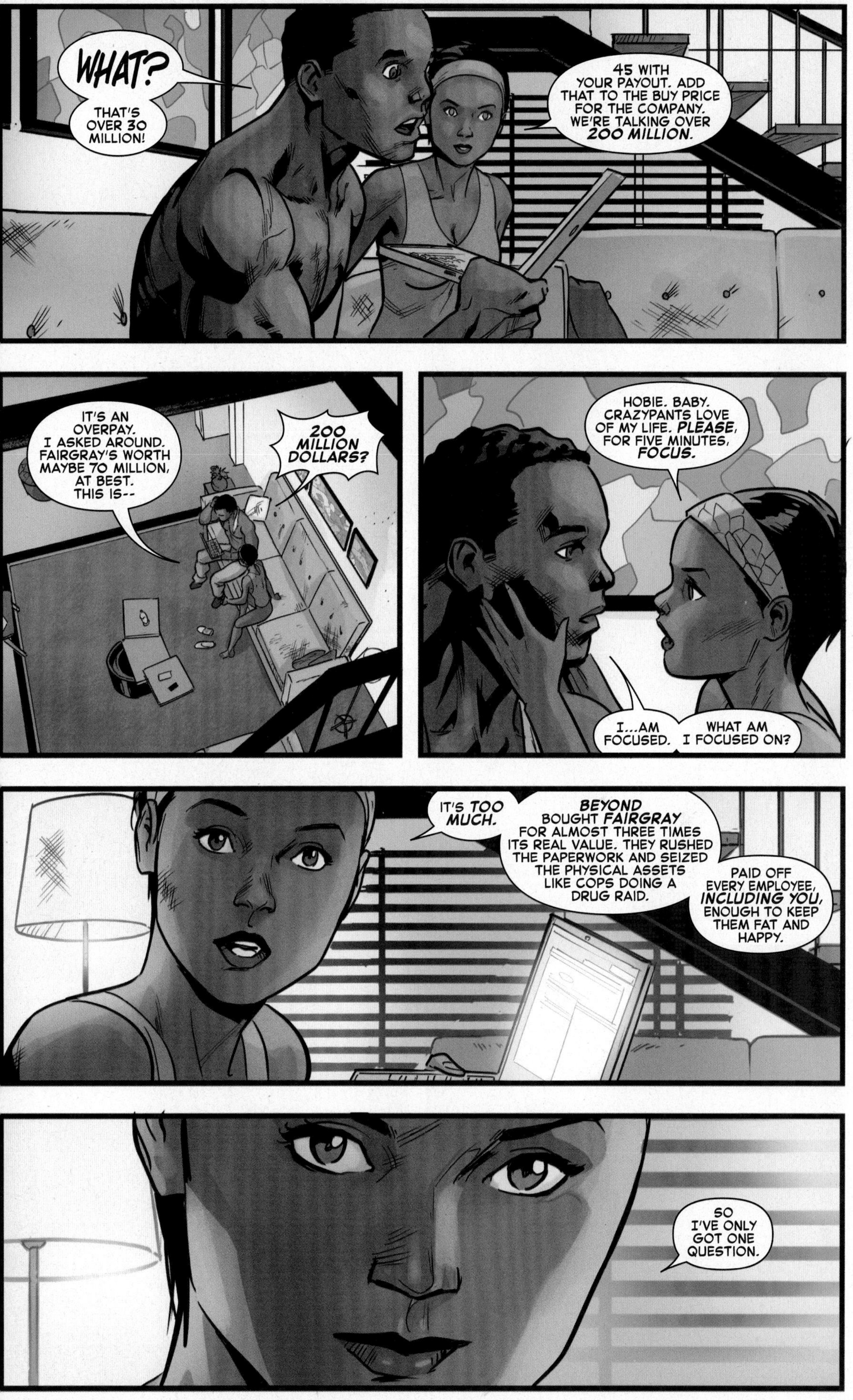
WHAT?
THAT'S OVER 30 MILLION!
45 WITH YOUR PAYOUT. ADD THAT TO THE BUY PRICE FOR THE COMPANY. WE'RE TALKING OVER 200 MILLION.
IT'S AN OVERPAY. I ASKED AROUND. FAIRGRAY'S WORTH MAYBE 70 MILLION, AT BEST. THIS IS--
200 MILLION DOLLARS?
HOBIE. BABY. CRAZYPANTS LOVE OF MY LIFE. PLEASE, FOR FIVE MINUTES, FOCUS.
I...AM FOCUSED.
WHAT AM I FOCUSED ON?
IT'S TOO MUCH.
BEYOND BOUGHT FAIRGRAY FOR ALMOST THREE TIMES ITS REAL VALUE. THEY RUSHED THE PAPERWORK AND SEIZED THE PHYSICAL ASSETS LIKE COPS DOING A DRUG RAID.
PAID OFF EVERY EMPLOYEE, INCLUDING YOU, ENOUGH TO KEEP THEM FAT AND HAPPY.
SO I'VE ONLY GOT ONE QUESTION.

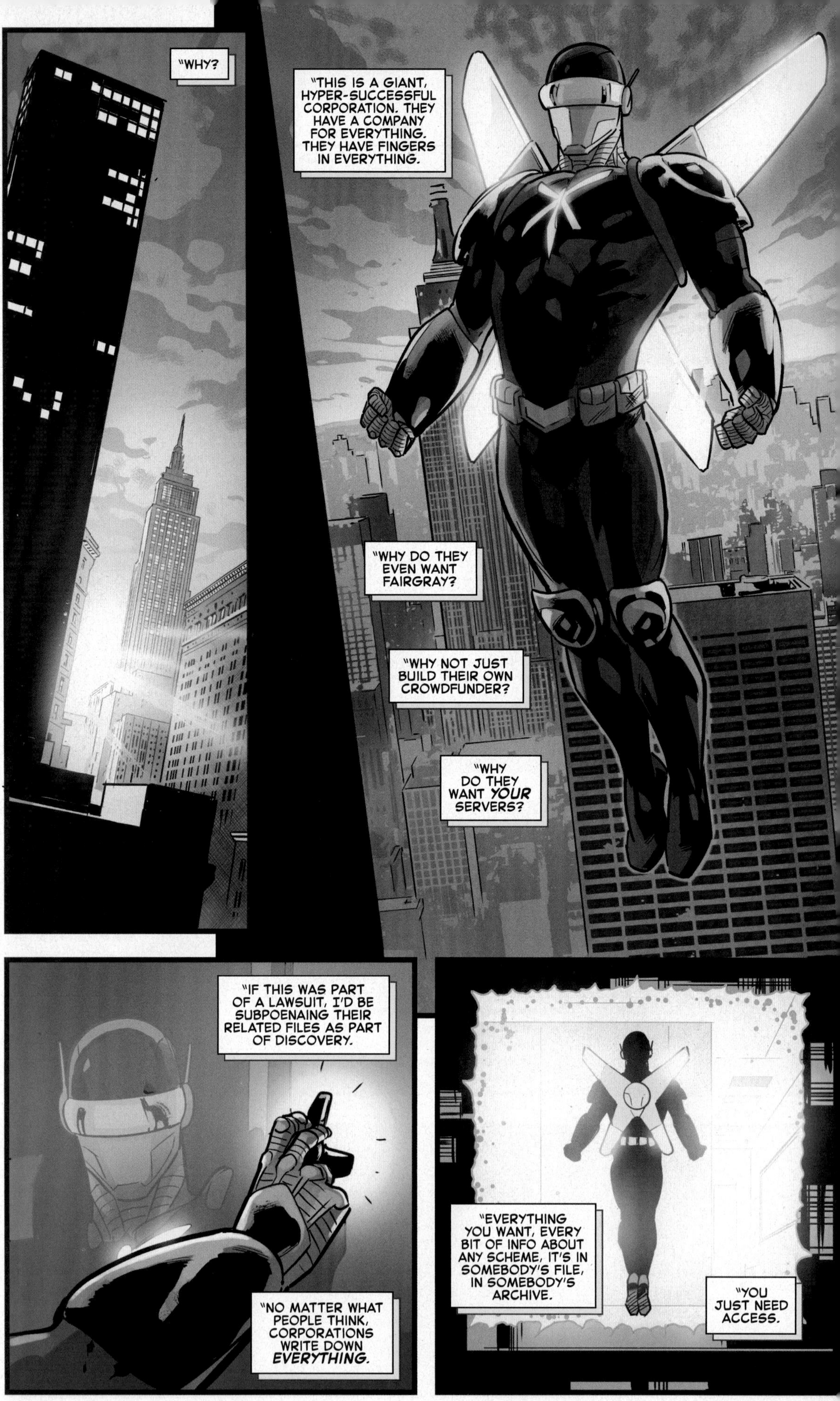
"WHY?
"THIS IS A GIANT, HYPER-SUCCESSFUL CORPORATION. THEY HAVE A COMPANY FOR EVERYTHING. THEY HAVE FINGERS IN EVERYTHING.
"WHY DO THEY EVEN WANT FAIRGRAY?
"WHY NOT JUST BUILD THEIR OWN CROWDFUNDER?
"WHY DO THEY WANT *YOUR* SERVERS?
"IF THIS WAS PART OF A LAWSUIT, I'D BE SUBPOENAING THEIR RELATED FILES AS PART OF DISCOVERY.
"NO MATTER WHAT PEOPLE THINK, CORPORATIONS WRITE DOWN *EVERYTHING.*
"EVERYTHING YOU WANT, EVERY BIT OF INFO ABOUT ANY SCHEME, IT'S IN SOMEBODY'S FILE, IN SOMEBODY'S ARCHIVE.
"YOU JUST NEED ACCESS.

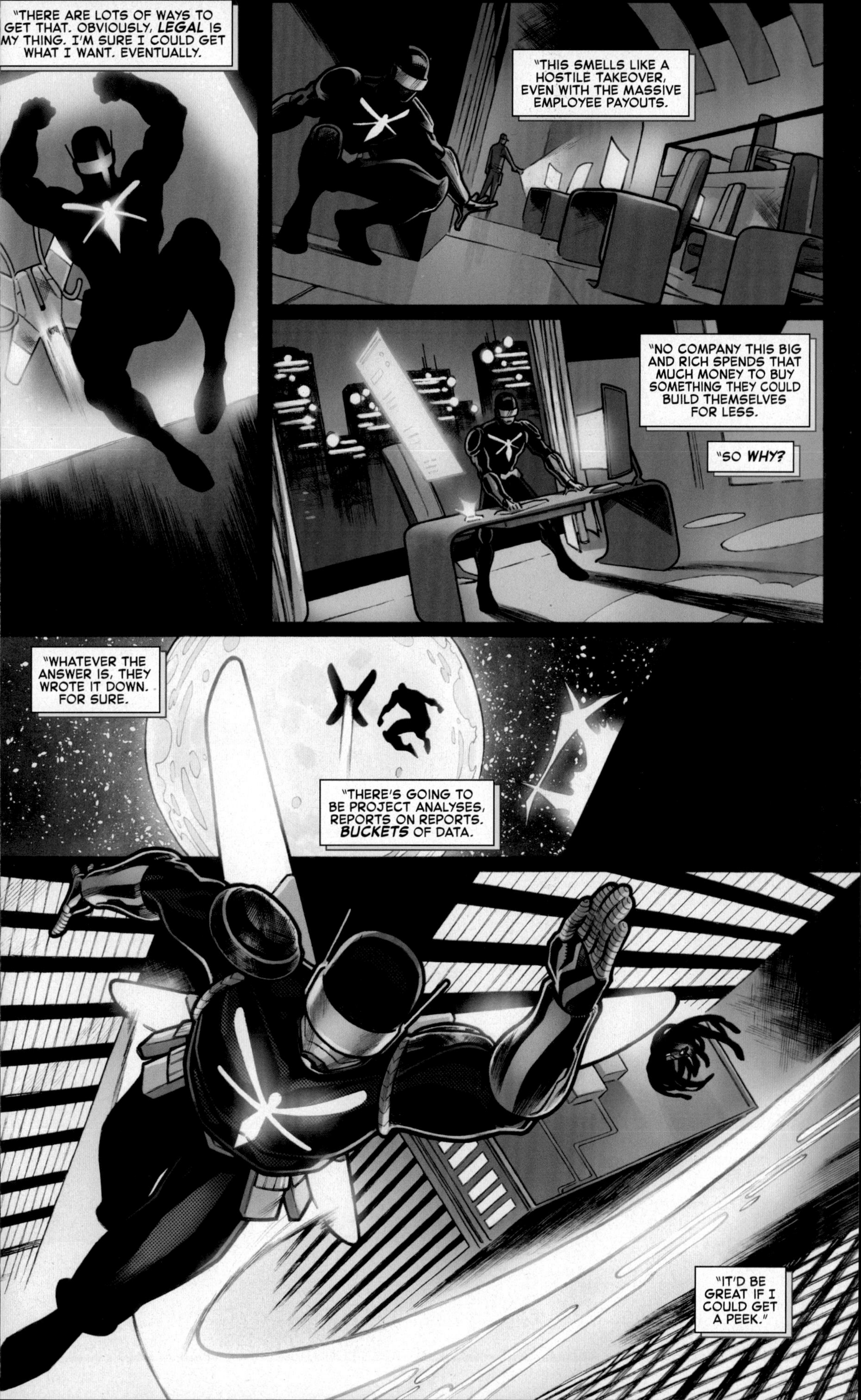
"THERE ARE LOTS OF WAYS TO GET THAT. OBVIOUSLY, *LEGAL* IS MY THING. I'M SURE I COULD GET WHAT I WANT. EVENTUALLY.
"THIS SMELLS LIKE A HOSTILE TAKEOVER, EVEN WITH THE MASSIVE EMPLOYEE PAYOUTS.
"NO COMPANY THIS BIG AND RICH SPENDS THAT MUCH MONEY TO BUY SOMETHING THEY COULD BUILD THEMSELVES FOR LESS.
"SO *WHY?*
"WHATEVER THE ANSWER IS, THEY WROTE IT DOWN. FOR SURE.
"THERE'S GOING TO BE PROJECT ANALYSES, REPORTS ON REPORTS. *BUCKETS* OF DATA.
"IT'D BE GREAT IF I COULD GET A PEEK."

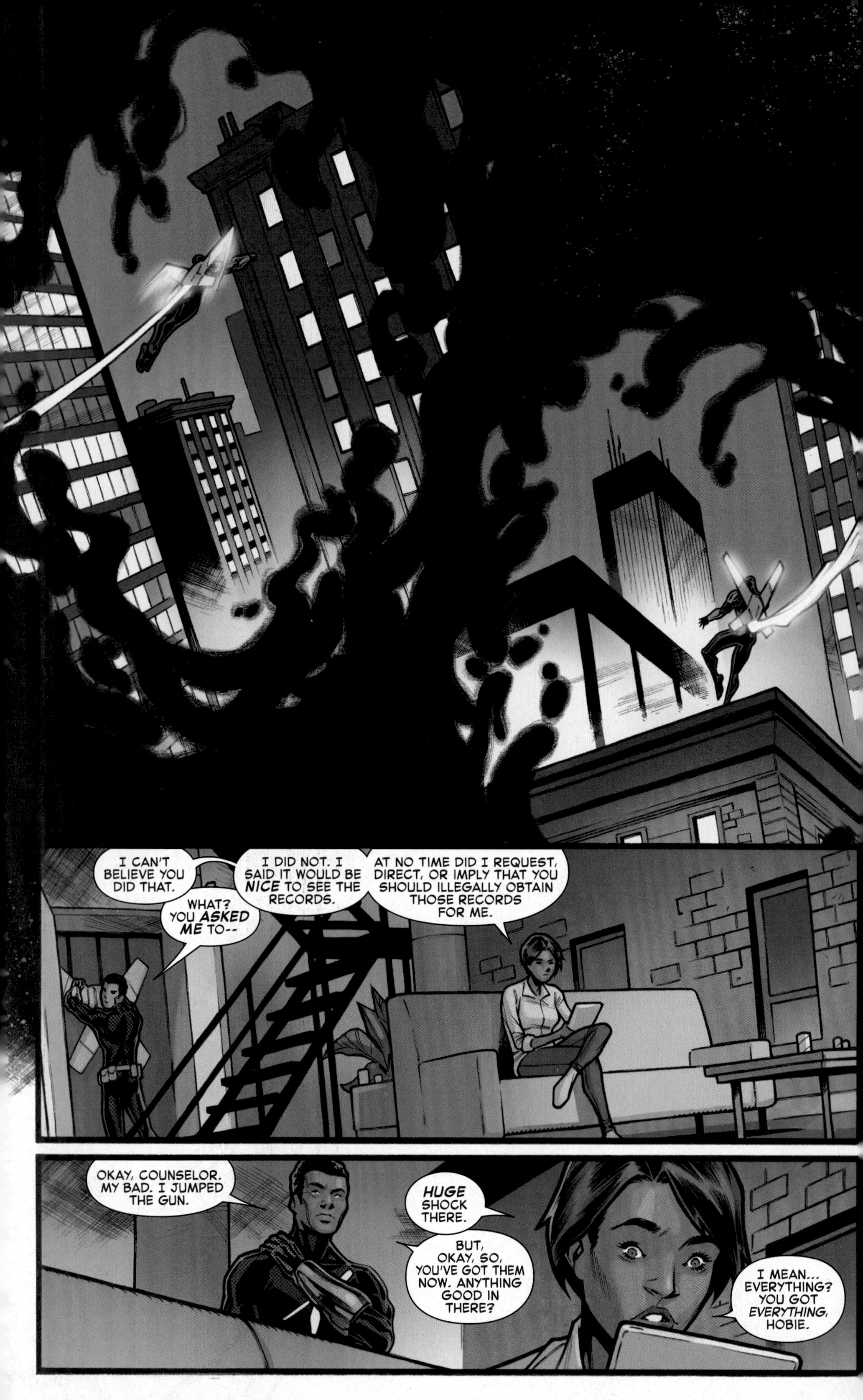
I CAN'T BELIEVE YOU DID THAT.
WHAT? YOU ASKED ME TO--
I DID NOT. I SAID IT WOULD BE NICE TO SEE THE RECORDS.
AT NO TIME DID I REQUEST, DIRECT, OR IMPLY THAT YOU SHOULD ILLEGALLY OBTAIN THOSE RECORDS FOR ME.
OKAY, COUNSELOR. MY BAD. I JUMPED THE GUN.
HUGE SHOCK THERE.
BUT, OKAY, SO, YOU'VE GOT THEM NOW. ANYTHING GOOD IN THERE?
I MEAN... EVERYTHING? YOU GOT EVERYTHING, HOBIE.

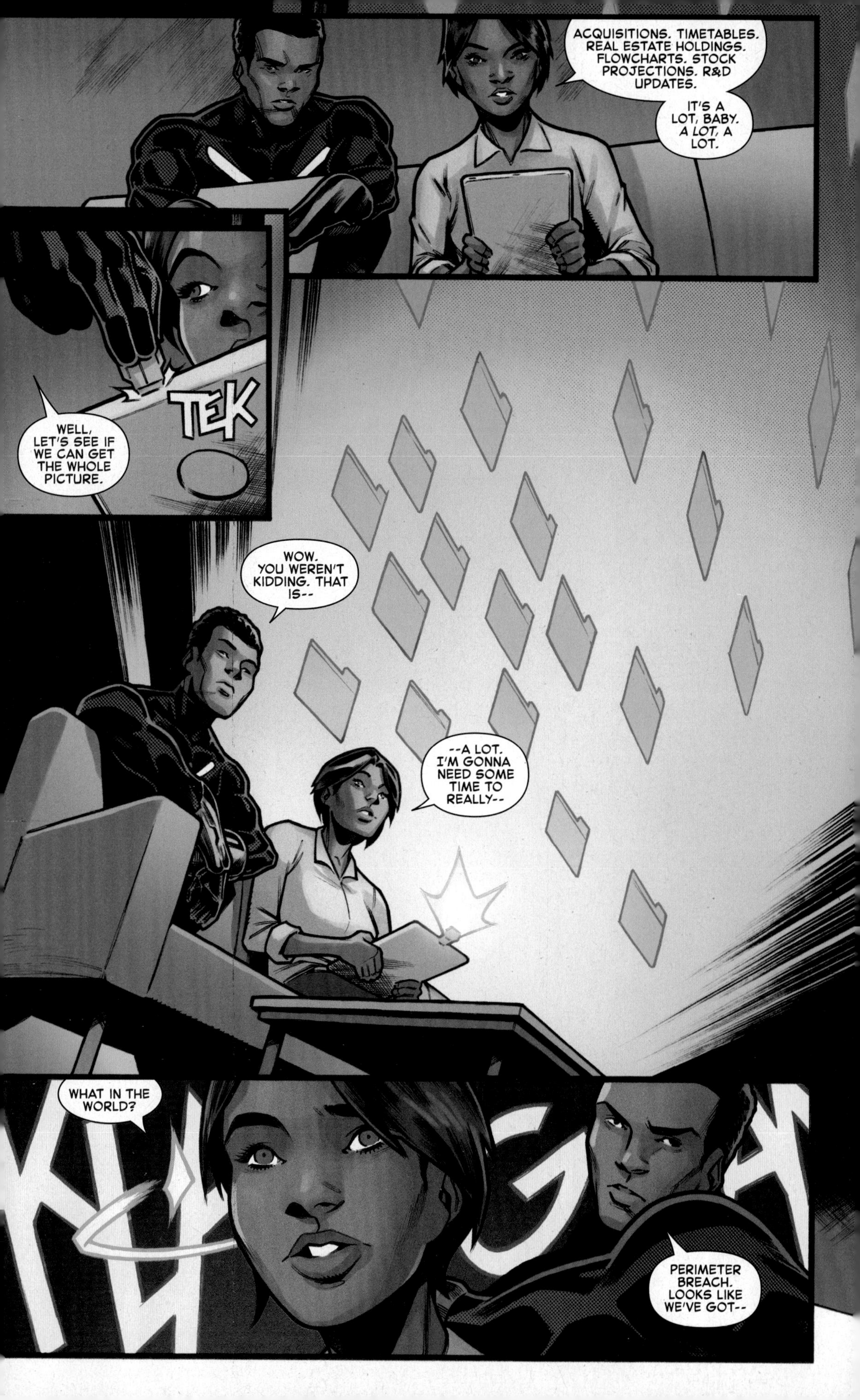
ACQUISITIONS. TIMETABLES. REAL ESTATE HOLDINGS. FLOWCHARTS. STOCK PROJECTIONS. R&D UPDATES.
IT'S A LOT, BABY. A *LOT*, A LOT.
TEK
WELL, LET'S SEE IF WE CAN GET THE WHOLE PICTURE.
WOW. YOU WEREN'T KIDDING. THAT IS--
--A LOT. I'M GONNA NEED SOME TIME TO REALLY--
WHAT IN THE WORLD?
PERIMETER BREACH. LOOKS LIKE WE'VE GOT--

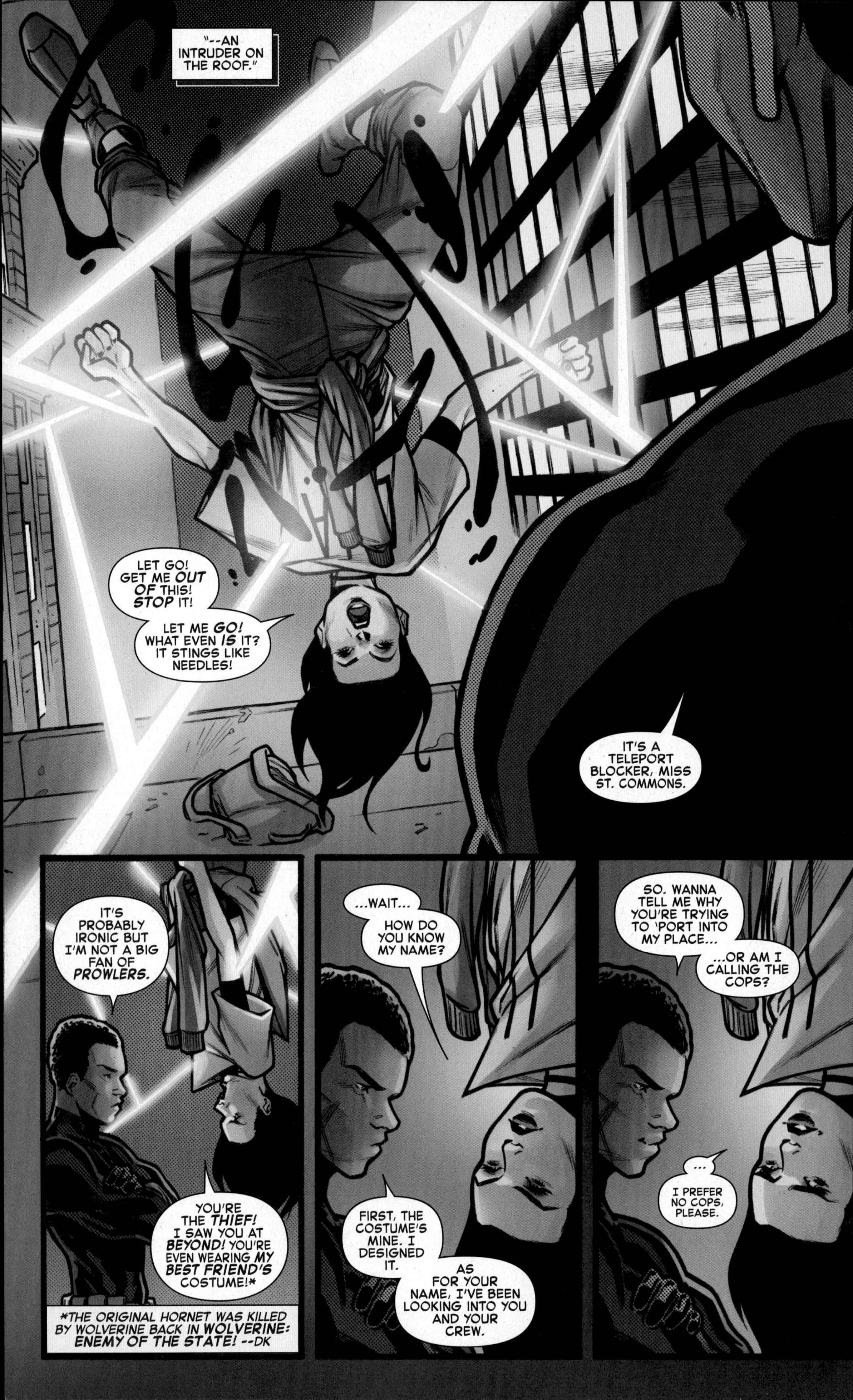
"--AN INTRUDER ON THE ROOF."
LET GO! GET ME OUT OF THIS! STOP IT!
LET ME GO! WHAT EVEN IS IT? IT STINGS LIKE NEEDLES!
IT'S A TELEPORT BLOCKER, MISS ST. COMMONS.
IT'S PROBABLY IRONIC BUT I'M NOT A BIG FAN OF PROWLERS.
YOU'RE THE THIEF! I SAW YOU AT BEYOND! YOU'RE EVEN WEARING MY BEST FRIEND'S COSTUME!*
*THE ORIGINAL HORNET WAS KILLED BY WOLVERINE BACK IN WOLVERINE: ENEMY OF THE STATE! --DK
...WAIT...
HOW DO YOU KNOW MY NAME?
FIRST, THE COSTUME'S MINE. I DESIGNED IT.
AS FOR YOUR NAME, I'VE BEEN LOOKING INTO YOU AND YOUR CREW.
SO. WANNA TELL ME WHY YOU'RE TRYING TO 'PORT INTO MY PLACE...
...OR AM I CALLING THE COPS?
...
I PREFER NO COPS, PLEASE.

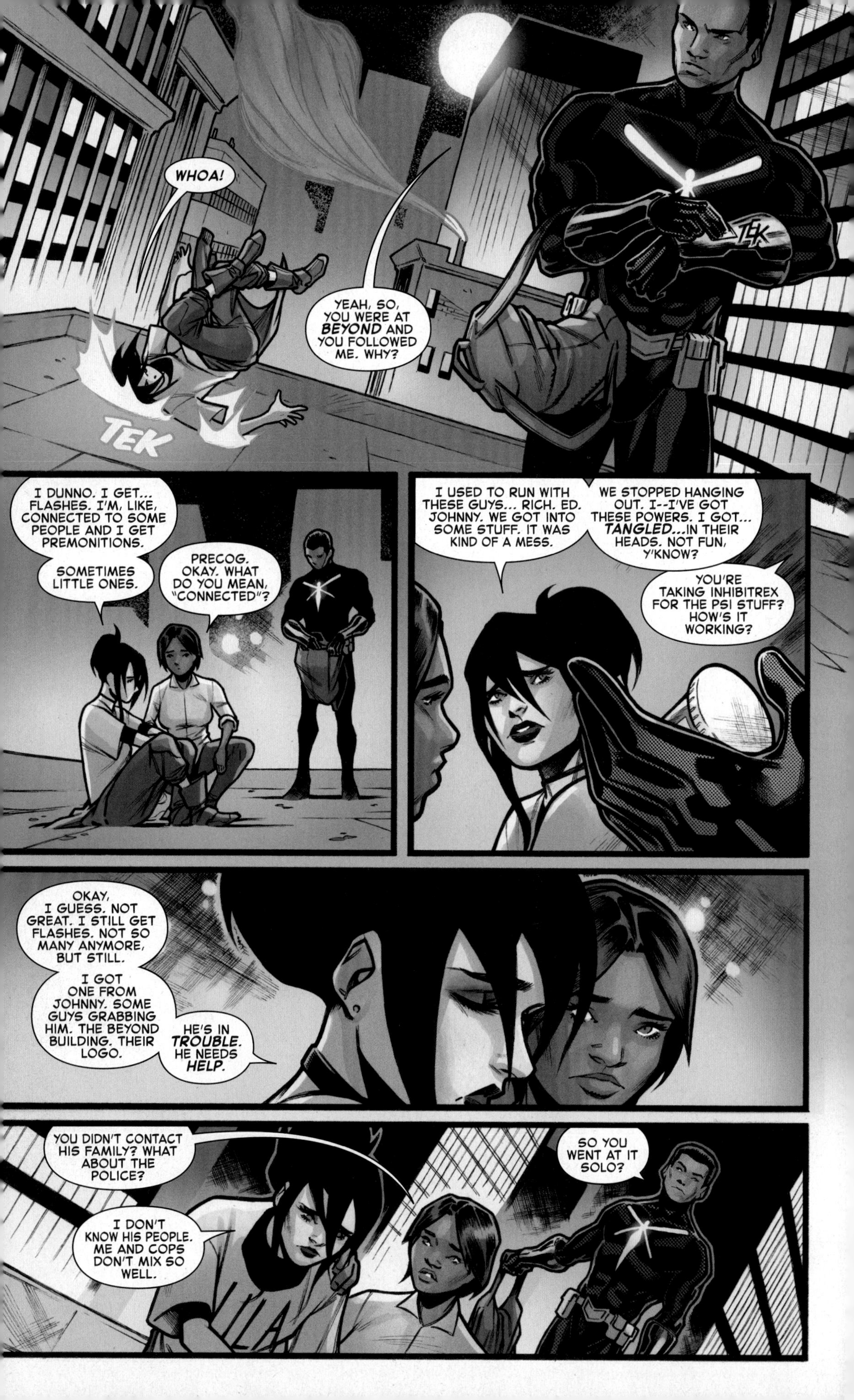
WHOA!
YEAH, SO, YOU WERE AT BEYOND AND YOU FOLLOWED ME. WHY?
TEK
TEK
I DUNNO. I GET... FLASHES. I'M, LIKE, CONNECTED TO SOME PEOPLE AND I GET PREMONITIONS.
SOMETIMES LITTLE ONES.
PRECOG. OKAY. WHAT DO YOU MEAN, "CONNECTED"?
I USED TO RUN WITH THESE GUYS... RICH. ED. JOHNNY. WE GOT INTO SOME STUFF. IT WAS KIND OF A MESS.
WE STOPPED HANGING OUT. I--I'VE GOT THESE POWERS. I GOT... TANGLED...IN THEIR HEADS. NOT FUN, Y'KNOW?
YOU'RE TAKING INHIBITREX FOR THE PSI STUFF? HOW'S IT WORKING?
OKAY, I GUESS. NOT GREAT. I STILL GET FLASHES. NOT SO MANY ANYMORE, BUT STILL.
I GOT ONE FROM JOHNNY. SOME GUYS GRABBING HIM. THE BEYOND BUILDING. THEIR LOGO.
HE'S IN TROUBLE. HE NEEDS HELP.
YOU DIDN'T CONTACT HIS FAMILY? WHAT ABOUT THE POLICE?
I DON'T KNOW HIS PEOPLE. ME AND COPS DON'T MIX SO WELL.
SO YOU WENT AT IT SOLO?

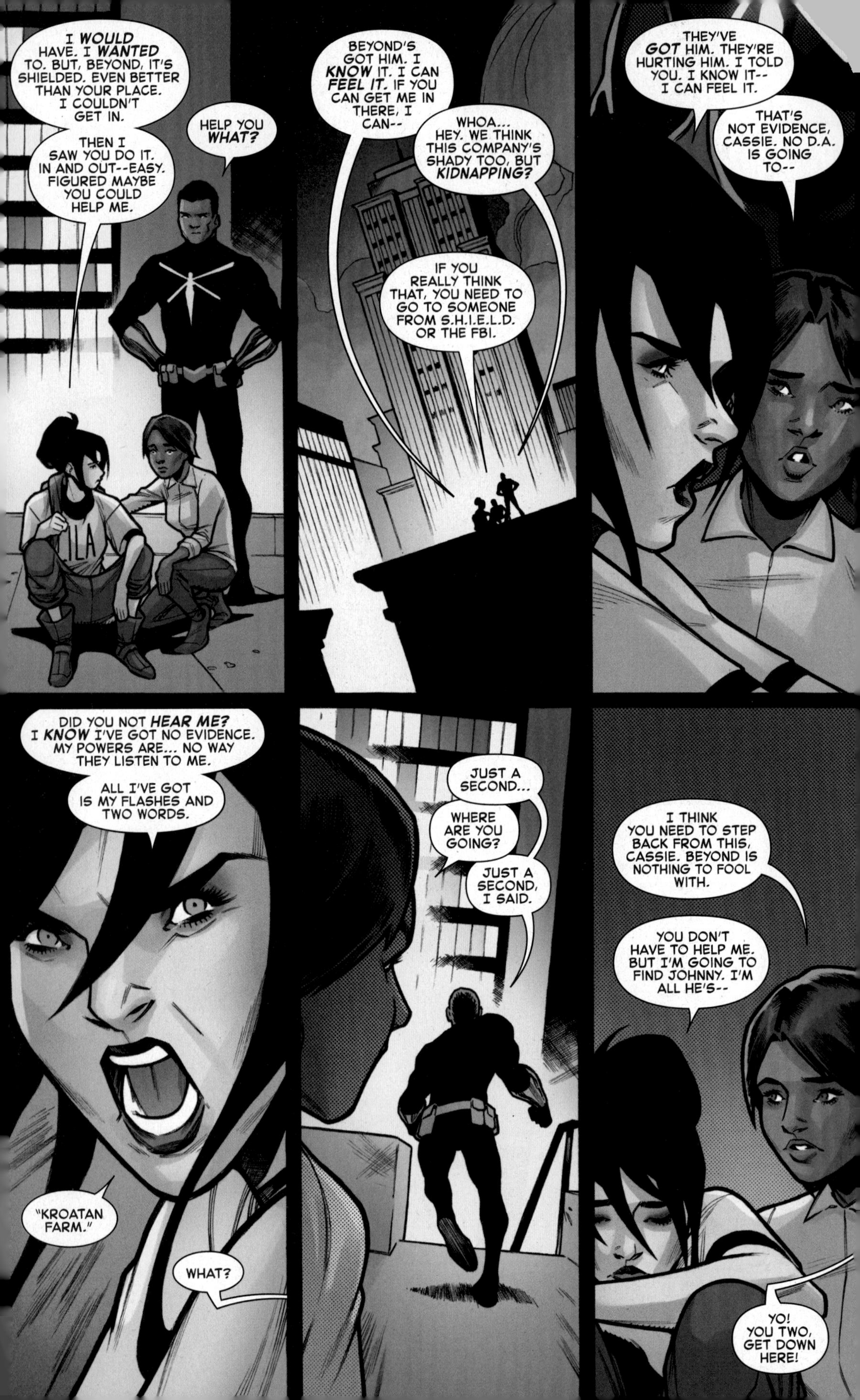
I WOULD HAVE. I WANTED TO. BUT, BEYOND, IT'S SHIELDED. EVEN BETTER THAN YOUR PLACE. I COULDN'T GET IN.
THEN I SAW YOU DO IT. IN AND OUT--EASY. FIGURED MAYBE YOU COULD HELP ME.
HELP YOU WHAT?
LILA
BEYOND'S GOT HIM. I KNOW IT. I CAN FEEL IT. IF YOU CAN GET ME IN THERE, I CAN--
WHOA... HEY. WE THINK THIS COMPANY'S SHADY TOO, BUT KIDNAPPING?
IF YOU REALLY THINK THAT, YOU NEED TO GO TO SOMEONE FROM S.H.I.E.L.D. OR THE FBI.
THEY'VE GOT HIM. THEY'RE HURTING HIM. I TOLD YOU. I KNOW IT-- I CAN FEEL IT.
THAT'S NOT EVIDENCE, CASSIE. NO D.A. IS GOING TO--
DID YOU NOT HEAR ME? I KNOW I'VE GOT NO EVIDENCE. MY POWERS ARE... NO WAY THEY LISTEN TO ME.
ALL I'VE GOT IS MY FLASHES AND TWO WORDS.
"KROATAN FARM."
WHAT?
JUST A SECOND...
WHERE ARE YOU GOING?
JUST A SECOND, I SAID.
I THINK YOU NEED TO STEP BACK FROM THIS, CASSIE. BEYOND IS NOTHING TO FOOL WITH.
YOU DON'T HAVE TO HELP ME. BUT I'M GOING TO FIND JOHNNY. I'M ALL HE'S--
YO! YOU TWO, GET DOWN HERE!

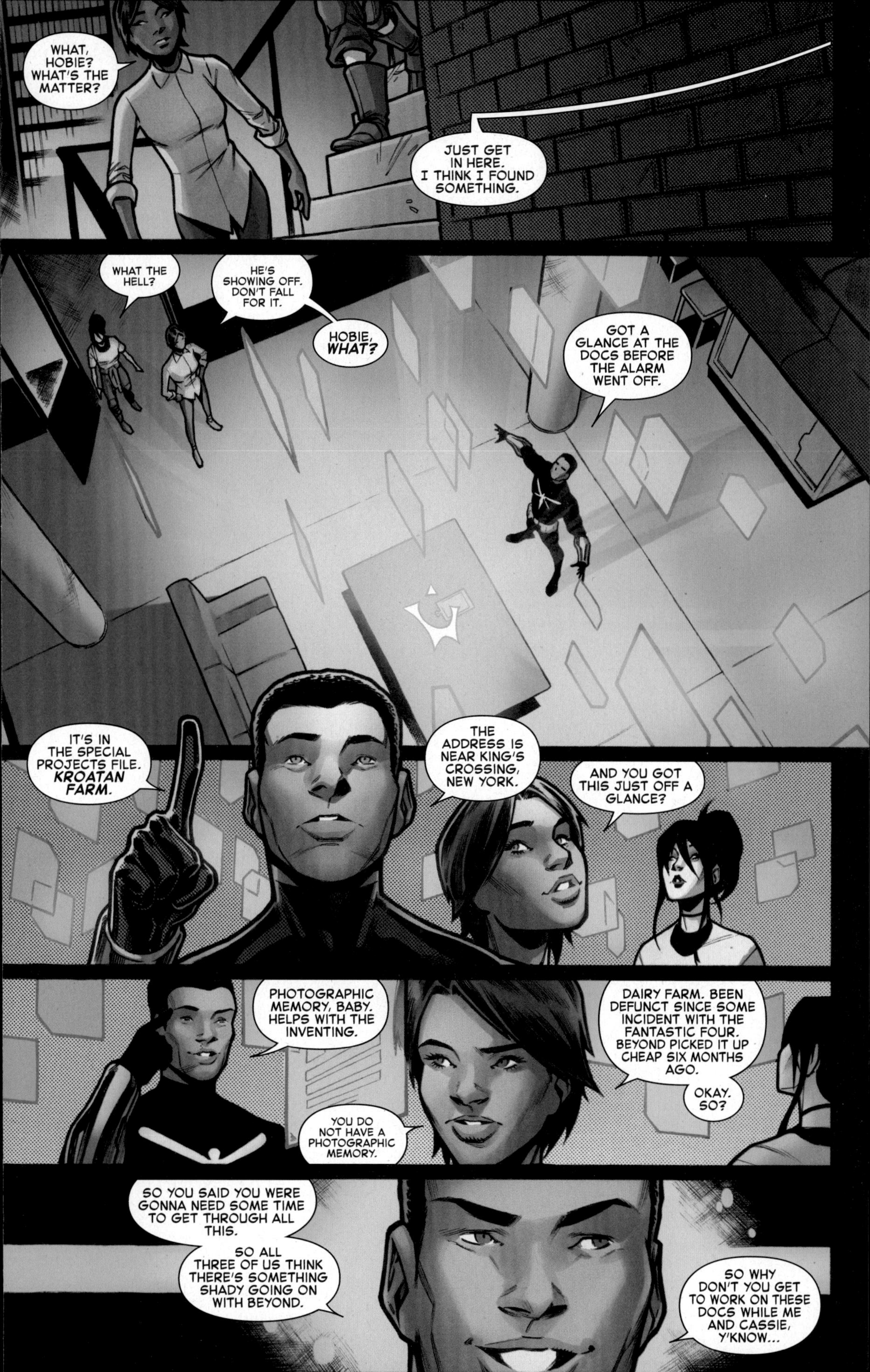
WHAT, HOBIE? WHAT'S THE MATTER?
JUST GET IN HERE. I THINK I FOUND SOMETHING.
WHAT THE HELL?
HE'S SHOWING OFF. DON'T FALL FOR IT.
HOBIE, WHAT?
GOT A GLANCE AT THE DOCS BEFORE THE ALARM WENT OFF.
IT'S IN THE SPECIAL PROJECTS FILE. KROATAN FARM.
THE ADDRESS IS NEAR KING'S CROSSING, NEW YORK.
AND YOU GOT THIS JUST OFF A GLANCE?
PHOTOGRAPHIC MEMORY, BABY. HELPS WITH THE INVENTING.
YOU DO NOT HAVE A PHOTOGRAPHIC MEMORY.
DAIRY FARM. BEEN DEFUNCT SINCE SOME INCIDENT WITH THE FANTASTIC FOUR. BEYOND PICKED IT UP CHEAP SIX MONTHS AGO.
OKAY. SO?
SO YOU SAID YOU WERE GONNA NEED SOME TIME TO GET THROUGH ALL THIS.
SO ALL THREE OF US THINK THERE'S SOMETHING SHADY GOING ON WITH BEYOND.
SO WHY DON'T YOU GET TO WORK ON THESE DOCS WHILE ME AND CASSIE, Y'KNOW...

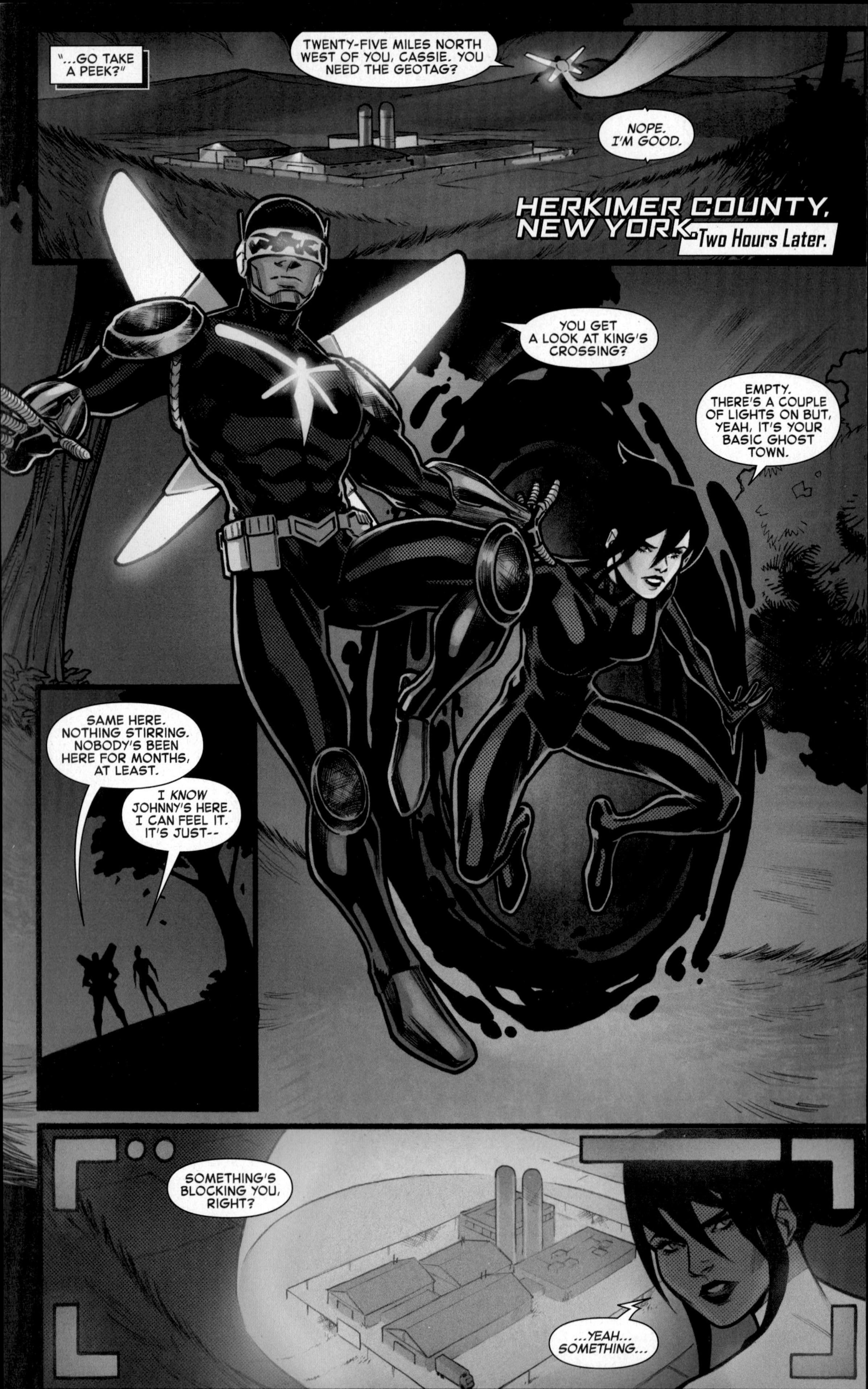
"...GO TAKE A PEEK?"
TWENTY-FIVE MILES NORTH WEST OF YOU, CASSIE. YOU NEED THE GEOTAG?
NOPE. I'M GOOD.
HERKIMER COUNTY, NEW YORK. Two Hours Later.
YOU GET A LOOK AT KING'S CROSSING?
EMPTY. THERE'S A COUPLE OF LIGHTS ON BUT, YEAH, IT'S YOUR BASIC GHOST TOWN.
SAME HERE. NOTHING STIRRING. NOBODY'S BEEN HERE FOR MONTHS, AT LEAST.
I KNOW JOHNNY'S HERE. I CAN FEEL IT. IT'S JUST--
SOMETHING'S BLOCKING YOU, RIGHT?
...YEAH... SOMETHING...

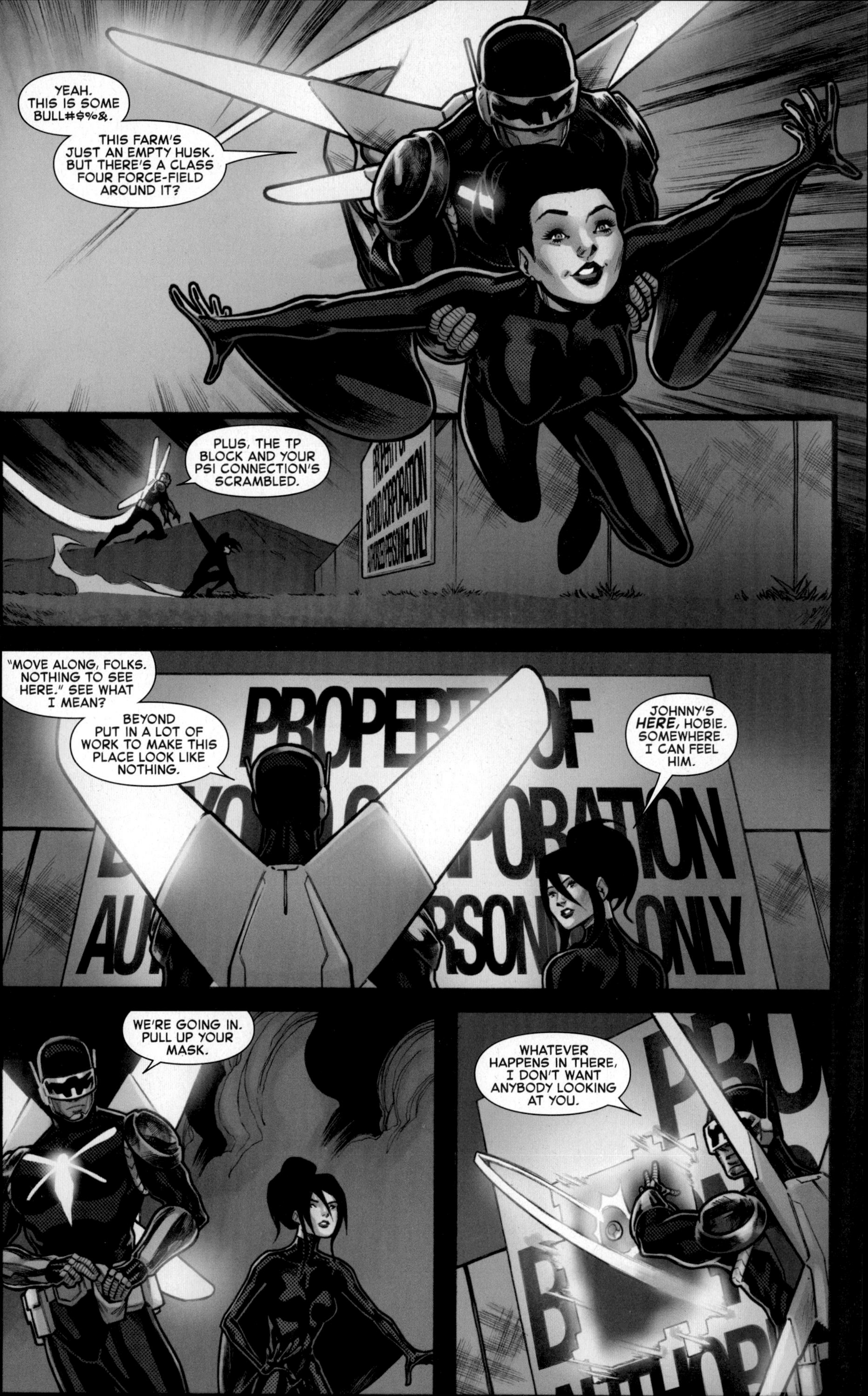
YEAH. THIS IS SOME BULL#$%&.
THIS FARM'S JUST AN EMPTY HUSK. BUT THERE'S A CLASS FOUR FORCE-FIELD AROUND IT?
PLUS, THE TP BLOCK AND YOUR PSI CONNECTION'S SCRAMBLED.
PROPERTY OF BEYOND CORPORATION AUTHORIZED PERSONNEL ONLY
"MOVE ALONG, FOLKS. NOTHING TO SEE HERE." SEE WHAT I MEAN?
BEYOND PUT IN A LOT OF WORK TO MAKE THIS PLACE LOOK LIKE NOTHING.
JOHNNY'S *HERE*, HOBIE. SOMEWHERE. I CAN FEEL HIM.
WE'RE GOING IN. PULL UP YOUR MASK.
WHATEVER HAPPENS IN THERE, I DON'T WANT ANYBODY LOOKING AT YOU.

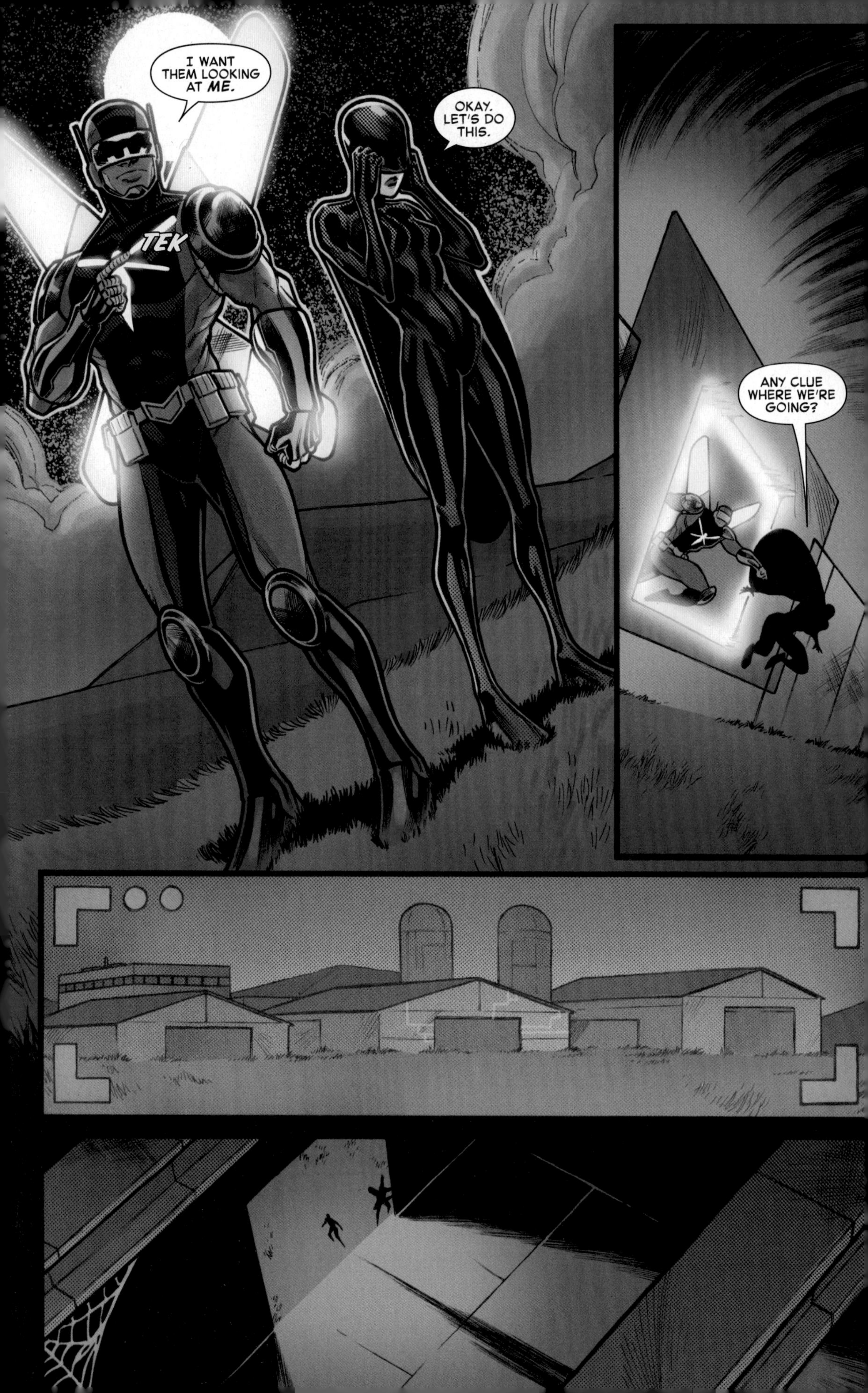
I WANT THEM LOOKING AT ME.
TEK
OKAY. LET'S DO THIS.
ANY CLUE WHERE WE'RE GOING?

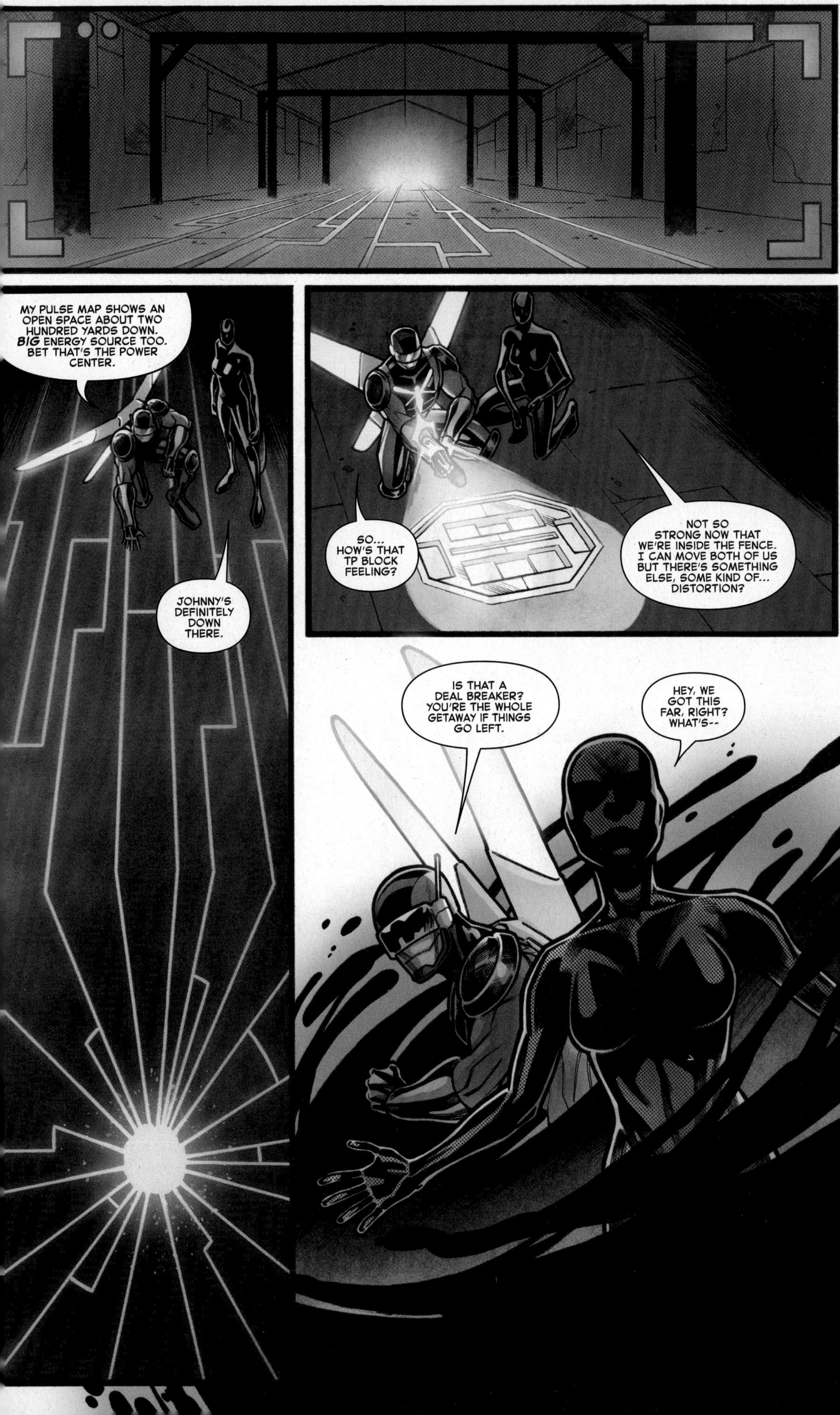
MY PULSE MAP SHOWS AN OPEN SPACE ABOUT TWO HUNDRED YARDS DOWN. BIG ENERGY SOURCE TOO. BET THAT'S THE POWER CENTER.
JOHNNY'S DEFINITELY DOWN THERE.
SO... HOW'S THAT TP BLOCK FEELING?
NOT SO STRONG NOW THAT WE'RE INSIDE THE FENCE. I CAN MOVE BOTH OF US BUT THERE'S SOMETHING ELSE, SOME KIND OF... DISTORTION?
IS THAT A DEAL BREAKER? YOU'RE THE WHOLE GETAWAY IF THINGS GO LEFT.
HEY, WE GOT THIS FAR, RIGHT? WHAT'S--

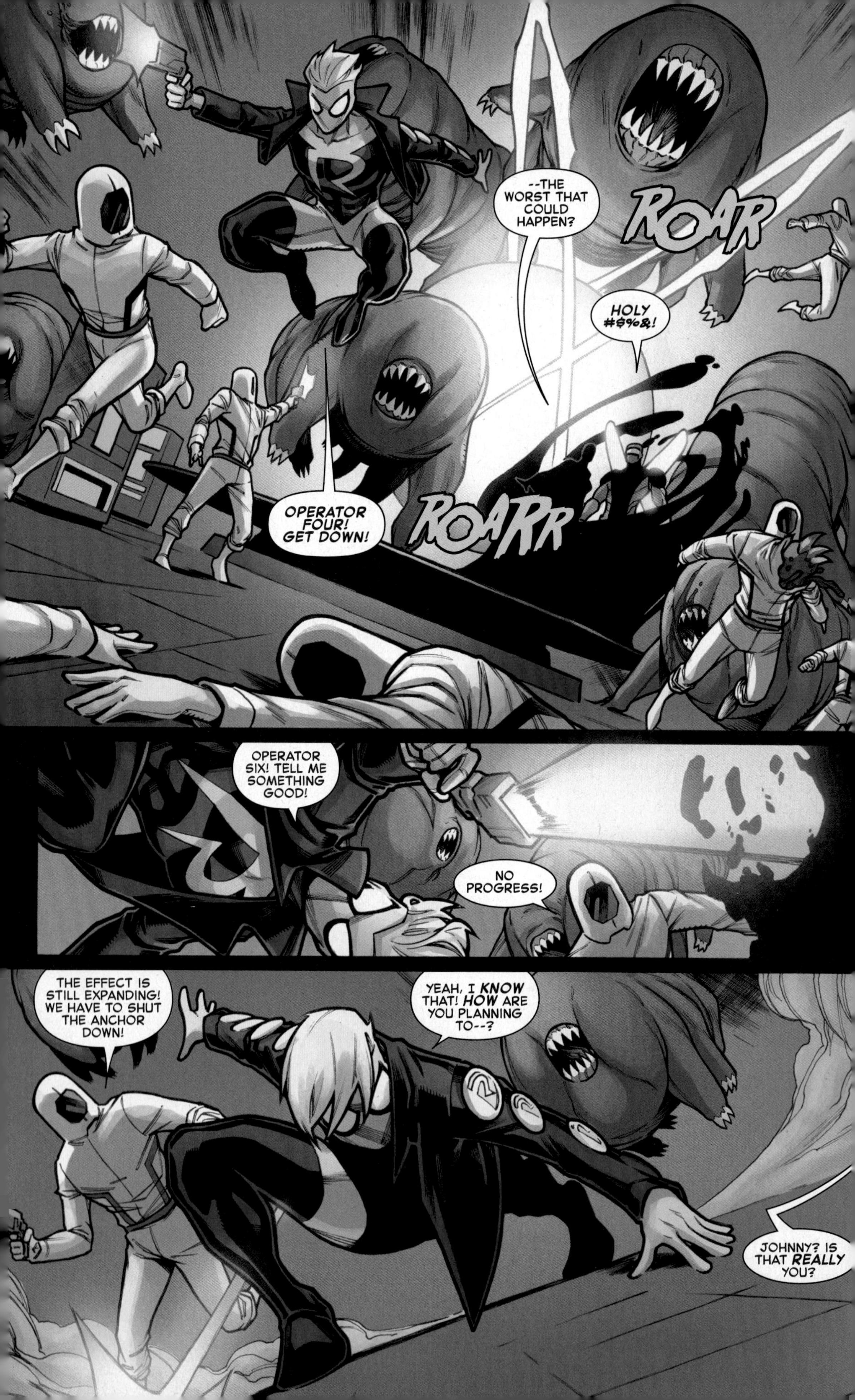
--THE WORST THAT COULD HAPPEN?
ROAR
HOLY #$%&!
OPERATOR FOUR! GET DOWN!
ROARR
OPERATOR SIX! TELL ME SOMETHING GOOD!
NO PROGRESS!
THE EFFECT IS STILL EXPANDING! WE HAVE TO SHUT THE ANCHOR DOWN!
YEAH, I KNOW THAT! HOW ARE YOU PLANNING TO--?
JOHNNY? IS THAT REALLY YOU?

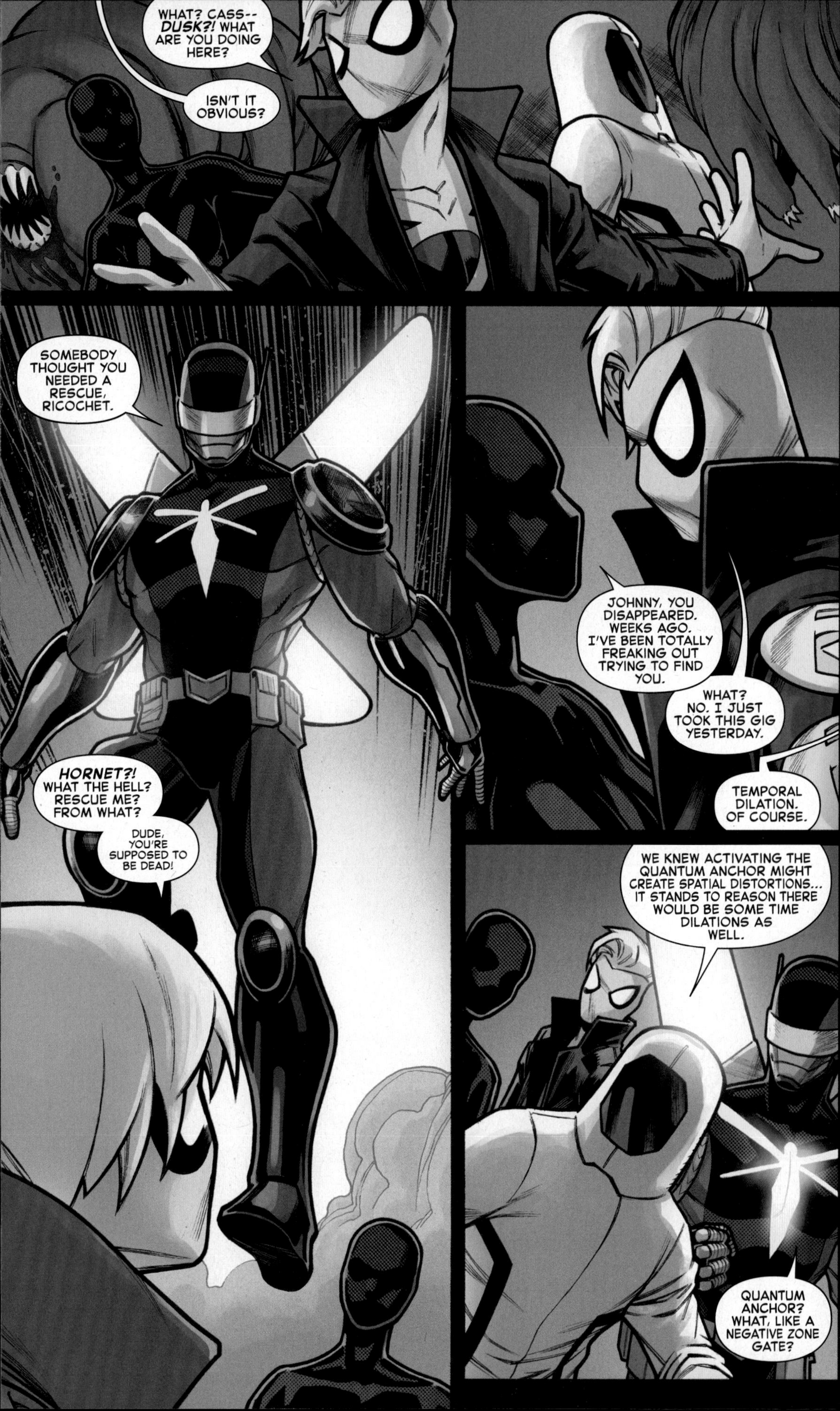

WHAT? CASS-- *DUSK?!* WHAT ARE YOU DOING HERE?
ISN'T IT OBVIOUS?
SOMEBODY THOUGHT YOU NEEDED A RESCUE, RICOCHET.
HORNET?! WHAT THE HELL? RESCUE ME? FROM WHAT?
DUDE, YOU'RE SUPPOSED TO BE DEAD!
JOHNNY, YOU DISAPPEARED. WEEKS AGO. I'VE BEEN TOTALLY FREAKING OUT TRYING TO FIND YOU.
WHAT? NO. I JUST TOOK THIS GIG YESTERDAY.
TEMPORAL DILATION. OF COURSE.
WE KNEW ACTIVATING THE QUANTUM ANCHOR MIGHT CREATE SPATIAL DISTORTIONS... IT STANDS TO REASON THERE WOULD BE SOME TIME DILATIONS AS WELL.
QUANTUM ANCHOR? WHAT, LIKE A NEGATIVE ZONE GATE?

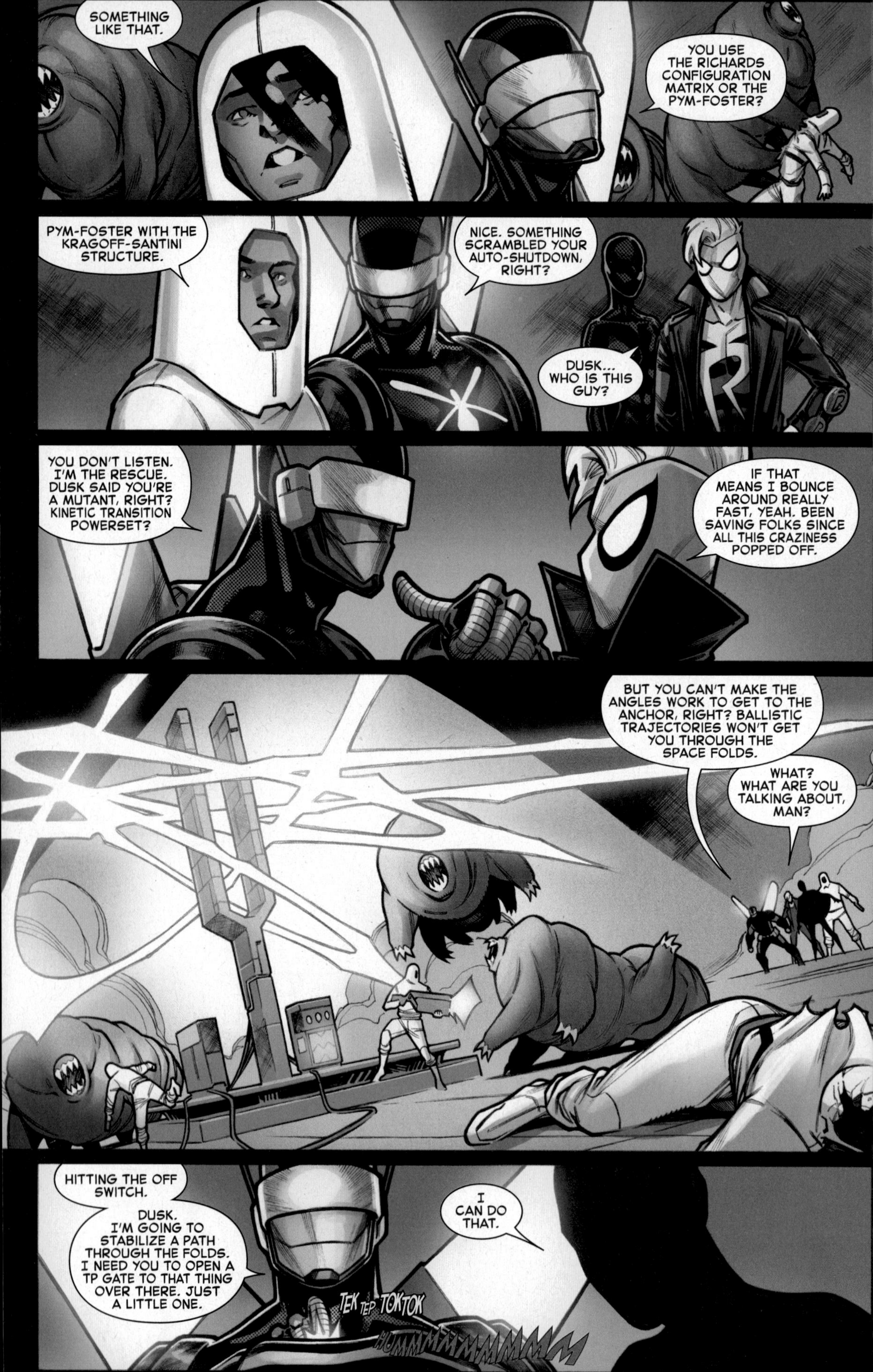
SOMETHING LIKE THAT.
YOU USE THE RICHARDS CONFIGURATION MATRIX OR THE PYM-FOSTER?
PYM-FOSTER WITH THE KRAGOFF-SANTINI STRUCTURE.
NICE. SOMETHING SCRAMBLED YOUR AUTO-SHUTDOWN, RIGHT?
DUSK... WHO IS THIS GUY?
YOU DON'T LISTEN. I'M THE RESCUE. DUSK SAID YOU'RE A MUTANT, RIGHT? KINETIC TRANSITION POWERSET?
IF THAT MEANS I BOUNCE AROUND REALLY FAST, YEAH. BEEN SAVING FOLKS SINCE ALL THIS CRAZINESS POPPED OFF.
BUT YOU CAN'T MAKE THE ANGLES WORK TO GET TO THE ANCHOR, RIGHT? BALLISTIC TRAJECTORIES WON'T GET YOU THROUGH THE SPACE FOLDS.
WHAT? WHAT ARE YOU TALKING ABOUT, MAN?
HITTING THE OFF SWITCH.
DUSK. I'M GOING TO STABILIZE A PATH THROUGH THE FOLDS. I NEED YOU TO OPEN A TP GATE TO THAT THING OVER THERE. JUST A LITTLE ONE.
I CAN DO THAT.
TEK TEP TOKTOK
HUMMMMMMMMMMM

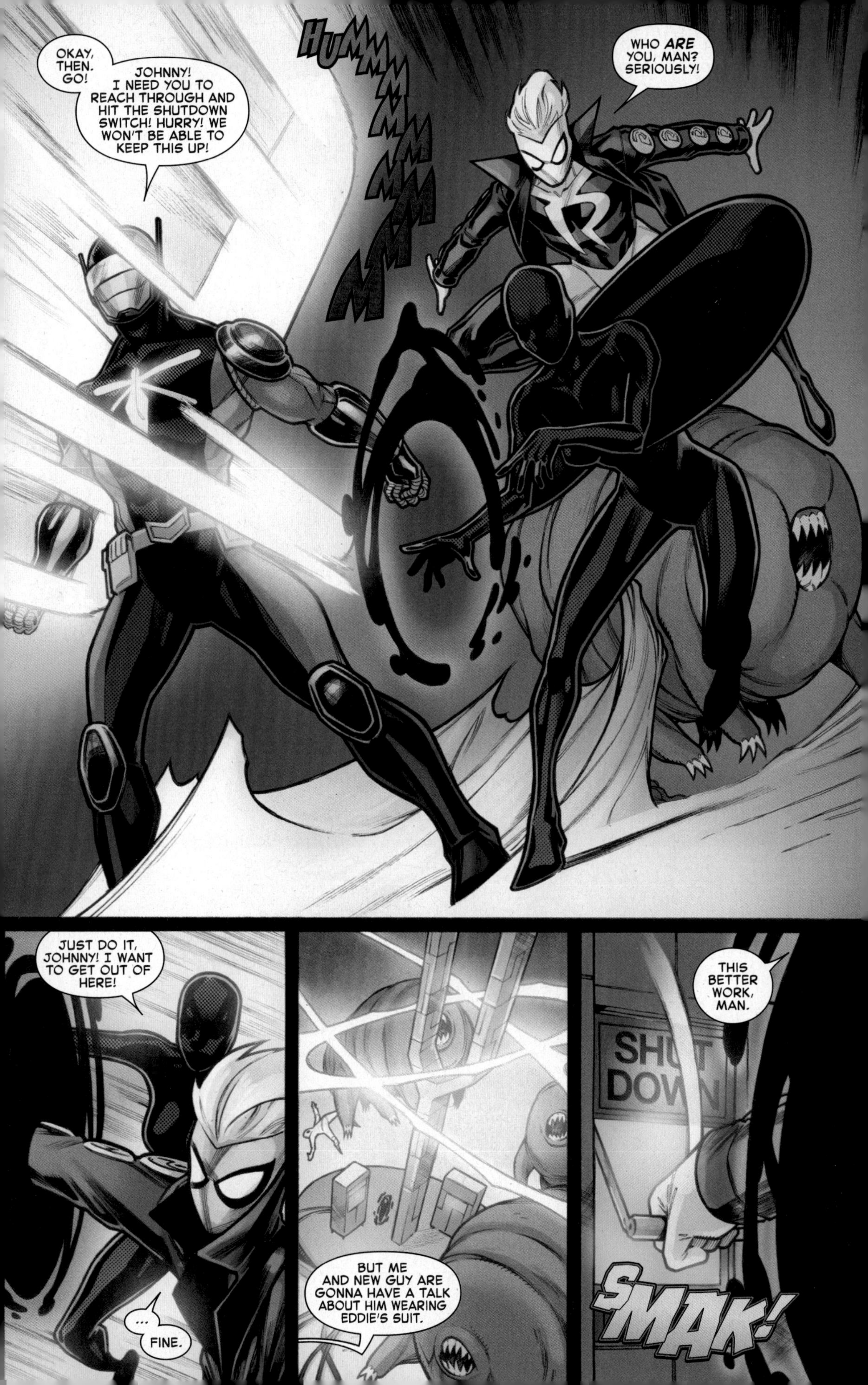
OKAY, THEN. GO!
JOHNNY! I NEED YOU TO REACH THROUGH AND HIT THE SHUTDOWN SWITCH! HURRY! WE WON'T BE ABLE TO KEEP THIS UP!
HUMMMMMMMMMMM
WHO ARE YOU, MAN? SERIOUSLY!
JUST DO IT, JOHNNY! I WANT TO GET OUT OF HERE!
...
FINE.
BUT ME AND NEW GUY ARE GONNA HAVE A TALK ABOUT HIM WEARING EDDIE'S SUIT.
THIS BETTER WORK, MAN.
SHUT DOWN
SMAK!

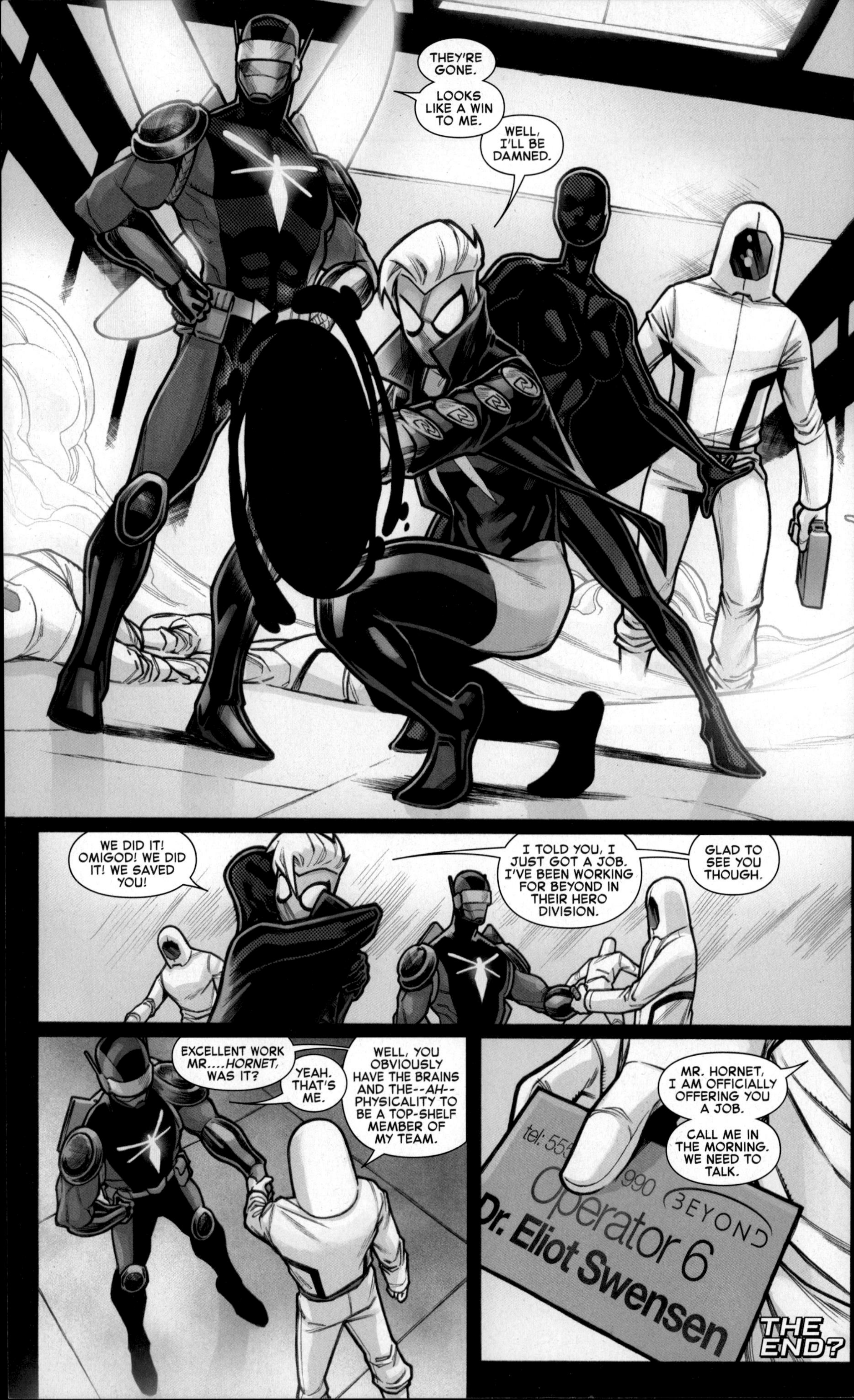
THEY'RE GONE.
LOOKS LIKE A WIN TO ME.
WELL, I'LL BE DAMNED.
WE DID IT! OMIGOD! WE DID IT! WE SAVED YOU!
I TOLD YOU, I JUST GOT A JOB. I'VE BEEN WORKING FOR BEYOND IN THEIR HERO DIVISION.
GLAD TO SEE YOU THOUGH.
EXCELLENT WORK MR....HORNET, WAS IT?
YEAH. THAT'S ME.
WELL, YOU OBVIOUSLY HAVE THE BRAINS AND THE--AH--PHYSICALITY TO BE A TOP-SHELF MEMBER OF MY TEAM.
MR. HORNET, I AM OFFICIALLY OFFERING YOU A JOB.
CALL ME IN THE MORNING. WE NEED TO TALK.
BEYOND
Operator 6
Dr. Eliot Swensen
THE END?

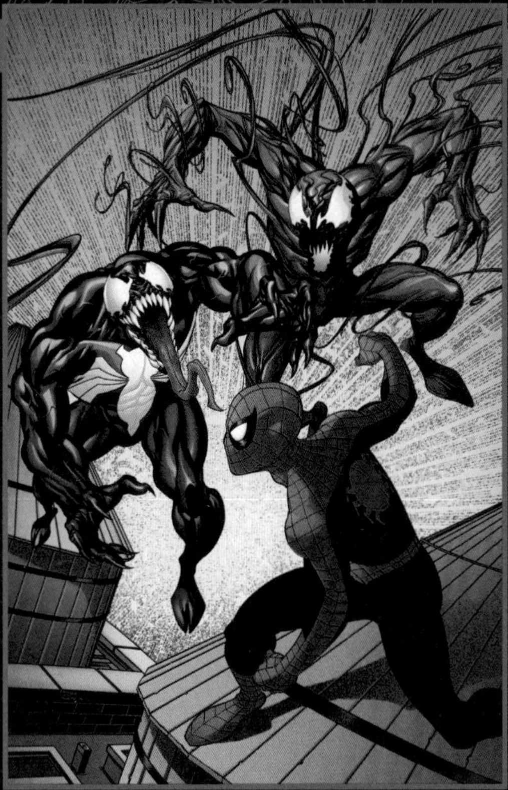

#86 CLASSIC HOMAGE VARIANT BY
MIKE McKONE & **CHRIS SOTOMAYOR**

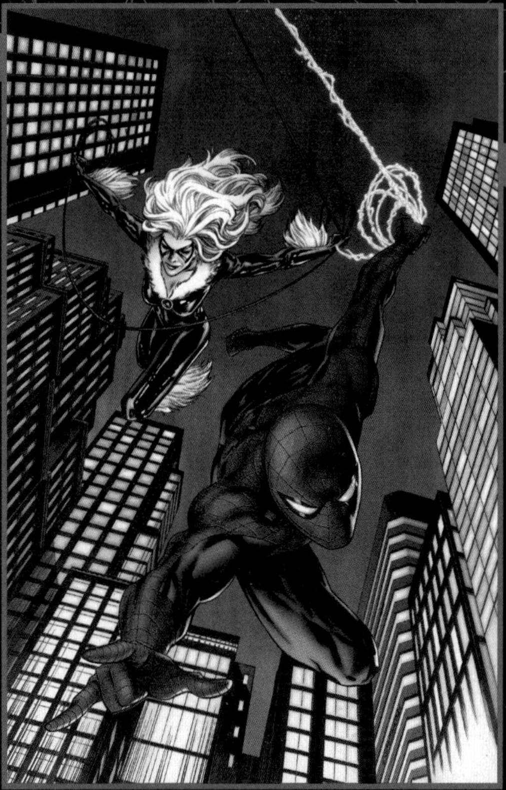

#87 VARIANT BY
CORY SMITH & **MORRY HOLLOWELL**

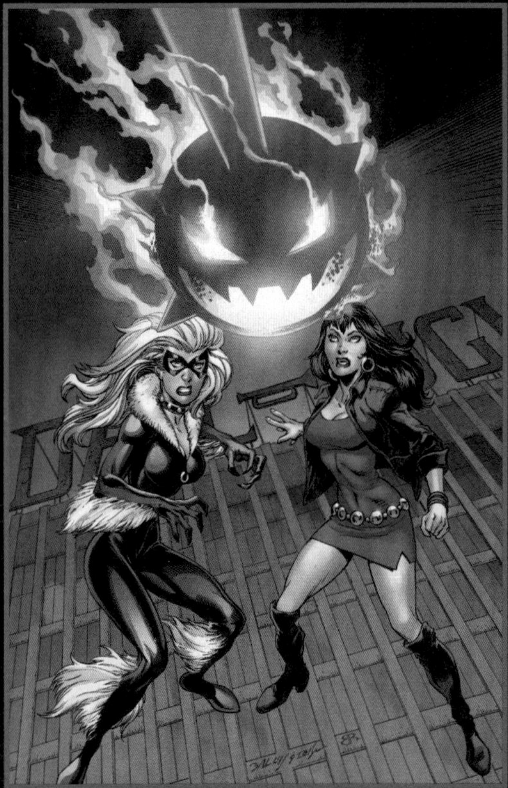

#88 VARIANT BY
MARK BAGLEY, **JOHN DELL** & **BRIAN REBER**

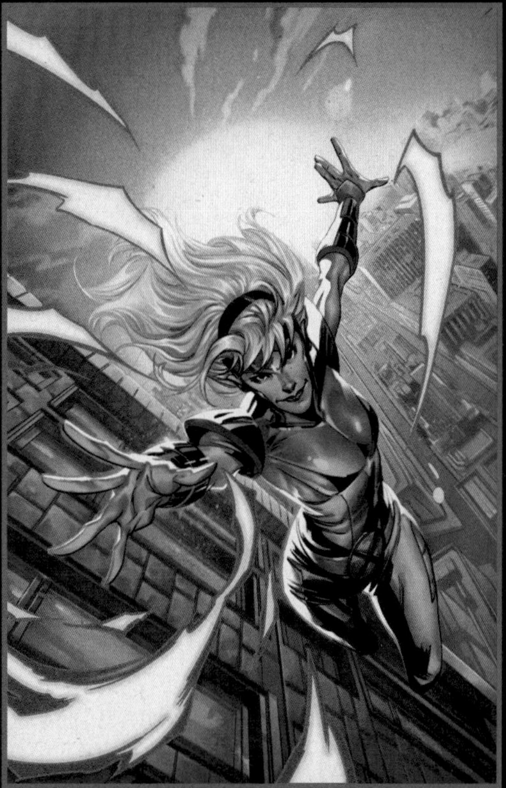

#88 X-GWEN VARIANT BY
FRANCESCO MANNA & **FLAVIO DISPENZA**

BEYOND CORPORATION

#88 DESIGN VARIANT BY
PATRICK GLEASON

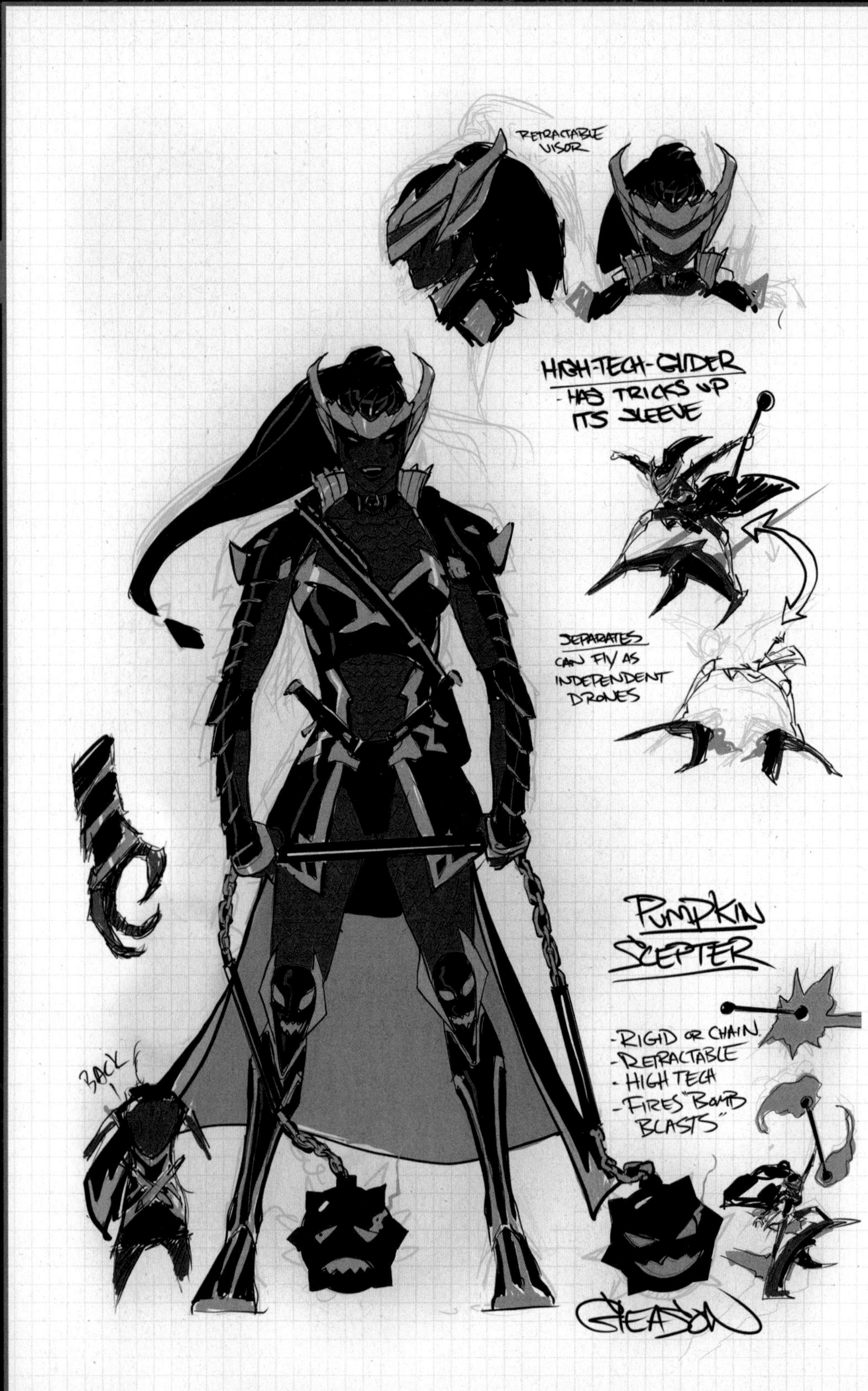
RETRACTABLE VISOR
HIGH-TECH-GLIDER
- HAS TRICKS UP ITS SLEEVE
SEPARATES
CAN FLY AS INDEPENDENT DRONES
PUMPKIN SCEPTER
- RIGID OR CHAIN
- RETRACTABLE
- HIGH TECH
- FIRES "BOMB BLASTS"
BACK
GLEASON

BEYOND
CORPORATION

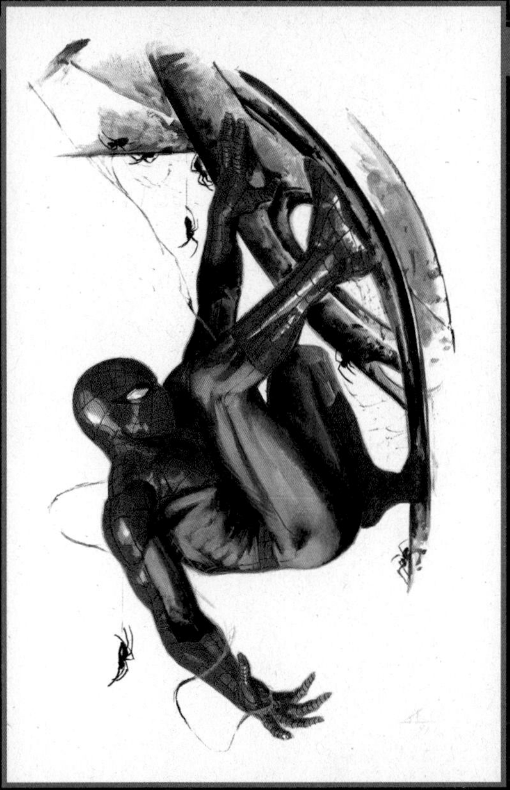

#88 2ND-PRINTING VARIANT BY
CARLOS GÓMEZ & **EDGAR DELGADO**

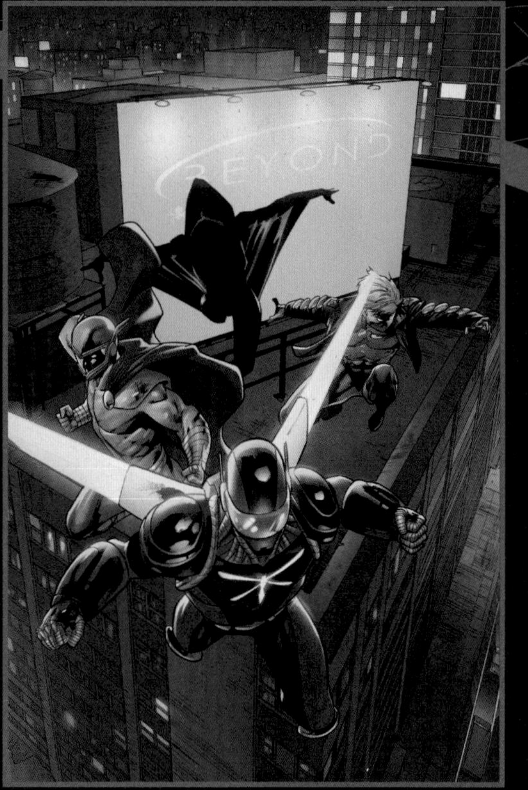
BEYOND

#88.BEY VARIANT BY
JAN BAZALDUA & **JESUS ABURTOV**

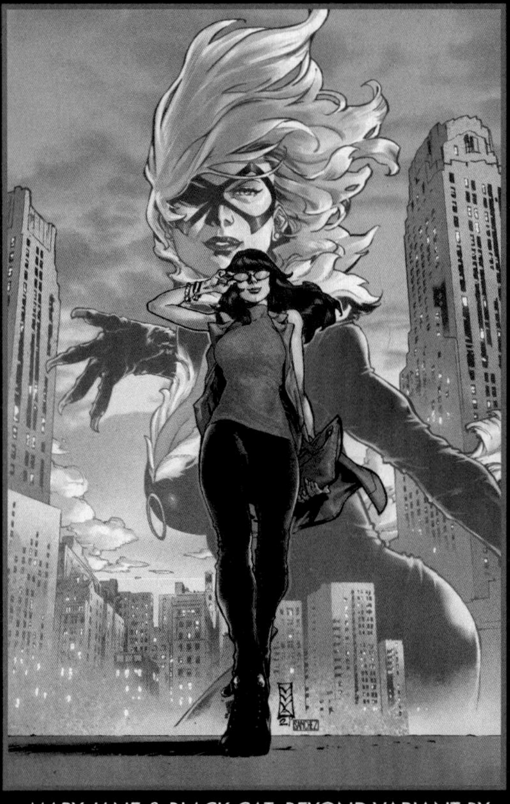

MARY JANE & BLACK CAT: BEYOND VARIANT BY
C.F. VILLA & **ALEJANDRO SÁNCHEZ**

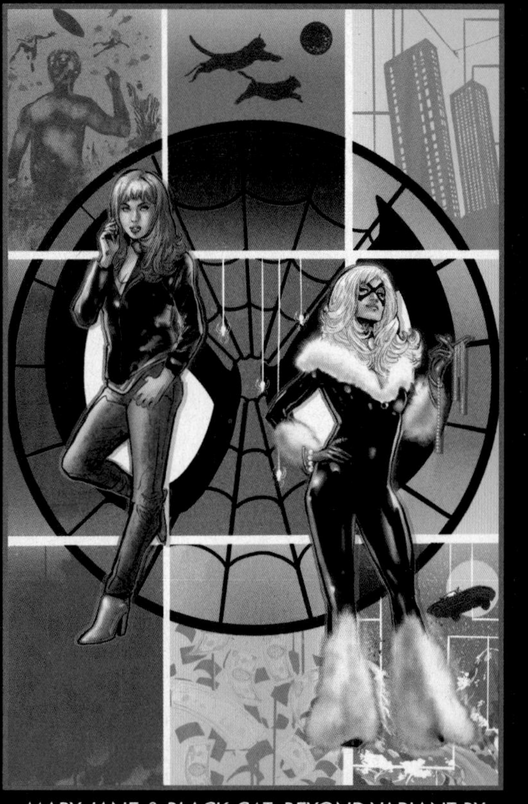

MARY JANE & BLACK CAT: BEYOND VARIANT BY
PHIL JIMENEZ & **EDGAR DELGADO**

BEYOND CORPORATION

MARY JANE & BLACK CAT: BEYOND VARIANT BY
HUMBERTO RAMOS & **EDGAR DELGADO**

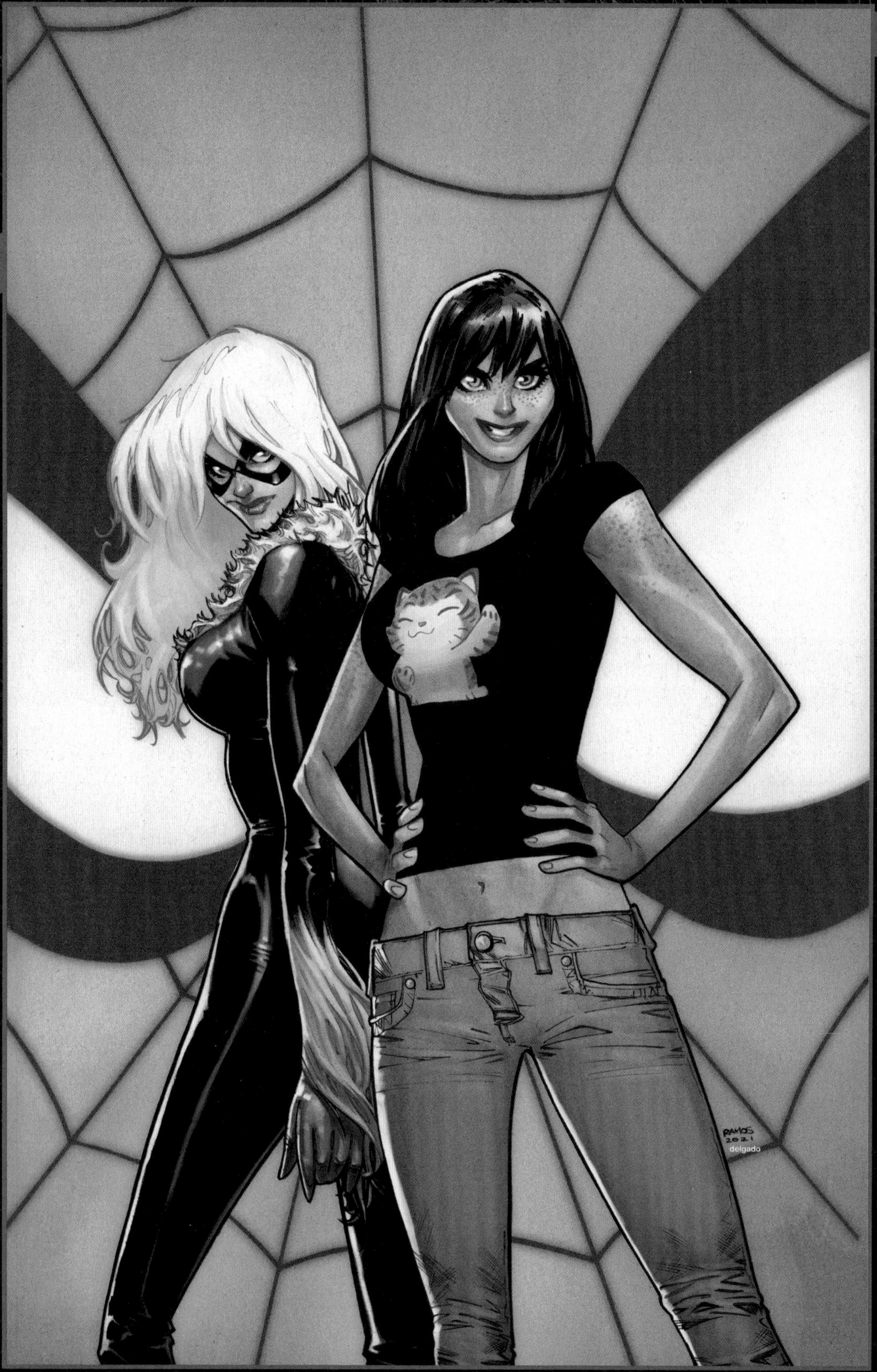
RAMOS
2021
delgado

MARY JANE & BLACK CAT: BEYOND VARIANT BY
NABETSE ZITRO & **MORRY HOLLOWELL**

BEYOND
CORPORATION

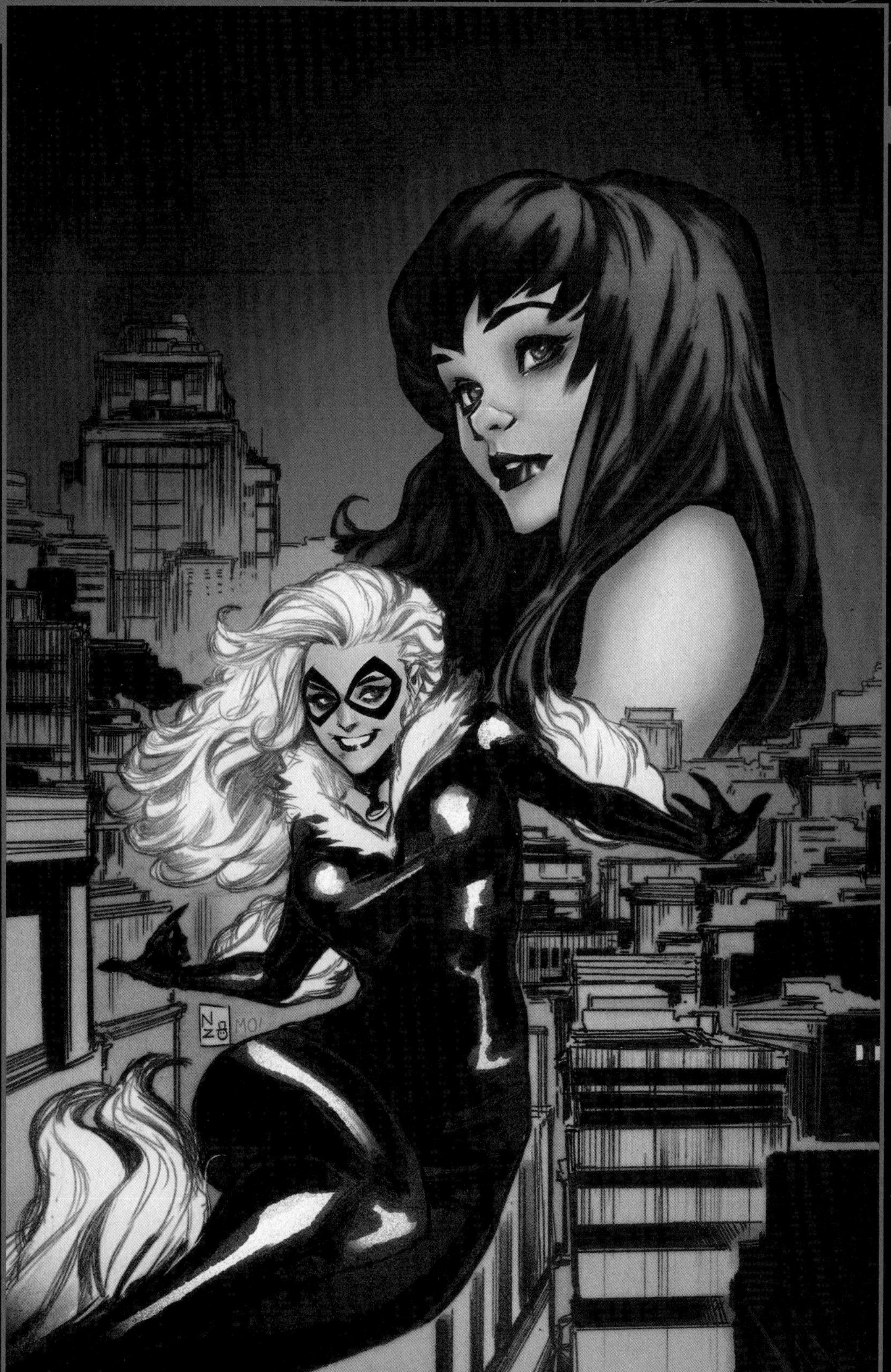

MARY JANE & BLACK CAT: BEYOND VARIANT BY
ADAM HUGHES

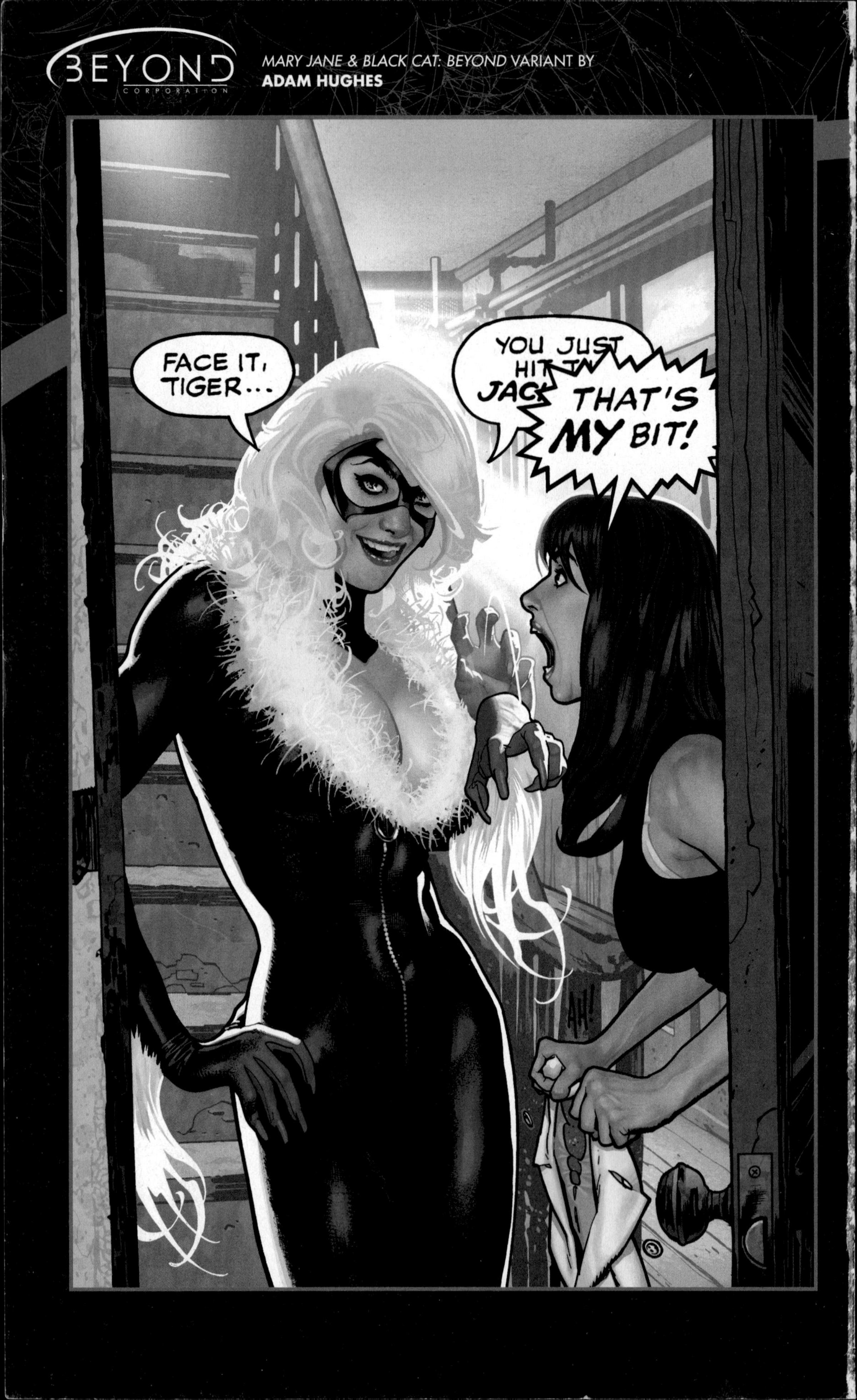
FACE IT, TIGER...
YOU JUST
THAT'S MY BIT!
AH!